Peace in the Mountains

Peace in the Mountains

Northern Appalachian
Students Protest the Vietnam War

Thomas Weyant

Legacies of War
G. Kurt Piehler, Series Editor

The University of Tennessee Press
Knoxville

The Legacies of War series presents a variety of works—from scholarly monographs to memoirs—
that examine the impact of war on society, both in the United States and globally.
The wide scope of the series might include war's effects on civilian populations,
its lingering consequences for veterans, and the role of individual nations and the
international community in confronting genocide and other injustices born of war.

LIBRARY OF CONGRESS CATALOGING-IN-PUBLICATION DATA
Names: Weyant, Thomas, 1979– author.
Title: Peace in the mountains: northern Appalachian students protest the Vietnam War /
Thomas Weyant.
Description: First edition. | Knoxville: The University of Tennessee Press, 2020. |
Series: Legacies of war | Includes bibliographical references and index. | Summary:
"This book explores student war protests at three northern Appalachian universities during the
Vietnam War era: Ohio University, the University of West Virginia, and the University of Pittsburgh.
All three universities had robust ROTC programs, and Thomas Weyant looks at these programs,
its students, and the war protests surrounding them. He discusses how ROTC student dissent and other
student protests—far removed from the widely known atrocities at Kent State and the nationally
covered student protests at American universities in the DC area—illuminates our understanding
of the Vietnam War and its lingering effects on American society"—Provided by publisher.
Identifiers: LCCN 2020004254 (print) | LCCN 2020004255 (ebook) | ISBN 9781621905714 (hardcover) |
ISBN 9781621905721 (adobe pdf)
Subjects: LCSH: Student movements—Appalachian Region—History—20th century. |
Vietnam War, 1961–1975—Protest movements—Appalachian Region | Ohio University—History. |
West Virginia University—History. | University of Pittsburgh—History. |
United States. Army. Reserve Officers' Training Corps—History.
Classification: LCC LA230.5.A6 W48 2020 (print) | LCC LA230.5.A6 (ebook) | DDC 371.8/10974—dc23
LC record available at https://lccn.loc.gov/2020004254

To Amy, Paul, Ralph, and Blanche

Contents

Illustrations

Following page 123

Peace Movement Member with Large Letter to Richard Nixon,
West Virginia University (1970)

War Resisters League Marches against Death and the Vietnam War,
West Virginia University (Winter 1969–1970)

Students Protest the State Road Commission and Arch Moore,
West Virginia University (1969)

Students Urge Participation in Vietnam Moratorium Day,
West Virginia University (1970)

Vietnam Moratorium Day Protest in Courthouse Square,
West Virginia University (October 15, 1969)

State Police Attempt to Break Up Anti-War Demonstration on University
Avenue, West Virginia University (May 7, 1970)

Freedom March Protester Hold "OU Local Student Peace Union"
Sign at Ohio University, 1963

Crowd at Ohio University Mock Republican Convention, 1964

Bird's-Eye-View of Ohio University's Mock Republican
Convention Speaker, 1964

Jim Steele Speaks from the Center of Martin Luther King Jr.
Memorial Ceremony Blocking Intersection, April 7, 1968

Students Protest against Fee Increase in Cutler Hall, 1970

National Vietnam Moratorium Day, October 15, 1969, Athena Yearbook

Students at Grover Center Rally, May 1970, Athena Yearbook

Grover Center Student Rally, May 1970, Athena Yearbook

National Guardsman in front of Baker Center (Old),
Students Looking On, May 1970

Class Gateway (New) in Early Spring, Early 1960s

U.S. President Lyndon B. Johnson Speaks from the West Portico
of Memorial Auditorium, May 7, 1964

U.S. President Lyndon B. Johnson Speaks at Ohio University, May 1964

Foreword

War has played a crucial role during the development of higher education in America in the twentieth century. Through ROTC and other programs, colleges and universities educated a significant number of commissioned officers needed for the armed forces. Beginning in World War II, the federal government bestowed vast sums of money to institutions of higher learning to undertake research with military application. Even before final victory was secured, the federal government made provisions through the Servicemen's Readjustment Act of 1944 (the GI Bill of Rights) that provided a range of benefits to financially disabled and abled bodied veterans, including funds to attend vocational school, college, or earn an advance degree. Federal research dollars and the later influx of veterans studying under the GI Bill led to immense growth in the size and prestige of private and public universities in the late 1940s and early 1950s.

The Cold War that soon followed the defeat of Germany and Japan ensured a permanent federal role as a patron of research. The Soviet Union's successful launch of Sputnik in 1957 fostered an unprecedented influx of federal involvement in education in order to meet the challenges posed by this leap into outer space. Beginning with the National Defense Education Act (NDEA) of 1958, the U.S. Congress provided a record increase in support for education on all levels. For college and universities, this legislation created a student loan program along with graduate fellowships in fields deemed essential to meet the challenges posed by the Soviets achievements in space.

Prior to World War II, only a small fraction of the American population had the opportunity to attend college. Economic prosperity in the postwar period combined with increased state and federal support of higher education fueled an exponential growth in the size and prestige of state universities. As children of the middle class flocked to higher education, they encountered institutions undergoing a transition in both the student culture and curriculum. As the decade opened, many public universities continued to promote student culture that still was anchored around football and fraternities. Under *loco parentis* universities still regulated the personal conduct of students. In the case of women, curfews remained the norm and co-educational residence halls did not yet exist. By the same token, while expanding research opportunities and curricular options, class sizes at public universities soared, and students often had less contact with their professors.

In the 1960s, student activists would challenge the established order seeking to engage their fellow classmates and the wider public in support of the civil rights struggle, protest against the war in Vietnam, and back a range of other causes. Politically, college students were divided, but there existed a significant increase in liberal and leftist activism in the form of public marches, teach-ins, and other acts of protest. Activists also sought a greater voice for students in the institutional policies (with varying degrees of success). Although *loco parentis* eventually faded, the role of students in shaping institutional policies remained circumscribed.

The story of student activism is often told through the lens of elite public and private universities on the East and West Coast. Thomas Weyant seeks to expand this story to take into account the often-stereotyped region of northern Appalachia. His study offers a nuanced perspective by focusing on public universities in three different states: Ohio University, University of Pittsburgh, and West Virginia University. For his evidence, Weyant draws heavily on the college newspapers of these institutions to capture the dynamic quality of the political debate on all three campuses. Newspapers remained an essential source for uncovering the history of student organizations and their activities that did not leave behind an archival record. Student activism in the form of public protests petered out in the early 1970s at all three universities, but the student as an engaged citizen endured and is best reflected in the constitutional amendment lowering the voting age to eighteen in 1971.

G. Kurt Piehler
Florida State University

Acknowledgments

The journey to this book has been in turns difficult, fun, trying, awe-inspiring, cringe-worthy, frustrating, and introspective (often all in the same day). A dozen years ago, I could never have imagined it would be possible to complete this work. I felt lost and untethered, my future obscured by the crushing realities of present failures. This is not a story of triumph nor of overcoming adversities, rather this book represents a stubbornness of purpose and an intransigent desire to see my project through to the conclusion it deserved. It stands as a testament to obstinacy and an abiding belief that one cannot measure oneself on another's yardstick. Countless people have supported, pushed, pulled, restrained, compelled, and assisted me in this long and difficult process. No amount of words of thanks here can in any meaningful way adequately express my gratitude, though I will try. Furthermore, it should go without saying—though I will say it anyway—any mistakes, errors, problems, issues, inaccuracies, or other concerns are my fault, not theirs.

First, I must thank the University of Akron History Department. All of it. This was my home for nearly a decade. Its people were my family. I have had the great and awesome experience of working and studying alongside some of the most dedicated and caring people the academy has produced. In no particular order, I cannot let this moment pass without thanking the following faculty members: Gregory Wilson, Stephen Harp, Martha Santos, Michael Levin, Martin Wainwright, Janet Klein, Walter Hixson, Michael Graham, Kevin Kern, Lesley Gordon, Zachary Williams, Toja Okoh, and Rose Eichler. Equally important, the graduate students at the University of Akron provided an intellectual community that was nurturing and supportive. I must recognize the following for their many acts of fellowship and friendship: Abby Bernhardt, Nathaniel Bassett, Tom Barefoot, Jonathan Sapp, Anne Maltempi, Daniel Hovatter, Angela Riotto, Katie Brown, and Ian Campbell. Further, I would like to thank the School of Mathematics & Social Sciences at Black Hills State University for welcoming me into their family and providing me with the support and encouragement to see this project through to completion.

I could not have completed this work without the generous support and efforts of various organizations and institutions. First, let me thank Black Hills State University for providing generous funds for research and support that helped this book project come to its conclusion. Additionally, thanks go to the University of Akron, Department of History for awarding me the Robert W. Little Graduate Fellowship in 2014-2015, which allowed me to write the majority of the dissertation from which this book arises. The University of Akron's Graduate Student Government awarded me a Professional Enrichment Grant in 2012 to present some of my initial research at two conferences in a single weekend (one in Illinois and the other in California). Additionally, I need to thank the Ohio Academy of History for providing me with not only the Junior Faculty Research Grant in 2018 but for allowing me to present my research at several conferences over the past decade. Similarly, I would like to thank most graciously the various organizations, symposia, and conferences that have allowed me to present and from which I have gained valuable insights and received necessary and helpful feedback, including the Society of Appalachian Historians, the Historians of the Twentieth Century United States, the Pennsylvania Historical Association, the Ohio Valley History Conference and graduate conferences at Kent State University, North Carolina State University, Northern Illinois University, Ohio University, and the University of California at Los Angeles. I would like to thank Marsha Robinson and Cambridge Scholars Publishing for (a) allowing me to publish my first run at some of this material back in 2012 in *Lesser Civil Wars: Civilians Defining War and the Memory of War*, and (b) for granting permission to use, in modified form, that material. Similarly, a thank you goes to the editors of *Ohio Valley History* for publishing a portion of these ideas in their Summer 2019 edition. Furthermore, without the help of the archivists and staffs at the Archives Service Center of the University of Pittsburgh, the Mahn Center for Archives and Special Collections at Ohio University, and the West Virginia and Regional History Collection housed at West Virginia University, none of this project would be possible. Finally, to the wonderful editors and staff at the University of Tennessee Press who have worked so hard and been so forgiving of a first time author, my many thanks.

The greatest thanks are reserved for my family (sorry everyone else). It is with a full heart that I thank my family in Pennsylvania, Massachusetts, and North Carolina. The holidays and random weekend visits were much needed respites. The warmth, love, and joy shared during those encounters sustained me through this process in incalculable ways. I want to say a special thank you to Mollie, Hannah, Noah, Jacob, Paxson, and Adeline—your wonder and amazement at the world around you is refreshing and inspiring. Thank you Matt and Lizzi for your words of encouragement, love, and unwavering support. Finally, to Lee and Char: you have your own special brand of crazy and I love you for it. It is from my parents that I learned certain important lessons, including the idea that one should never give up one's dreams, that pride should never get in the way of asking for help, and doing what one loves is worth any hardship to achieve.

Peace in the Mountains

Citizens of the University and the Nation

On May 31, 1967, Dr. David H. Kurtzman, the retiring chancellor of the University of Pittsburgh, delivered a short but pointed commencement address in which he called on the recent graduates to serve as their own advocates and to continue to pursue their own course of excellence. Kurtzman reflected on the changes the students had faced since they arrived at the University in the fall of 1963, stating poignantly, "your years here have been most unreal." He asked the students to remember the lessons they had learned during their time at the University, those from both inside and beyond the classroom walls, and to "put them together constructively within the fabric of society." In these pursuits, Kurtzman challenged the students to confront stereotypes, break down assumptions, and overcome barriers that artificially separated individuals. The chancellor urged students to "discern and protest against oppression, intolerance, and injustice," as well as "keep faith with the democratic system." However, he stated he would "not caution [them] to be patient with the process of government, for the great changes in society are not made by people who are patient." Kurtzman ended his address by charging the graduating class with a mission as citizens to improve society and make new again the promises of the nation in service to all humanity.[1]

The graduating class of 1967 addressed by Chancellor Kurtzman that May had seen several dramatic changes both at Pitt and in the nation. Before their freshman year began, the March on Washington drew more than a quarter-million people to the nation's capital to call for jobs and racial equality and by the end of the semester an assassin had struck down President Kennedy in Dallas, Texas. The students left campus the following spring amid Beatlemania; some traveled to Mississippi for Freedom Summer, and when they returned to campus for the fall the United States was at war in Vietnam. Before they finished their sophomore year, some students would travel to Selma, Alabama, to march with Dr. King. Others participated in the first Pitt campus teach-in on Vietnam, and others even traveled to Washington to march in the Students for a Democratic Society (SDS) antiwar rally. Throughout their junior year, they leveled challenges against women's hours and both pro- and anti-war demonstrations grew in frequency. By their senior year, they witnessed an escalation in both the war and resistance to it with an Angry Arts against the War program and peace vigils, as well as a growing black empowerment movement locally and nationwide. Much about the world they had known when they graduated high school in 1963 had changed for Pitt's class of 1967, and in ways they could not have foreseen. Through it all, students sought to expand their influence and control over the events that directly and indirectly affected them. They claimed their right as citizens of the University and of the nation.

Analyzing events at the University of Pittsburgh, along with Ohio University and West Virginia University, provides a gateway to broadening and deepening the work of scholars trying to understand the origins, ideas, methods, actions, and legacies of student social and political activism during the Vietnam War era. By seeing the actions of students during the upheavals of the 1960s as part of a larger negotiation of citizenship, within which notions of student identity developed, one can better understand the student experience of the decade. At northern Appalachian universities particularly, this approach helps explain why the students did what they did rather than fault them for not doing what other student communities did.

Drawing largely from participant narratives, the scholarly understanding of Sixties student activism has, until recently rested on several key frameworks and assumptions. First, they centered the narrative on white, middle-class men at elite universities. Second, they established the sense of a decade of optimism torn asunder by despair, frustration, and violence. Third, they offered a top-down, organizationally defined narrative of activism. While the organizations squabbled over strategies and tactics, the narrative suggested, they shared a similar vision of what the problem was that confronted the nation.[2] Scholars throughout the 1990s and early 2000s assailed these assumptions expanding the definition of participants, strategies, and localities of activism.

Much of the expansion of historical analysis occurred in the wake of Kenneth

Heineman's groundbreaking *Campus Wars*. Heineman argued that non-elite state universities like Pennsylvania State University and Michigan State University were important sites of student activism as they demonstrated the broad base of activism and shifted the focus from large, nationally recognized events.[3] Since the publication of *Campus Wars* in the early 1990s, the literature has continued to expand beyond the elite state and private schools to analyze activism at a host of other universities and colleges.[4]

The definition of agents of change broadened as the scholarship on Sixties student activism expanded to include increasing numbers of potential actors. White, male students have dominated the historiography of student activism, especially antiwar activism, because of the disproportionate amount of emphasis given to New Left organizations, such as SDS, and the history-memoirs of these groups' leaders. Though this book does retain a focus on white, middle-class, male students—in part due to the student body make-up of the institutions under investigation—it recognizes and takes steps to integrate, when possible, connections to additional constituencies, including women and people of color.

Building from the expanded base of Sixties studies post-Heineman, this book shines the historical spotlight on Appalachia, an often-overlooked region of the country. Far too often Appalachia enters the collective consciousness, especially in terms of the Sixties, as a site of poverty programs and coal-mining unrest; however, Appalachia did not escape the Vietnam War era without directly engaging with the central issues that stirred activism and upheaval throughout the nation. Further, the students attending universities in northern Appalachia were neither more nor less disinterested or apathetic than their counterparts around the nation. Northern Appalachian universities may not have made the national news as often as schools on the coasts, but that did not mean they lacked student engagement with political and social issues.

The students of northern Appalachian universities engaged in social and political activism in part as a response to the events and trends they witnessed in Cold War American society. By looking at how Appalachian youth interacted with their campus, local, state, and national communities, and the similarities with the larger national activities of students, it becomes clear that the young people of Appalachia must have experienced the same socio-cultural, political, and economic changes as the rest of the nation, at least on some level. To date, scholars of Sixties student activism have left Appalachia out of this discussion, assuming that, as the President's Appalachian

Regional Commission report stated in 1964, "Appalachia is a region *apart*."[5] The notable exception to this gap in the historiography is Thomas Kiffmeyer's *Reformers to Radicals*. Kiffmeyer explores the radicalization of students in the Appalachian Volunteers as they strove to fight poverty and deprivation in Kentucky.[6]

The schools chosen for this study include Ohio University, the University of Pittsburgh, and West Virginia University. Selections were made based on several factors, including (1) whether they fit within the geographically defined northern Appalachia; (2) whether, by the mid-1960s, they existed as a doctoral-granting state university (or state-related university); and, (3) whether they had some level of connection with one or more of the other schools in the region (athletics rivalry, regional organizations, etc.).[7] For my purposes, I collapse the most recent Appalachian Regional Commission designations of "northern" and "north central" into a singular "northern" that, while anachronistic, more closely reflects the colloquially defined subregion within Appalachia.[8]

While Athens, OH, and Morgantown, WV, are undoubtedly within Appalachia, some people may question whether urban and industrial Pittsburgh fits within the parameters of Appalachia, most often conceptualized as a region of shack-dwellers living in a Dickensian nightmare of poverty deep in some remote hollow. Pittsburgh sits well within the geographical boundaries of Appalachia; federal officials have defined all the surrounding counties for at least 80 miles in any direction as Appalachia, thus it seems incongruous to suggest that Pittsburgh is somehow not a part of Appalachia given its obvious geographic connection. Pittsburgh, whether consciously aware of it or not, is an Appalachian city—by far the largest Appalachian city. However, one need not be consciously aware that one is in Appalachia for the narrative constructions of Appalachia to have effect. Additionally, Pittsburgh serves as a counter to the existing narrative of Appalachia as southern, rural, and poor, by suggesting that the region was also northern, urban, and industrial.

The popular image of Appalachia constructs a conflicted vision of the effects of modernity in the region, seeing a place where individuals stubbornly cling to their antiquated ways in the face of progress while simultaneously becoming victims of development, all of which results in crushing poverty, ignorance, and despair. In this imagining, Appalachia symbolizes both the negatives of development and the intransigence of tradition. Appalachian scholar Allen Batteau described this view when he stated that for many "Appalachia represented poverty ennobled and perfected."[9] Appalachia therefore struggled within a culture of poverty and a colonial relationship with absentee corporations. Within the historiography, Appalachia has played the role of the "other," often appearing as a counterpoint to arguments about slave power in the antebellum South, as a backdrop for discussions of unionization and the effects of natural resource extraction, and as the chief battleground in the federally directed War on Poverty. Themes such as poverty, exploitation, development, and labor unrest, have reappeared frequently in the historiography often to reinforce a sense of Appalachian victimhood.[10]

The Sixties imaging of Appalachia emphasized its economic, political, and social shortcomings in comparison to the booming, modern American society alongside which it existed. In a February 1960 article for the *Saturday Evening Post* entitled "The Strange Case of West Virginia," reporter Roul Tunley depicted West Virginia—and thereby, the region of Appalachia—as America's paradox. The article's title, a play on Robert Louis Steveson's 1886 novel *The Strange Case of Dr. Jekyll and Mr. Hyde*, suggested the region had a deviant nature; Appalachia was the brutish Mr. Hyde to modern America's Dr. Jekyll.[11] A similar evaluation of the region appears in a survey undertaken by the Ford Foundation in the late-1950s and published in 1962. The survey chronicled the substandard conditions in education, health services, and local government in the region while identifying a peculiar traditionalism and a weakness in both coal mining and agriculture as the main factors causing the region's deficiencies.[12]

In 1963, Harry Caudill's *Night Comes to the Cumberlands* established the narrative framework for much of Appalachian scholarship as well as official and popular images of the region during the following few decades. His passionate prose painted a vivid portrait of Appalachia that reached a national audience, depicting a region victimized by malevolent corporations bent on natural and human resource exploitation. He described the mountaineers as stoic and tragic heroes locked in a virtually inescapable debt spiral.[13] Caudill's work inspired other accounts of the region's deprivations and provided a guiding framework for federal efforts at regional development. The influence of Caudill's narrative echoes in J.D. Vance's *Hillbilly Elegy* and the responses it generated from scholars determined to push back against this narrative.[14]

Established by President Kennedy following his experiences in West Virginia during the 1960 presidential election, the President's Appalachian Regional Commission (PARC) argued that isolation and backwardness had caused poverty to linger in the mountains despite national prosperity. At its core, the commission's 1964 report suggested applying modernization theory to Appalachia. This theory held the view that "traditional" societies required assistance to become "modern" societies through the benevolent assistance of democratic capitalist nations, and was used as the basis for America's development aid to the so-called Third World. In this view, Appalachia was an internal third world nation populated by the poorest Americans deprived of all the conveniences of modern American society. The 1964 PARC report called for an application of "that part of our international development program which fosters capital investment . . . into Federal programs that affect the regional development program for Appalachia."[15] Thinly veiled within this solution was a sense of Appalachian inferiority and backwardness amongst those coming into the region to lift up its residents. However, these programs did not address the underlying structural inequalities and shortcomings—they addressed the symptoms but not the illness—and therefore failed.

Although northern Appalachia's characteristics stand as relatively representative of the larger region, scholars have focused little attention on the subregion. The bulk of the historiography focuses on Kentucky or southern Appalachia. When it does address West Virginia, it largely ignores connections with northern Appalachia.[16] While northern Appalachia was more urban, industrialized, and prosperous than the other subregions of Appalachia, in part because of the benefits of an extensive railroad network, the region faced the same devastating effects wrought by post-World War II economic dislocation, especially as the highway boom slowed rail traffic. The deterioration of the railroads, decaying industry, and the mechanization of extraction-based labor sapped northern Appalachia's economic vitality resulting in the same struggles in the region as existed throughout the central and southern subregions.[17]

Simultaneously, the popular imagination constructed Appalachia as a Southern region. Regional movements and organizations such as the Council of the Southern Mountains, a community action agency headquartered at Berea College in Kentucky (which had begun its existence in 1913 as the Southern Mountain Workers Conference), reinforced this image.[18] Such organizations penetrated West Virginia but could go no farther north because of the centuries-old division; the Mason-Dixon Line continued to serve as an imagined and symbolic border. Thus, even though intellectually one may have recognized Pennsylvania, Ohio, or even New York as part of Appalachia at the time, the popular imagination erased these states from its construction of the region because they were not Southern. This false division continues to pervade Appalachian historiography.

The false image of Appalachia as disconnected from the rest of the nation has created a faulty impression that some of the fundamental concerns of the early Cold War era did not affect Appalachia. Baby Boomers who grew up in northern Appalachia did not live in an alien world devoid of the impulses and activities that affected the rest of their generation. If student activism during the Sixties was a response to the Cold War world they experienced, then the fact that northern Appalachian students engaged in similar activities as their national counterparts should suggest they were responding to similar stimuli. Thus, despite assumptions of Appalachian otherness and a dearth of scholarly studies that expand beyond poverty, unions, and migration during the period of 1945 to 1960 in Appalachia, the student activism of the Sixties suggests a greater continuity with the national narrative.

In fact, or in their imagination, Baby Boomers grew up in the new suburban subdivisions of Cold War America in part because of the vast reach of the Serviceman's Readjustment Act of 1944. The G.I. Bill, as the act became known, provided money for schooling and to start businesses, but equally important, it allowed veterans to buy a home through its loan program.[19] Raised in the Depression Generation's white suburban "American Dream" of security in an age of anxiety, the Baby Boom Generation emerged. By the early 1950s, America appeared to be awash in babies. Young families littered the landscape of the new suburban subdivisions of ranch houses. Child-rearing advice flowed from all directions and the stores brimmed with the newest trends, gadgets, and necessities for the babies of today to grow into the citizens of tomorrow. However, not all Americans who wanted to could participate in this middle-class, white, suburban bliss that television programming and advertisements pumped around the nation.[20] Regardless, from birth, those around them conceived Baby Boomers as part of a new era in American history.

As Boomers grew, the conception of a generational coherency grew as well, inculcated among them from various sources: political, economic, and cultural. Young people united in a generational sense through their shared youth and liminal space in American political society. The Baby Boom Generation often found that politicians called them the "future leaders of America," and were encouraged to participate in political activities, like pen pal programs, that served to widen the national security needs of the nation.[21] In an economic sense, youth represented an increasingly important target market. Culturally, the Boomer generation shared the same entertainment outlets across the nation, whether it was music, movies, or television—all of which, by the middle of the 1960s, reinforced a supposed youth generation.[22] As the theme song from *The Monkees*, a popular television show aimed at Sixties youth, said, "We're the young generation, and we've got something to say."[23] Ultimately, a wide variety of socio-cultural and political sources helped to forge the idea of the Baby Boom Generation and provided a framework for their worldview as they began to populate the nation's college campuses in the early 1960s.

Scholars, administrators, students, and the general population have long debated the purpose and nature of the university in American life. In this sense, the Cold War years and the Sixties, in particular, were not unique. From the colonial era to the mid-twentieth century, the dominant view in the United States held that the central role of college was to create and sustain the upper classes of American society. However, industrialization and Populist-Progressive reform impulses in the late-nineteenth and early-twentieth centuries fostered curricular changes from the classical liberal arts to specialized technical and professional training.[24]

World War II and the Cold War shifted the debates again: the advent of the military-industrial-academic complex altered the relationship of colleges with the government, students, and society. Tensions emerged from the pressures and possibilities associated with the Cold War and enrollments ballooned thanks to the G.I. Bill and the Baby Boom. Enrollments at colleges and universities doubled as veterans stormed the campuses leading to a few logistical problems: from housing, to classroom spaces, to finding qualified instructors. In the end, large class sizes, mechanically graded exams, graduate-student-led discussion sections, and several other innovations became standard procedures maintained even after the flood of World War II student-veterans receded from campuses.[25]

The G.I. Bill also altered the relationship between institutions of higher education and the federal government. Schools relied on federal funds to build the facilities necessary to accommodate the student-veterans at the same time that the federal government sought to stimulate research beneficial for winning the Cold War. Large sums of money flowed into schools, which helped reinforce the expansionism stimulated by the G.I. Bill. By 1960, universities drew nearly $1.5 billion from the federal government, largely from the Department of Defense.[26] Some administrators and political leaders expressed trepidation at linking university and military research agendas fearing it had a corrupting influence on the mission of higher education in America.[27]

During a series of lectures in 1963, later published as *The Uses of the University*, Clark Kerr laid out a detailed analysis of the state of the modern American university, which he argued was created in part through the innovations adopted to respond to the influx of student-veterans and expanded federal funding opportunities. Kerr, the chancellor of the University of California at Berkeley and president of the University of California system at the time, argued that the modern American university did not represent one, unique campus culture but rather had multiple constituencies, functions, and centers of power and thus represented a "multiversity." Further the expansion of many campuses' physical footprint and curricular offerings over the previous decade created a greater physical and intellectual distance between students, faculty, and administrators, while adding a new constituency—that of the Department of Defense or another federal funding agency.[28]

Divided campuses and conflicting notions of mission made college campuses ripe for unrest. With increasing distance between students, faculty, and administrators, and as each sought to address various needs and constituencies, the social bonds that had once created a sense of a singular college community frayed leading to increased tension and animosity between the various groups. On top of the internal divisions growing within universities one must add the pressures wrought by the Cold War: the fear of Communist subversion led to investigations, dismissals, or forced resignations of faculty and administrators as well as large sums of federal monies flowing into university coffers to support research deemed necessary for national security.[29] Claims of rightful access to the collegiate campus space grew in number as an ever-widening array of constituencies came under the multiversity's umbrella making it increasingly difficult to discern the mission of the university and the meaning of studenthood.

The multiversity concept in action created a level of anxiety amongst students, as they felt increasingly distant and disenfranchised. Further, it left them to try to define themselves, their roles, and their community within an increasingly faceless university society. In response to the diverse web of impulses and expectations that pulled students in myriad and contradictory directions, a contested student community developed.[30] Students invented their own culture in which they imagined a united campus based on shared experiences, frustrations, and aspirations. Though never fully unified, student communities emerged—of students of a particular university or field of study, for instance, but also a shared trans-campus community identity that spanned the United States and, especially in the 1960s, the world. They attempted to define themselves in dialectic opposition to faculty and administrators and the campus newspapers served as the conduit that perpetuated this forged identity.[31]

One of the largest sources for this project is student newspapers, due in part to limited additional sources to get at student voices. Most of the archival sources that provide student voices address a period post-1967. These limitations are perhaps the result of the ephemeral nature of short-lived, and often ad-hoc, student organizations, or the lack of a bureaucratic nature among some New Left and New Left-inspired student groups. Further, the student newspapers offer some insight into the conflicted nature of campus through what they deemed worthy to discuss and present.

There are flaws inherent in using student newspapers, chief among these problems being a question of bias. They obviously do not present an unfiltered view of campus life—external restrictions of various forms exist (such as advisors and administration censors) as well as self-censorship and student editorial control. However, the student newspapers offer one of the few ways, if not the only way in some cases, to determine what was happening on campus, things one cannot find through reading the academic bulletins and yearbooks. Additionally, they offer insights that differ from official administration sources.

The papers help to highlight cross-causal development of student activism as one sees similar names and groups appearing in a variety of contexts. Also, since campus papers often address, if only in a cursory way at times, national and international events, seeing what they present, and how, can offer some insights into why or how students formulated their views. In part, using the newspapers offers a way to get at the student voice, and to that end my goal is to analyze the language deployed in the articles, editorials, and letters to the editor.

Admittedly, many of the chief actors engaged in political and social activism at northern Appalachian universities were white and male. In the case of antiwar activism, the immediacy brought by possible conscription—one failed exam could lead to induction and on to the Mekong Delta—made many men attuned to the war, and increased their likelihood to engage in public demonstrations. Though white men were both vocal and visible within the antiwar movement on northern Appalachian campuses, they were not the sole actors. When one contextualizes antiwar activism within the larger panorama of student activism, the leadership and contributions of female and black students emerges. The same impulses that drove civil rights and women's rights activities inherently connected to antiwar rallies and demonstrations.

Students saw direct connections between local, state, national, and collegiate communities—an effort to improve one served as an effort to improve all, through the notion of the student-citizen. This conception of the student-citizen was not limited to white men but emerged within the diverse population of the universities. While this book does often present the words and actions of white male students, it also attempts to integrate women and people of color, to show cross-cause development and the breadth of student activism.

Furthermore, for the sake of brevity in the following chapters, the term "students" serves as a shorthand for a subset of students on college campuses. It would be too simplistic to refer to them simply as "radical" students because many liberal and moderate (and a few conservative) students shared some of these impulses. Perhaps "active" students would be appropriate; though, again there is a great deal of nuance within who one does and does not consider "active." Is letter-writing active? Or, must one engage in demonstrations? Or, is it not merely participating in but planning rallies that defines active? Further, "antiwar," "anti-ROTC," or "antidiscrimination," fail as adequate descriptors because students' views were not always constructed in negative terms; thus, they were equally, "peace," "academic freedom," or "equality" students.

Helen Lefkowitz Horowitz, a scholar of undergraduate cultures, provided a tripartite division of college students that offers some insights. She divides students into those who embraced the extracurricular activities of college life yet not academics, those who focused on grades and professional preparation rather than the social facets of college life, and those who cared about learning if not grades and wanted to refocus campus social life away from frivolity and toward matters of moral conscience.[32] Often, it is this last subset of students the following chapters refer to when using the generic "students" term. These individuals frequently were, though not exclusively, part of or inspired by the New Left.[33] Further, given the very small minority populations on northern Appalachian campuses during these years, there is also an assumed whiteness to the term "student," though the following chapters do attempt to make racial distinctions when appropriate. Thus, to keep the chapters from bogging down with parsing the word "student" at every turn, the book consciously uses a more ambiguous term, "students," despite its potential flaws or oversimplifications.

At the core of this study are questions surrounding how young people debated the definitions of "student" and "citizen" in a time of unrest and why, despite the limited successes of protest and dissent, students felt compelled to act. Further, how did the conflicted nature of college campuses in the Sixties facilitate or hinder the development of student activism? Ultimately, one question that became a central focus around which the rest of the book developed was: What united student activism on national issues like the war in Vietnam and civil rights to activism on campus issues such as action against *in loco parentis*? In other words, what was it that led students to get involved in the first place and then led them into other areas of activism, how did they justify their actions, and why did they feel such a sense of obligation to become active?

Through their words and actions, the students of northern Appalachian universities forged a dual-identity as students and citizens, arguing that the obligations of each required them to act to improve their communities. Like millions of other young people around the nation during the Vietnam War era, they confronted conflicting meanings of patriotism, dissent, and citizenship, and tied these debates directly to the role of the university in American society and to their rights as students. For these students the national and local intertwined significantly. Throughout it all, student activists argued that an individual could have a positive impact on society and it was their obligation as students and citizens to do their part to make the world a little better than they had found it. Thus, to understand better the Sixties, one must recognize not only the cross-causal connections of activism and dissent, but also the interplay between the local and national as encoded in the student-citizen identity. Many saw the college campus as the nation in microcosm, what was happening at one level directly influenced and connected with the other and that through the dual-identity as student-citizens, young people of the Vietnam War era united the local and the national. To explore this further, this book specifically sets out to explore cross-causal connections of activism on civil rights, antipoverty, antiwar, and campus policies—such as in loco parentis.

The conclusion drawn from this research is that the reoccurring and unifying theme is that of citizenship. Students who became involved in activism did so because of their definition of the proper role of a citizen. The citizenship they envisioned involved active participation and sought to reform society, and, on occasion, revolutionize it. They argued that as citizens of the United States and citizens of the university, they had an obligation to act.

Citizenship, the set of duties and obligations of a member of a political community, rests on the notion that all constituent members of the political community exist and act as equals and therefore have equal right to offer or deny consent to the activities of the political community.[34] By constructing an image of the university as civic society, wherein all constituent members—administrators, faculty, and students—were equal partners, students made a claim to university citizenship. Lacking the vote, most students were not full members of the American citizenry, yet they believed they possessed the requisite qualities and temperament to be full citizens; thus, participating in and expanding the civic functions of the university afforded students opportunities to demonstrate their abilities and make claims for full citizenship within the nation. The conception of citizenship as active underscored the New Left vision of participatory democracy and grew from long-standing notions of the moral obligation of citizens to engage in the civic process.

Student activism used many tactics and strategies, adopted and adapted from other movements. Sometimes students sought to build communities of activist-agents who would possess the skills necessary to fight for and retain some level of control in the decision-making process. At other times, they attempted to harness a general sense of disgust and frustration through mass marches and demonstrations. The problem came when the size of the crowd and the volume of their chants became the measure of success rather than access to decision-making power.

Although none of the campuses under investigation drew sustained national attention, nor did the students generate dramatic or foundational shifts in student-administration relations, these campuses represent contested grounds as students of the Vietnam War era negotiated their dual identities as students and citizens amongst themselves and with other university constituencies. In conceptualizing their definition of student as analogous to citizen and the university as the nation in microcosm, students established parallels for defining and justifying an expanded and increasingly active participation in the decision-making processes of the university. By viewing the university as a civil society, an entity that exists to perform civic functions, students built a form of citizenship that afforded them an opportunity to experience and experiment with the meaning and obligations of citizenship within the wider American community.

Students during the Sixties forged a new identity as student-citizens in a time of war and unrest. They argued that one could not easily separate one facet of their selves from another and that being a student did not absolve one from their obligations as a citizen. However, the students debated and negotiated what those obligations were and how one should interact with authority, whether in the form of the university or the state. They sought to define also the role of the university itself within the context of American society. By examining how students engaged in campus politics and larger social concerns, one can see how they defined citizenship and patriotism. Thus, through investigating the activities of northern Appalachian university students we gain a window into the multiple ways in which young people experienced the Sixties. We also gain a more complex understanding of Appalachia during the period as well as a more nuanced vision of the concepts of student identity and activism during the Vietnam War era. As students and citizens, young people felt compelled to act to improve their communities and their nation.

Chapter 1

Background

Cold War Universities in Northern Appalachia by the Early 1960s

During the Sixties, millions of Baby Boomers flooded onto college campuses around the nation, several thousand to schools in northern Appalachia. College campuses became a central stage for the performance of political and social activism by American young people. Simultaneously, the campus environment was in transition as ever-increasing populations, as well as expanding physical footprints and curricular offerings, combined with a widening array of constituencies to form the "multiversity." Further, the Cold War fueled the development of a military-industrial-academic complex. The changing spatial and administrative relationships of the Cold War American university became yet another impulse that stimulated student activism, as students increasingly conceived of themselves as citizens of both the nation and the university.

In the early years of the 1960s, the campus newspapers chronicled the events and experiences that supposedly tied the expanding northern Appalachian campus communities together, such as parades, dances, and extracurricular activities. These invented traditions and rites of passage served to initiate new students into the student community and allowed existing members to reaffirm their connection, all within the framework of "school spirit." At Ohio University, the University of Pittsburgh, and West Virginia University, Homecoming represented one of the largest campus-wide events of the fall and drew together both returning alumni with current students as well as uniting upperclassmen with freshmen. Football played a pivotal role in helping to forge aspects of the student community, representing a ritual experience that identified all participants as members of the community. Football rituals happened early in the school year and served as points where supposedly all of the student body came together, subsuming their own distinct identities and pouring themselves into the larger vessel of "student" and university partisan.[1]

While football seemingly provided an opportunity for the entire student body to unite, both physically at the games or associated dances and mentally by creating a shared experience that individuals who may not have previously met each other could reminisce about, these events also helped highlight the fractures within the student community on northern Appalachian campuses. Participants in the games, dances, and parades saw those who did not attend as outsiders, as not part of the majority "student" identity, because they did not fraternize and create shared memories. Ultimately, the competing visions of studenthood created by the students are important for understanding their political and social activism during the Vietnam War era.

The shared experiences of going to class, studying, and doing homework generally linked all various student identities, though even here there were some who considered themselves outsiders. Often the distinctions of student-ness came from what happened outside the classroom: who one's friends were, where one lived, and in what extracurricular activities one participated. As Baby Boomers came of age in the Vietnam War era, they confronted an American society fraught with major and important transitions, and they sought to define their place within and their relationship to this changing society. In the end, the universities chosen for this study were not immune to the transitions and upheavals affecting higher education and college life in the early Cold War years nor to the socio-economic realities of Appalachia. Ohio University, the University of Pittsburgh, and West Virginia University all drew students from eastern Ohio, western Pennsylvania, and northern West Virginia as well as from urban centers on the East Coast. During the Sixties, all three schools faced major challenges and conflicts between increasing numbers of students and definitions of studentness, as well as expanding numbers of constituencies and questions regarding the very mission of their institution. In the end, Appalachian universities were much like their counterparts around the nation. The students at the three northern Appalachian schools explored here faced the same questions and frustrations as their counterparts around the nation, thereby helping to erase some of the sense of Appalachian aloofness. However, they also show that while Appalachia fully engaged with national events and impulses, the region had its own internal concerns that affected students.

The post-World War II era saw important shifts in American higher education. A rising careerist emphasis coincided with strengthening domestic anticommunism and ballooning federal funding of research to create a new campus culture. During the immediate postwar wars, university enrollments expanded significantly, as hundreds of thousands of returning veterans took advantage of Title II of the Serviceman's Readjustment Act of 1944 (or G.I. Bill). By 1960, enrollments totaled 3.5 million students around the nation as the first wave of Baby Boomers entered college.

University life in America has been in a constant state of flux from its beginning and in that regard, the Cold War era (and the Sixties in particular) were not entirely new. Much of what Americans considered standard collegiate life by the mid-twentieth century had its roots in the student literary and debating societies, which slowly morphed into social fraternities (and sororities). This emphasis on extracurricular social activities was an important component of late nineteenth and early twentieth century notions of college as a means by which the upper middle class forged the bonds and alliances necessary to maintain and advance their vision of democratic capitalism.[2] However, the twin forces of industrialization and Progressive reform impulses at the turn of the twentieth century caused curricular changes away from the classical liberal arts model and toward specialized technical and professional training necessary for industrial society.

By the middle decades of the twentieth century, the debates surrounding higher education in America were between those who saw the goal of college as career preparation, in one way or another, and those who believed the institution should foster an independent and general desire for learning. According to undergraduate cultures historian Helen Lefkowitz Horowitz, by the mid-twentieth century a second type of student emerged who viewed college as a preparation for admittance to the professional classes and rejecting the traditionalist college experience of Greek societies and juvenile antics, creating a new "careerist" student on campus. These were students unconcerned with social organizations and focused on scholastic achievement. Eventually, a third grouping of students emerged, unconcerned with grades but not wanting to participate in the extended adolescent antics of the Greek social organizations. This group saw the role of the university as providing a basis for social change, empowerment, and individual growth, embodied in notions of learning for the sake of knowledge rather than to earn degrees.[3] Thus, as the Sixties dawned a tripartite structure of student cultures existed on college campuses.

Many of the changes identified during the early Cold War years have links to the G.I. Bill and the growing military-industrial-academic complex spawned by the Cold War. Enrollments at colleges and universities doubled in only a few months after World War II ended as veterans flooded the campuses. This influx of new students led to a number of logistical problems from providing housing and classroom spaces, to finding qualified instructors. In accommodating the swell of student-veterans, many universities built new facilities and expanded faculty sizes, suggesting they intended to pursue a policy of recruitment that would prevent enrollments from dropping to prewar levels. Thus, the large physical footprint and distant professorate that were essential components of what some later labeled as the "multiversity" grew because of massive veteran enrollments facilitated by the G.I. Bill.[4]

The G.I. Bill also altered the relationship between institutions of higher education and the federal government, an alteration that would resonate in the development of the military-industrial-academic complex. By 1960, universities had drawn nearly $1.5 billion in federal funds (largely from the Department of Defense), which they used to build the facilities necessary to accommodate the student-veterans as well as to stimulate research beneficial for winning the Cold War.[5] While critics of the new relationship feared the military-industrial-academic complex would prove a corrupting influence on the mission of higher education, others defended expanded Defense Department research as a patriotic duty undertaken by American universities. Since the universities were now part of the national security apparatus, they had to be secured from the creeping hand of Communist saboteurs and instigators, which gave license to anticommunist crusaders to penetrate into the college campus and purge faculty members they deemed subversive.[6]

The sprawling new campuses, the exploding class sizes, and the swell of the collegiate bureaucracy to manage these new systems helped American universities in the Cold War era forge new identities as "multiversities." The term comes from the work of Clark Kerr, the chancellor of the University of California at Berkeley and president of the University of California system in the early 1960s, who argued that the modern American university did not represent one, unique campus culture but rather had multiple constituencies, functions, and centers of power.[7] With increasing distance between student, faculty, and administrators, and as each seeking to address various needs and constituencies, the social bonds that had once created a sense of a singular college community frayed, leading to increased tension and animosity between the various groups.[8] More and more claims were made of rightful access to the collegiate campus space by this expanding array of constituencies that it became increasingly difficult to discern the mission of the university and the meaning of studenthood.

These contested definitions of studentness saturated student newspapers as they reported on activities and events around campus. Homecoming and Greek social events echoed with the assumed definitions of student as one associated with a fraternity or sorority, a largely traditional vision of student-ness by the 1960s. The student government and campus-wide events, such as Homecoming Court, often divided the campus community into two factions: Greek and "independent." The moniker "independent" represented an inherently biased term that lumped together vastly different sets of people who may not necessarily have seen themselves as sharing anything in common beyond not being members of a Greek social society. The newspapers often encouraged students to attend sporting events and show their support for the school's athletic teams, especially the football team, and in doing so they set up the dichotomy of those who cheered on their school's teams as true students whereas those who did not were false or weak students lacking necessary school spirit. The front pages were often awash in stories chronicling the events and experiences that supposedly tied the expanding campus communities together, such as parades, dances, and extracurricular activities. These invented traditions and rites of passage served to initiate new students into the student community and existing members reaffirmed their connection, all within the framework of "school spirit."

The changes wrought by the Cold War to American universities made them ripe for unrest by the 1960s. College campuses became a central stage for the performance of political and social activism by American young people. Simultaneously, ever-increasing populations and expanding physical and curricular boundaries combined with a widening array of constituencies to form the multiversity. The growing military-industrial-academic complex combined with these changing relationships to fuel student impulses toward activism and provided opportunities for new conceptions of students as citizens of both the nation and the university.

As the Ohio Territory progressed to statehood in the first decade of the nineteenth century, it was also in the process of establishing a university in the recently settled town of Athens. Initially known as the American Western University, the college adopted the name Ohio University in celebration and commemoration of the new state it resided in; it opened in October 1808 with three enrolled students. From these inauspicious origins, Ohio University would grow to over thirteen thousand students across several different campuses by 1962.[9]

Despite a temporary closure in the mid-1840s due to low enrollment, Ohio University, its students and faculty, and the city of Athens have participated in many of the major events and debates of American history over the past two hundred years. In 1828, barely twenty years after it opened its doors, OU graduated its first black student, John Newton Templeton (it would be another ninety years for the first black female graduate of OU). Several of the University's trustees served as conductors of the Underground Railroad, and during the Civil War students, as well as faculty, volunteered for service in the Union Army—some even defended Athens during Confederate General John Hunt Morgan's 1863 raid into Ohio. Though the University had three black members on the board of trustees between the 1870s and 1910s, the University adopted policies in the first decades of the twentieth century that limited the inflow of black students from southern states and offered only lip service to the efforts to address discrimination in the Athens community. Not until the 1960s, did the University hire its first black faculty member, E. Curmie Price, a professor in the English department.[10]

Though OU lost its bid for funding under the Morrill Land Grant College Act (the state instead used the monies to establish what the Ohio State University in Columbus became), the University continued to expand in both physical footprint and course offerings, eventually adding a normal school at the turn of the twentieth century. During these years student activities expanded dramatically as well. Greek social organizations for both men and women formed, a variety of student publications emerged, and organized university athletics began. Although baseball and football teams routinely played during the 1890s and the student body adopted green and white as official school colors in 1896, the sports teams did not adopt the bobcat as their nickname and mascot until 1925. Ohio University students served in the military during both world wars while the University established facilities and curricula to train soldiers. The creation of military training programs received significant debate during both wars; however, during World War I students backed a compulsory training course, while during World War II students protested the creation of a voluntary Reserve Officers Training Corps (ROTC) program. Following World War II, the student population swelled with enrollments, more than doubling between 1945 and 1946, with the bulk of the more than seven thousand students coming from veterans using their G.I. Bill benefits. The result was to force the University to find innovative ways to house and teach the new mass of students; in the end, Quonset huts littered the campus often serving double purposes as classrooms and living space.[11]

By the 1950s, Ohio University stood deceptively calm in the bucolic setting of the rolling hills of Athens, Ohio. In a 1954 history of the University, the author noted the "peaceful and somewhat sequestered tranquility" of Athens and hoped that the coming changes wrought by industrial development would not rob Ohio University of the quiet serenity "in which the learning process thrives." According to this 1950s vision of academia in Athens, "at no time since the founding of the university have relations among the students, the faculty, the administrators, and the trustees been more cordial."[12] The 1958–1960 Student Bulletin echoed this rosy assessment by stating, "Ohio University is a friendly university. The faculty and administration strive to give students an education and to make life as pleasant for them as possible while they are doing it."[13] Perhaps this was an overly optimistic (and paternalistic) view of these relationships; regardless, within a decade the relations between these various constituencies would become strained in a way that they had not been since the University's founding.

By the early 1960s, Ohio University sat on the edge of the new multiversity concept of higher education. Vernon Alden, the new, young, energetic president of OU, guided the University and its thousands of predominately white students through the many ups-and-downs of the decade. Not even forty when he became president in 1962, Alden exuded a sense of optimism reflective of President Kennedy's New Frontier and was hopeful that he could help OU blaze new trails into a better future. By 1964, Alden would become a key player in President Lyndon Johnson's War on Poverty, suggesting the importance of OU to the larger plan for regional and national development.[14]

In 1787, as disgruntled Americans met in Philadelphia to draft a new Constitution for the fledgling nation, the school that would become the University of Pittsburgh was coming into existence on the other end of the commonwealth of Pennsylvania. Initially established as a secondary school serving the 7,000-person city of Pittsburgh, the Pittsburgh Academy would become the non-denominational Western University of Pennsylvania (WUP) by 1819. The University temporarily suspended operations because of a series of fires in the mid-to-late 1840s; however, by the mid-1850s, the WUP trustees sought to reestablish the school in downtown Pittsburgh, a city that had reached a population of nearly 100,000. In 1882, fire again struck the University forcing it to move from its downtown buildings to a temporary residence across the Allegheny River (in the then separate city of Allegheny) for fourteen years. Eventually, the University moved to its current campus in the Oakland section of Pittsburgh in 1909 where it quickly adopted the name the University of Pittsburgh and chose the panther as its mascot.[15]

Even as a private university, the early decades of the twentieth century saw a steady growth in Pitt's size in terms of acreage, student population, and course offerings. In 1898, WUP had an enrollment of nearly 700 students, which would balloon to several thousand in a quarter century. These years also saw the birth of a football tradition at the University. After several losing seasons the football team eventually saw three national championships in the 1910s, twenty-seven consecutive winning seasons from 1913 to 1939, and four Rose Bowl visits, all before World War II. The wealthy steel and industrial magnates of the city provided large sums of money to fund the University's growing athletics programs as well as its endowment. In return the University added greater emphasis on science, engineering, and technology. World War I provided a spark for University growth, as over 1,300 officer trainees flooded the campus as part of the Student Army Training Corps, necessitating the construction of seven wooden barracks. These barracks would remain a part of the University campus for the better part of a decade as the increasing student population required new dormitories and classrooms. During the mid-1920s, the University planned and constructed the most iconic building of the campus—the forty-two-story tall Cathedral of Learning—creating the largest educational structure in the United States. In 1931, the Cathedral of Learning opened for classes when the student population of the University reached its pre-World War II peak of over 14,000 students.[16]

During World War II and the subsequent Cold War, Pitt opened its doors to the military. The Cathedral of Learning became a temporary dormitory for many enrolled in Pitt's Army Specialist Training Program (ASTP) and Civil Affairs Training Schools at the University of Pittsburgh (CATSUP) during World War II. In all, the University trained over seven thousand Army and Navy personnel and saw several thousand students, faculty, staff, and alumni serve in the war—including over 250 women. However, the connection between the University and the military did not dissipate with the end of hostilities in 1945. Thousands of vets flooded into Pitt in the wake of the war and by 1947 more than half of Pitt's 25,700 students were veterans on the G.I. Bill. Pitt became a major research university by the mid-twentieth century providing facilities for a number of important projects including research on the polio vaccine. As a private institution, Pitt had limited access to state funds, but by the early 1960s it was among the top twenty schools receiving federal funds for research and development.[17]

When 41-year-old Edward H. Litchfield arrived at Pitt in 1955 as its twelfth Chancellor, he immediately sought to elevate the University's prestige and grow its physical footprint. Litchfield won national praise for his response to Soviet premier Nikita Khrushchev during the premier's September 1959 visit to the University. Litchfield stated, "The search for truth is our mutual and constant objective. . . . The winner in such a competition will not be your country, or ours, but all mankind." To achieve such success Litchfield undertook an ambitious building project and curricular expansion, for which he believed a growing economy would help provide the necessary support for and into which local elites would be willing to invest. By the early 1960s, despite the large sums of federal research dollars, Pitt was on the brink of financial collapse. In the end, the Board of Trustees decided to turn, in part, to the Pennsylvania legislature, transitioning Pitt from a private university to a state-related institution. However, administrators did not want to become fully a state university for fear that one day the state may refuse to provide adequate funding. With its new state-affiliated status, the University opened to wider numbers of people who would not previously have been able to attend, such as the sons and daughters of the city's steelworkers. By the end of the 1960s the student demographics of the University almost perfectly mirrored the city population.[18]

Pitt students had a history of political activism and dissent. During the Great Depression, students protested wrongful imprisonments of labor activists, the institution of loyalty oaths, and the activities of General Douglas

MacArthur. However, what drew the greatest level of student outrage was the dismissal of popular professor Ralph E. Turner in 1934 for his political support for a radicalization of the New Deal programs of Franklin D. Roosevelt. The University's handling of the Turner affair and its early initiation of anti-communist loyalty oaths foreshadowed the coming McCarthyist scare and to some extent the University's later reaction to the troubles of Professor Robert Colodny in 1960–61. Despite Colodny's four years of service in the Pacific Theater during World War II, his enemies cited his service in the Abraham Lincoln Brigade during the Spanish Civil War (in 1937), his support for the Fair Play for Cuba Committee, and his leadership role in the Pittsburgh chapter of the Committee for a SANE Nuclear Policy as evidence of his Communist subversion and an excuse for his removal from the faculty. Students, and eventually Chancellor Litchfield, rallied around Colodny and helped defend the well-liked professor from the last gasps of McCarthyist attacks on higher education.[19] The Colodny episode demonstrated an active campus with students asserting their influence.

West Virginia University

West Virginia University came into existence in 1868 as a land-grant university under the Morrill Act of 1862. Several existing Morgantown academies and institutes provided the initial nucleus of the University, and the campus remained all male until 1889. As a land-grant institution, WVU housed a corps of cadets since its inception; however, during the First World War, the University began a separate Student Army Training Corps (the forerunner of the Reserve Officer Training Corps).[20]

Football also served as the basis for several of the major traditions and rituals of WVU society. In 1895, four years after their disastrous debut against Washington and Jefferson College (losing 71–0), WVU won the inaugural match against the Western University of Pennsylvania initiating a long-lived rivalry between the two institutions, which became known as "the Backyard Brawl." It was during a football game in 1936 that the University officially debuted the Mountaineer as the school's mascot (though the first version of this character played more on the image of the supposedly ignorant, hayseed mountainfolk of Appalachia than the later version which suggested an imagined, rugged pioneer from a heroic age in the Daniel Boone mold). The Homecoming game became a central component of campus life with the inaugural singing of the *alma mater* in 1938 and the first selection of Homecoming Queen in 1939; the game became the occasion for a parade and dance. Further, to indoctrinate new students into WVU society University policy required freshmen to wear a beanie cap for the first few weeks of the semester, until the Homecoming game.[21]

The students who populated WVU came from throughout the state and the region. Many of these students were the first in their family to attend college; many took part-time jobs to pay for expenses as well as carrying a full-time course load. Like most post-secondary institutions, WVU claimed the right of in loco parentis and sought to oversee the morality of the young people under its charge. The administration set dress codes, established guidelines for social functions that sought to limit unsupervised male-female interactions, and enforced curfews for women living on campus. However, no matter how watchful the administration eye, it could not see or prevent all infractions, and actions such as panty raids became staples of campus life. By-and-large, fraternities and sororities, which first appeared in the 1890s, dominated the campus social scene, as well as campus politics by the 1960s. The black student population on campus was very small, no more than 100 students in 1967; however, the administration engaged in efforts to recruit and retain increasing numbers of black students. Women at WVU, subjected to panty raids and restrictive regulations, participated in the various student activities including governance; however, it wasn't until 1974 that the students elected a woman to the position of student body president.[22]

West Virginia University in the early Cold War years, 1945 to 1960, experienced similar expansions and upheavals as their northern Appalachian counterparts. By 1948, with the assistance of the G.I. Bill, enrollments jumped to over 6,500, nearly doubling prewar figures. By the end of the Sixties the number would double again. The expanding enrollments meant a need for additional facilities to house and educate the growing masses, so the University acquired new property for this development. The University's footprint grew so large that by the early 1970s the University created a Personal Rapid Transit (monorail) system to ease student movement. The University sought to gain access to federal research funds; however, state regulations complicated these efforts, though professors did undertake research beneficial to the coal industry. Students throughout the 1950s and into the early 1960s not only participated in football traditions and panty raids but also questioned the necessity of compulsory ROTC and segregated housing, setting the stage for later activism.[23]

Conclusion

The universities of northern Appalachia have different origin stories; however, during the 1960s their students would wrestle with the same problems and issues. Whether they began their institutional lives as public or private schools, by the mid-1960s all three were public doctoral-granting universities embroiled in the dramatic changes of the decade. Each school experienced large building projects, overflowing student enrollments, and new research opportunities—all part of the Cold War University's shift to the multiversity. The very nature of the university and its role in society were open questions and students struggled to define their roles on campus and in society.

Part 1

1964–1967

In September 1964, freshmen (members of the class of 1968) at West Virginia University listened as the University President, Paul A. Miller, explained the role of the university in American society and the ways the college experience would affect them over and beyond the next four years. Miller argued that education was the key to citizenship and warned students against the traditional distractions of collegiate life—including Greek social organizations—which were good in moderation but in excessive doses could derail any educational endeavor. "You should leave here more ready to practice leadership than to hold a job," Miller argued, going on to encourage students to "Learn to work up to and beyond your ability. Yet be scornful of those who work simply for the grade." In the end, Miller argued students were not in college for a good time, nor to get a degree or simply to prepare for a career; grades, while important, did not matter as much as the pursuit of knowledge. He stated, "The college diploma measures the serving of time but it is never a measure of learning."[1]

Miller said the goal for students was to build the skills of lifelong learners, to challenge themselves, and to become their own advocates for their development as citizens. Universities, such as WVU, afforded opportunities to learn about one's world beyond the limitations of the classroom, but these opportunities only had value if students sought them out. Miller concluded by saying that the students controlled their futures and that they had the right and the obligation to make sure they were prepared to assume these leadership roles, declaring, "the ball is finally in your hands." If the University was not living up to their needs, he called on them to act to improve the University, thereby improving society. Miller implored students, "Stand up and be counted! Throw yourself into the place! . . . Don't be tame. Don't be silent. If you are, the University will grow complacent."[2]

In future years, students would take Miller's message to heart and, as student-citizens, act in ways perhaps beyond how he envisioned they should. They recognized that their limited ability to act could not in itself end all discrimination, stop the war in Vietnam, or erase poverty, yet students felt compelled to act. Further, students accepted that through their actions they helped generate what Robert F. Kennedy termed "tiny ripples of hope" that would amplify off each other and "build a current which can sweep down the mightiest walls of oppression and resistance."[3]

Student activism at northern Appalachian universities between 1964 and 1967 focused on several political and social issues, but grew from a central sense that students, as Miller argued, had an obligation to act and to improve their community. Whether it was the in loco parentis policies of the university, racial discrimination, poverty, or the war in Vietnam, students made direct and tangible links between what was happening on campus with what was going on in the country and the world. As the Students for a Democratic Society's Port Huron Statement made clear, "That student life is more intellectual, and perhaps more comfortable, does not obscure the fact that the fundamental qualities of life on the campus reflect the habits of society at large." This New Left call to action would go further to argue that the university and students represent crucial social actors with which to forge a movement to break down the racist and classist Cold War consensus that had used fear and economic manipulation to retain power. The principles of participatory democracy called for students to take greater control over the governance of their lives on campus and in so doing create a model for expanded citizen participation in the governance of society.[4] However, it was not just New Left students who engaged in political and social activism, rather wide swaths of students had to come to terms with changing definitions of studentness caused by the confluence of mass education, the military-industrial complex, and a widening challenge to the Cold War political consensus.

The period 1964 to 1967 represents a transitional period for student political and social activism as students sought to expand their power and influence over the decision-making structures of the university and society. Students around the nation and in northern Appalachia moved from supposedly acceptable modes of political expression, such as mock political conventions, and relatively passive participation in the political process—characterized by listening to, not participating in, lectures or debates by experts—to increasingly active, student-directed engagement with political and social issues, such as "bleed-ins," silent protests, and marches. In part, this transition stemmed from the growing centrality of the war in Vietnam in the lives of students and a sense of urgency about the war (through the institution of the draft).

Interconnectivity became one of the recurring themes essential to later activism. It manifested as student participation in multiple socio-economic, political, and cultural movements simultaneously, as well as through the college existence of these students, which they argued directly related to the wider world and vice versa. In other words, the college campus was not isolated from its local community or the nation-at-large, but vitally connected. In this way, as students challenged in loco parentis policies, they sought to challenge the sense of estrangement and isolation generated by the perceived dehumanizing conformity of American society. This empowerment to address campus issues directly correlated to the impulse to construct empowered poor and minority communities, able to serve as their own advocates in the halls of government of the nation.

The multiversity, like American society itself, had become so vast that students felt lost amongst the masses. Increasingly, students engaged in activism to force others to confront their individuality and through this personal liberation, they hoped to forge new communities based on the centrality of the individual. In his work on student activists in Texas, Doug Rossinow argued, "student dissenters leaned on the legitimacy enjoyed by universities as havens of free thought" for the construction of an authentic and radical response to the depersonalization of Cold War American society.[5] Thus, the student unrest that would define the entirety of the Vietnam War era, including at northern Appalachian universities, grew from this desire to forge new connections of the individual with society, and a sense of obligation inherent in the meaning of student and citizen drove this impulse.

The student-citizen identity represents the melding of two community associations within the individual of the student, that of citizen of the university and citizen of the nation. The rights, privileges, duties, and obligations of citizenship in one community intimately and directly tied to those of the other. In 1964, many students lacked the ability to vote, the ability to participate in the decision-making process of the nation, so too they felt that they lacked an adequate voice in the decision-making apparatus of the university. To build an empowered community able to influence the national community, students sought to foster a parallel, empowered student community to influence the university. Some saw victories in the university as more likely and therefore as necessary steps in wider enfranchisement.

By-and-large, the student-citizen identity rested on an active participation in the political process and drew inspiration from New Left conceptions of participatory democracy. The student-citizen identity was not simply another name for the New Left, though the New Left fully embraced this identity. Students all along the political spectrum began to accept, on some level, components of the student-citizen identity; although, predominately, it was individuals to the political left who took up this identity with the greatest zeal.

As social and political movements grew outside the university community, student-citizens found new outlets for their expressions of citizenship. Engaging in civil rights or antipoverty activism provided a bridge to other forms of activism with the same goals—the expansion of the political process and the social sphere to more and more people. In 1964, few students called for greater control over the decisions that affected their daily lives, a key component of the burgeoning student-citizen identity, despite participation in inherently political activities. By 1967, large numbers of students had come to embrace this identity on some level. The debates became not whether students should have a part to play in decision-making but how large the role should be and how to determine those who would play it. Increasingly, students were calling on their classmates to get off the sidelines and get involved, seeing earlier forms of student participation as too weak an expression of engaged citizenship.[6] Throughout the period 1964 to 1967, the language that students used showed that they saw themselves as legitimate stakeholders whose views and opinions shared as much weight as (perhaps, even more than) any other constituency in the university. Moreover, students argued that if they were members of one community—the university—they were equally members of the other—the nation.

Chapter 2

Claiming Control on Campus

Paternalism and Political Participation

In the years since the end of World War II, college campuses had seen little in the way of disruptive student activism for larger national and international issues despite the rapid changes brought to the universities by the Cold War, its expanding military-industrial-academic complex, and the development of the multiversity. A relatively quiescent status quo emerged, based in both the domestic anticommunism of the era and what scholar Beth Bailey identified as the dominant American view of college as a place to instill a culture of respectability and general middle-class ethos. College administrators saw their role as preparing good citizens with the proper middle-class moral values. The longstanding in loco parentis doctrine, the idea that college administrators stood in for parents in terms of ensuring specific moral or ethical behavior, served this mid-century cultural desire and led to the governing of such things as the hours female students kept and the implementation of dormitory visitation regulations. The resulting paternalistic relationship gave administrators the latitude to police the social mores of the young people at their institutions. The creation of good moral character and a respect for the status quo became important components of Cold War universities.[1]

Even when students played pranks or broke rules during these early Cold War years, administrators and the general public viewed these actions not as a threat to the larger stability of society, but rather as adolescent antics that students would grow out of as they matured. The popular imagination conceived of education as the path to eventual citizenship. Further, the generally accepted emphasis of extracurricular activities, like Greek social organizations, reinforced the notion that students should not challenge the overarching system.

The universities seemed to accept Greek social societies as a mechanism for acculturating new students and maintaining university traditions, given the mid-century Greek social system's reticence to challenge established norms. Greeks became the dominant force in campus politics, controlling student governments and serving as a central focus of campus newspapers. Their activities strained against though never broke with the parent-child antagonism of in loco parentis and never threatened to disrupt the existing social order of the university.[2] However, by the mid-1960s, groups of students had begun to challenge policies enacted by the universities to maintain and perpetuate that status quo, often using the same language of respectability and responsibility used by administrators to reinforce the system to make claims of citizenship within the university.

By 1967, one can clearly see the formation of a student conception of dual citizenship, that as a citizen of the university and of the nation. In an opinion editorial for Ohio University's *Post*, columnist Richard Pesin argued that the role of the University was to develop leaders who could speak for their communities—on campus and beyond. Pesin argued:

> Students here, like students across the nation, are dedicated to getting the grade, because society has set that as the most sought-after goal. Without grades it is difficult to make it into the world of security after graduation. But education has not been developing enough leaders. . . . But to be a leader, one must do something. A student must have the responsibility to develop his own abilities to organize and create. . . . But most education is lecture-oriented, text directed. Courses are isolated from one another. Developments in politics, economics, and the arts are treated separately in different courses. And everything is taught in the classroom. But the true laboratory for the leader cannot be the classroom at all times. For a real and contemporary experience, the opportunity to work with the real and the contemporary must be present. . . . Students who involved themselves in the community action programs in the vicinity are learning to become leaders.[3]

Thus, according to Pesin, the state of education created false divisions between the multiple impulses that affected individuals daily. The emphasis on the classroom as the sole site of education on campus deprived students of important educational opportunities and stunted their development, especially as leaders. Pesin was making an argument not just for the recalibration of education but also for the rise of student-citizens, like those who had already begun to participate in community action projects.

The struggle against in loco parentis policies expanded into a wider critique of the university and into calls for greater student input on issues from ROTC to the rights of workers on campus. The attacks made on campus policies, such as dormitory rules and visitations (known as parietals), came through the sanctioned challenges of student government, the campus newspapers, and the circulation of petitions. There were virtually no disruptive demonstrations held during the years 1964 to 1967 over the issues related to in loco parentis. However, by 1966, the likelihood of disturbances had increased as students debated ROTC and added their strength to a disruptive labor strike at OU in 1967. There was, not surprisingly, no singular student position on parietals, ROTC, or other campus policies, but rather a wide spectrum of opinion ranging from full-throated support to utter disdain. However, most students who entered the fray over in loco parentis used similar language, that of respectability, citizenship, and security.

Women's Hours and Parietals

The challenge to universities' parietals policies revolved around a growing student vision of citizenship and calls for solidarity in their shared studentness. Some students argued that rather than divide themselves up along petty differences—over fashion or music tastes—students needed to come together and recognize what they had in common. Editorials and letters to the editor questioned whether any university could effectively take on a parental role to thousands of young people and complained about the supposedly archaic rules regarding women's dress and discipline. They challenged the duplicity of such policies, arguing that the university claimed students were adults but treated them like children.

The role of women on campus and in American society was a hotly debated topic by the mid-1960s, and northern Appalachia was not immune to these issues. Scholars such as Elaine Tyler May, Stephanie Coontz, and Beth Bailey have argued that the postwar emphasis on female domesticity came under increased scrutiny at this time, and the mechanisms for the distribution of these cultural modes of behavior—such as university's parietals policies—became targets for reform.[4] Further, the general tensions between young people and adults intermixed with a growing sense of political awareness amongst students to make the challenge to in loco parentis more than simple youthful rebellion but a call to societal change. Students argued they were adult enough to make their own decisions free from paternalistic administrators. Thus, the actions of northern Appalachian students to resist and change their campuses' parietals policies support Bailey's argument that "Those who disputed the doctrines of in loco parentis, however, polite, were engaged in revolution."[5]

In 1964, while making a national tour in support of her book, *The Feminine Mystique*, Betty Friedan made appearances at the University of Pittsburgh and West Virginia University. Her visits sparked wider debates on these campuses about the role of women in society.[6] At WVU, the *Daily Athenaeum* informed students of Friedan's impending lecture about the need to challenge the myths and accepted truths surrounding the subordination of female identity to husbands or families. In the same article announcing Friedan's talk, the author also instructed female students, with seemingly no sense of irony, to take care to sign out appropriately with their housemothers so as not to receive late penalties if the discussion ran later than curfew.[7]

Nearly two months after Friedan's lecture at Pitt, the *Pitt News* ran an opinion editorial written by a Pitt student, under the dubious title "A Forced Equality," that challenged several of Friedan's basic arguments and linked the issue of women's identity to the campus movement against in loco parentis. In her editorial, Nancy Fuchs argued that the University's parental role toward women was, if not wholly appropriate, at least acceptable. Fuchs argued that the type of liberation Friedan advocated was neither the goal nor the desire of all women. Many women, Fuchs included herself, preferred a future role as housewife and mother with no need for an independent life beyond these things. "If men resent the modern woman's attempt to set herself up as their equal, how much more so does a woman resent being forced into a position she does not want—that of equality with men. . . . I appreciate the opportunity of receiving a good education, but I resent being forced to accept it." Fuchs concluded by saying she did not want to move to "complete equality . . . I prefer to stand still," therein suggesting that she saw nothing amiss with restrictive women's hours.[8]

When and how students, especially female students, could come and go represented one way the university exercised in loco parentis, but administrators could also demonstrate authority by limiting housing options and restricting other activities of students. In a letter to the editor of the *Post*, Stu Sharpe noted a "double standard" in Ohio University's dealing with students—that the University declared students were adults but treated them like children. Sharpe attacked the University's housing policies as well as, indirectly, women's hours, suggesting that the regulations did not help students prepare to enter the larger society upon graduation, but rather suspended them in a prolonged stage of adolescence. "Our professors encourage us to challenge them in their classrooms, to question rather than accept on word alone," Sharp argued, "why should we not responsibly challenge our administrators." He concluded that "The responsible element of Ohio University's student population has time and again demonstrated that it can and will assume the responsibility of adulthood."[9] Sharpe's arguments and language of responsibility anticipated similar arguments made one year later at the University of Kansas, which historian Beth Bailey discusses at length in *Sex in the Heartland*. Bailey argued that administrators and society-at-large saw higher education as a conduit that inculcated students, as future citizens, with "the values of responsibility, maturity, and citizenship," and that students appropriated this language in their challenge of in loco parentis.[10]

Additional letters to the *Post* echoed Sharpe's criticisms. Ned Whelan's letter argued that "everyday, another liberty is usurped from us" and went on to articulate a direct connection between the rights of students on campus and the rights of citizens within the nation, drawing links to the call for solidarity amongst students as a class, through both Karl Marx and the Declaration of Independence. Whelan lamented that many of his fellow students were not concerned with learning but with earning a degree and that the University seemed "intent upon stamping out all deviation" from this path, noting, "There is no right to question whether the regulation is valid—just punishment for violation." Such authoritarian policies ran counter to the notion of citizenship in America and thereby the University, according to Whelan, who further insisted that as citizens, students had a right to have their voices heard in University decision-making or else "remain unquestioning slaves to this administration."[11]

Not all critiques of the University were as blatantly political as Whelan's, some preferred humor and satire to challenge administration policies. In a letter published on February 25, 1964, four female students offered a tongue-in-cheek evaluation of the University's in loco parentis policies. They emphasized the issue of student responsibility that Sharpe and Whelan spoke of saying, "As coeds, we feel secure in the protection given us through the generous hours system formulated by our benevolent administration. . . . We are not old enough to know how to behave." The letter included other sarcastic and ironic notes of "praise" for the administration's watchful eye over them.[12]

In all three cases, the authors' arguments seem to reflect the accepted view of college as a time when they developed respectable citizenship. Furthermore, they asked that administrators give students the opportunity to exercise the responsibility they were cultivating; in other words, their criticisms do not reflect radical political views but rather a logical outgrowth of mainstream views of higher education and citizenship. In addressing what they saw as a possible contradiction between the statements and actions of the University—that students were adults but treated like children—the students at OU were highlighting an issue that would become a central component of student activism for the next decade. Further, their demands for redress of these grievances stood on the grounds of the rights and privileges of adult citizens, that if not enclosed in the bubble of the college campus, these policies would not be a part of their lives. The arguments reveal a burgeoning notion of the student as a peculiar identity and yet somehow intimately linked with the idea of citizenship.[13]

Students at WVU leveled part of their criticism at the campus women's governance organization, the Allied Women Students (AWS), for being too ineffective in advocating for change or for being too zealous in maintaining the status quo. In October 1966, leadership of the AWS announced, "that unladylike conduct in the [residence hall] lounge will be dealt with severely." Furthermore, women who failed to accurately "record grace minutes when they are taken" would face restrictions, which meant confining them to their room. In response, an editorial in the *Daily Athenaeum* opined, "If AWS is going to send college women to their rooms as though they are children, it may as well start administering spankings, too." The editorial concluded that while "AWS has made much progress in adapting rules that acknowledge University women as adults. Let us hope that in the future, all AWS rules will be fashioned according to this principle."[14]

Meanwhile, in the fall of 1966, at OU, resident assistants created a petition calling for an end to women's hours. The RAs argued they had the right to issue such a petition because they served as "the extension of the administrative arm, in essence its fingertips, and in closest contact with the students." However, rather than confront officials with the petition and demand action, the students passed the petition up through the sanctioned channels of student government and publicly stated they were unconvinced that any real changes would be forthcoming while praising themselves for having confronted the issue in a responsible manner.[15]

Throughout the period 1964 to 1967, students increasingly linked the questions of students' rights and challenges to in loco parentis to wider political and social concerns, progressively losing distinct coverage in the campus newspapers. One of the earliest examples of this conflation appears in March 1964 when the *Post* ran an editorial imploring OU students to act to affect changes in their society, especially at the University, rather than simply talk about the issues. The editorial admitted that it was important to discuss the issues, but change would not come from talking, "action speaks more effectively." The editorial concluded by suggesting that activism was worth it: "It's worth it if our University grows with the times as well as on the drawing board. It's worth it if every student gets from his education as much in the way of a learning experience as is possible. It's worth it if we can leave Ohio proud of ourselves for taking a stand and proud of the University for listening."[16] The plea was nonpartisan and suggested that students could find a sense of fulfillment and pride that was missing from their current lives and that through actively engaging with their society they were enhancing their education and breaking down the barriers of isolation within modern American society. The call to action made no specific policy prescriptions, only that students should not shy away from taking an active role in their community, such as participating in the 1964 presidential election—at least, to the extent that young people without a right to vote could participate.

Politics on Campus

Between 1964 and 1967, northern Appalachian students engaged with politics, adapting their existing participation in approved activities to more confrontational activities. In 1964, Mock Republican conventions provided a legitimate and approved space for students to demonstrate their ability to be respectable, responsible citizens. The debating skills honed here would carry over to the campus issues of military training and whether the unique situation of the Reserve Officer Training Corps (ROTC) program made it consistent with the university's mission. Finally, in the spring of 1967, students at OU participated in and supported a unionization effort by its nonacademic staff, claiming a right to weigh in on the issue as an effected constituency. From mock convention to real strike, students at northern Appalachian campuses were becoming more assertive in their expression of citizenship at the university and in the nation.

The largest political activity on the campuses of northern Appalachia during 1964 revolved around the impending presidential election. Several campuses held mock Republican conventions, part of a larger nationwide phenomenon, which served as an approved arena for political expression. Students only held mock Republican conventions, not surprising given the openness of the race for the GOP nomination and President Johnson's nearly assured acclamation by the Democrats. Students served as delegates, heard campaign speeches, and voted in an orderly (as orderly as a convention can be) fashion, selecting presidential and vice-presidential nominees.

Interestingly enough, none of the northern Appalachian schools selected Barry Goldwater as the standard-bearer for the Republican Party, a trend consistent with the nationwide state mock conventions. Rather, students supported more moderate to liberal candidates such as Nelson Rockefeller, Henry Cabot Lodge, William Scranton, and George Romney. The organizers of the conventions stressed that they hoped to raise political awareness as well as recognition for the process of electoral politics.[17]

The conventions suggested a limited interpretation of political expression and certainly did not support the chaotic participatory democracy already at the root of organizations such as Students of a Democratic Society or the Student Nonviolent Coordinating Committee. The mock conventions were consistent with the existing Cold War political participation this generation had engaged in: symbolic of American patriotism and promoting civic engagement.[18] While they could attend political rallies or debates, for many students, too young to vote in the upcoming election, these mock conventions served as their only direct connection to the political process.

Throughout the fall, the approaching presidential election continued to be the major political concern on campus as the two major candidates crisscrossed northern Appalachia making stops in Athens, Morgantown, and Pittsburgh, with their surrogates making several more appearances. The student papers were alive with election coverage, discussing the candidates' positions on a variety of issues of concern to students. Although students attended rallies and speeches held by the candidates or their respective parties, there was little other political participation, aside from a random letter or two to the editor. Students occasionally invited a surrogate for one of the candidates to speak, but they did not hold their own rallies or demonstrations to try to encourage direct participation in the political process—things that would later become an essential component of Sixties political activism. Rather, in 1964, students made claims to citizenship through adhering to the respectable and responsible modes of political expression deemed acceptable by the wider society.[19]

A longstanding issue brought up prior to the 1960s but gaining renewed traction in the growing debate over students' citizenship and the role of the university in American society by mid-decade was that of the Reserve Officer Training Corps.[20] Although obviously a question of American militarism, students framed the mid-1960s ROTC debates on northern Appalachian campuses within notions of the role of the university in American society and whether ROTC fulfilled that mission. Connected, often as an auxiliary argument, was the link between ROTC and the American war effort. This is seen most clearly in the actions of Pitt's Students for Peace (SFP) in the summer of 1966 when they undertook a campaign targeting the University's ROTC program.

Barely a year old at Pitt, SFP had gotten into a tussle with the administration three months earlier over the distribution of literature to incoming freshmen and its supposed links to "subversive organizations" like Students for a Democratic Society (SDS). Students for Peace distributed literature about the International Days of Protest (in March 1966) at a freshmen preview weekend, which some students and administrators felt violated a series of rules against organizations recruiting pre-freshmen. Members of SFP argued that asking potential students to attend a rally coordinated by groups at multiple local colleges was not a recruitment effort. When Helen P. Rush, Vice Chancellor for Student Affairs, contacted SFP, the person answering the telephone identified the office as both SFP and SDS. The University had not officially recognized SDS as a student organization on the Pitt campus. As a result the administration questioned whether SFP was simply a front for the unofficial SDS chapter. In the end, SFP received a minor punishment for its actions and administrators found no improper connection in the shared office space with SDS as the administration recognized SFP as a separate organization from SDS.[21]

The issue SFP raised against ROTC during the summer of 1966 targeted the supposedly special position afforded the program on campus. Students for

Peace argued that military education was antithetical to the mission of the University. Unlike any other program at the University, ROTC had the right to solicit students during orientation, which SFP felt was inappropriate at best. Frank Couvares, Treasurer of SFP, argued that the role of the university was to help students "form opinions, to articulate them, and to defend and advocate them," especially regarding such things as America's war in Vietnam. However, Couvares argued that ROTC's mission was military indoctrination not the promotion of free thought necessary for citizenship, saying, "The University must realize the contrariety of military indoctrination and training on the college campus."[22]

Students for Peace wondered aloud how it could be that the University argued that students were too immature to make informed decisions about housing or what hours to keep but mature enough to learn the lessons of war. Such a contradiction meant either parietals or ROTC had to go because they could not coexist logically. Couvares argued students had an obligation to challenge those things they believed were inconsistent with the mission of the university in society, such as ROTC, saying: "Students, becoming less and less convinced of the soundness of consensus policy, have responded to their obligation, though for some, perhaps, belatedly. They must continue to meet their commitments and maintain their integrity. They will, hopefully, clearly proclaim that agreement is not truth, popularity is not soundness and consensus is not democracy."[23] For Couvares, and others in SFP, already existing on campus with little concern for its status was not sufficient reasoning for ROTC to continue as it had. Pitt's ROTC fight joined an expanding anti-ROTC movement growing around the nation as involvement in Vietnam consumed more attention. For now, though, one feels a growing sense, among some at Pitt, of a student-citizen identity; however, a wide range of campus issues helped forge this notion of student-citizenship.

The campus issue at OU that sparked the greatest discussion of student roles as citizens of the University and the nation occurred in spring 1967 when a question of union rights, amongst non-academic employees at the University, entangled students. In early March, the University administration refused to accept a request for employees to have union dues deducted from their paychecks, launching a series of protests that stretched nearly ten days. Students participated in this dispute from its earliest stages and in so doing suggested a that there was a greater connection between students and organized labor, in some circumstances, than perhaps the assumed narrative of the period would suggest. For some students, the question of labor rights was an obviously personal issue, having relatives in various miners', teamsters', and industrial workers' unions.

Early in the standoff, Ohio University's student government passed resolutions supporting the strikers and calling on the University administration to recognize the employee union. They organized efforts to collect funds for striking workers and even coordinated efforts to bring coffee and donuts to picketers. Many students marched the picket lines, signed statements of solidarity, or walked away from their work-study jobs to symbolize their support.[24] Student government president Daniel DeNicola argued that students had a role to play in the union debate not only as members of the University community but also as responsible citizens of the United States. DeNicola had become the first independent president of OU's student government, challenging the status quo power of Greek organizations on campus. The union issue represented another challenge to entrenched power.[25]

A sustained weeklong campaign by non-academic workers and students, forced the University to capitulate. By the third day of the strike, March 8, University President Vernon R. Alden advised students that if they persisted it might force the University to close, at which point students would lose their activities fees and receive no academic credit for the partial session. However, the threat backfired. Rather than stopping their efforts, the students pushed harder after the threat, attempting to call the administration's bluff. Campus rallies and a march drew upwards of four thousand students—slightly less than half of the student body. Ultimately, the administration decided to move Spring Break two weeks earlier to relieve pressure caused by the striking workers and their student allies.[26]

In the end, the University gave into the employees' demands. The administration recognized the new union and returned workers to their positions without prejudice. Some students questioned whether the actions of the student government during the strike had served to harm its position relative to the student body and the administration. They worried that such a loss of confidence and respectability could make it harder for the organization to speak effectively for student concerns. Daniel DeNicola and his supporters, however, argued that the student government's relevance and authority were at an all-time high.[27] If nothing else, the events of March 1967 proved to some in the administration and the student body that OU students were not completely apathetic or without the ability to cause campus-wide disturbances.

In early April, the *Post* published a letter from student John T. Nixon that expressed a strong conviction that OU students had already forged a student-citizen identity, even if they did not march in massive protests across the College Green. Nixon argued that the "depersonalization" wrought by America's conformist culture and the isolation generated by mass education in the form of the multiversity had led students to "reject this whole life as it really is—phony." Nixon went on to argue:

> The university is seen as a microcosm of society, which the student views before he enters it, a culture characterized by impersonality in business, in living arrangements, even in social life—a culture in which nobody dares to be himself, and everybody wears a mask for fear he may be found to be in deviation at some point from conformity. . . . Part, indeed, of the adult restiveness in the face of student revolt is surely based on the disturbing accuracy with which the younger generation has unmasked the pretentiousness and insecurity of the older. . . . So, the wheel comes full circle, with the university being part of the establishment students reject. He sees too many trustees and administrators and faculty members working hand in glove with a society dedicated to human destruction and the denial of the meaning of personhood. . . . He sees the university training him to be an uncomplaining middle class person, adjusted to all the proper middle class mores, doing nothing to jar the well-oiled machinery called the Great Society.[28]

Nixon identified the struggle of students with a generational tension but mostly with a conformist establishment unwilling to allow young people to pursue their individuality. He argued that as students and citizens, young people had an obligation to challenge the stilted vision of personhood created by American society. He further questioned the role of the university in American society—whether it existed to generate technicians or to create thinkers. In total, Nixon presented the underlying issue at the center of much student protest and activism during the Vietnam War era, a discomfort with and desire to change the nature of American society from one that fears individuality to one that embraces the eclectic nature of humanity. For Nixon, education was not indoctrination but a gateway to the many possibilities of human endeavors. In the end, Nixon argued that students could not wait until they were older to try to affect change—by then they would be part of the system; thus, change could only come from the youth of America.[29]

Conclusion

Between 1964 and 1967, students at northern Appalachian universities became increasingly active in campus concerns. Students argued that as citizens of the university they had a right to participate in the decisions that affected their lives, including the hours they kept and the courses of study they pursued. They asserted a parallel structure between the rights of citizens within a democracy and that of students of the university.

A November 1965 article in OU's *Post* offers a fitting description of these years. The *Post* editor Joe Eszterhas took issue with a contemporary editorial in the *Pittsburgh Press* that blamed a permissive, liberal society for creating the situation in which youthful radicals could arise. Eszterhas lamented that editorials like this were all too common, and argued: "Our decade of college students has long been berated for its lack of activism. Now we find ourselves involving ourselves in serious issues, find ourselves playing a major role in issues like Civil Rights and Vietnam. And yet the same public which originally criticized us for lack of involvement is slashing into us, like the Pittsburgh PRESS, for the very involvement we are now demonstrating." Eszterhas went on to argue that the reason for the backlash from older generations was that young people were challenging foundational ideas held by the Depression Generation, which they never intended for college students to challenge. He stated, "Though we were supposed to think and act in college, we were supposed to think and act in predefined, preconceived ways." Eszterhas' critique spoke for his generation and concluded, "We have no need for elders who reject us simply because they disagree with us."[30]

Chapter 3

Building Empowered Communities

Civil Rights and Poverty Activism

The question of where, when, and why student activism developed across college and university campuses continues to occupy historians of the Sixties. Traditionally, the Free Speech Movement in the fall of 1964 at the University of California, Berkeley, has served as the starting point. Doug McAdam's *Freedom Summer* offered an alternative vision locating the origin of white, northern student activism in the Mississippi Freedom Project in the summer of 1964. He specifically noted how participation affected leaders of the Free Speech Movement, such as Mario Savio, by generating a confidence through what scholar Doug Rossinow would call "authenticity" of experience.[1] Unfortunately, McAdam's thesis that Freedom Summer represents the germinal moment of Sixties student activism does not fully account for the origins of student social activism in northern Appalachia. McAdam's work rightly points to a key element in the origins and development of northern, white student activism—the interconnectedness of various social and political movements and ideas. For some northern Appalachian students the entry point was anti-poverty activism, not civil rights. Noting these different initiators helps historians see that the movement was broader, and its beginnings much looser than any single event, however significant that event was.

The War on Poverty declared by President Lyndon B. Johnson focused a large portion of its firepower on the Appalachian front. Americans in the Sixties struggled to understand the continued existence of poverty in a country supposedly overflowing in abundance. Building from President John F. Kennedy's call to address the "unconquered pockets of ignorance and prejudice [and the] unanswered questions of poverty and surplus," President Lyndon Johnson turned to the nation's youth as the engine of change. Speaking to a crowd of students in Athens, Ohio, Johnson called the eradication of poverty "the glory of your generation," if students were willing to take up the burden of expanding opportunity to their fellow citizens. Through the Economic Opportunity Act of 1964 and the Appalachian Redevelopment Act of 1965, the Johnson administration provided the poor with the tools to organize and empower themselves politically, creating a countervailing force to that of local business and political elites. However, it would be the actions of individuals on the ground that would potentially win the war.[2]

Civil Rights

Since the mid-1990s, historians of the civil rights era have sought to contextualize the black freedom struggle within the Cold War framework, destabilize the King-centric narrative, and emphasize the role played by individuals at the grassroots, local level. Scholars such as John Dittmer, Mary Dudziak, and Nancy MacLean have been at the forefront of these efforts.[3] Moving beyond the attacks on Southern Jim Crow Laws, scholars such as Martha Biondi and Matthew Countryman have also begun to focus on the North and how civil rights activism addressed *de facto* segregation.[4] Increasingly, historians such as Michael Friedland and Simon Hall have explored the cross-causal nature of civil rights activism, especially in terms of antiwar efforts, and attempted to understand the relationship of northern, white college students to the wider movement for civil rights and black power.[5]

Before the Freedom Summer campaign of 1964, despite increasing calls for action, students at northern Appalachian universities still largely remained only tangentially connected to the expanding direct actions evolving around them. This distance appears in how students engaged with the movement for civil rights at Ohio University and the University of Pittsburgh in the spring of 1964. Students went to performances and lectures by activists and leaders in the freedom struggle, such as John Lewis (president of SNCC), comedian Dick Gregory, and the Freedom Singers. The students listened to the impassioned calls for action and the dire warnings of potential violence in the summer ahead.[6] At a performance in Pittsburgh at Carnegie Tech (sponsored by the college's Liberal Club), students from both Tech and Pitt listened as the Philadelphia-based Freedom Singers sang protest songs and spoke about the upcoming Freedom Summer event. The group's spokesperson, Matthew Jones, sent chills through those assembled when he warned them that, "There are no two ways about it, someone is going to die there this summer. Someone is going to die."[7]

Despite this participation, few northern Appalachian students took any action to confront racism and discrimination in their communities, and only a handful would later join the Freedom Summer campaign. One of the few instances of active student involvement in the civil rights movement came when WVU students traveled to North Carolina during their Easter Break in 1964 to help register black voters. Participant Dan Stubbs recalled his motivation for going, "It's hard to sit at home and gain insight into the civil rights dilemma of today. So we didn't. We came to find out the why and wherefore, to get the experience and through doing, understand."[8] For Stubbs and his companions, active participation on their part had greater meaning than simply talking about issues.

As spring moved into summer, the focus of the campus newspapers was still largely on the Greek social groups and other extracurricular fun, not social or political activism. Behind this reflection of traditional college experiences came calls for students to participate in new activities. Students and faculty asked fellow campus community members to get involved politically, including in summer civil rights projects. The editors of the *Pitt News* admonished students to "Go South!" and join the Freedom Summer campaign "challenging the white power structure [in Mississippi.]"[9] This duality between what the paper covered and what the editors advocated demonstrates the conflicted nature of campuses in the mid-1960s.

The city of Pittsburgh had a strong civil rights movement by the early 1960s, yet for the most part students did not directly participate in local civil rights activism. Joe W. Trotter, Eric Ledell Smith, Jared N. Day, and Ralph Proctor have provided several recent studies of Pittsburgh's civil rights activism highlighting the struggles against *de facto* segregation within the city.[10] However, it appears that students at Pitt largely did not involve themselves in these efforts until closer to the end of the decade. The *Pitt News* did report on, and a small handful of students seem to have supported, a local community action program in the Oakland neighborhood surrounding Pitt in late 1963. Participation in the Hill Education Program, a tutoring program aimed at disadvantaged black elementary and secondary students in the Hill District near campus, represented perhaps the largest off-campus civil rights activism Pitt students engaged in during the period 1964 to 1967. By-and-large, while the students made intellectual and rhetorical connections to the wider civil rights movement, they appear, in these middle years of the 1960s, to have focused their activism—when they were active—toward campus or by traveling to sites of national importance such as Freedom Summer in 1964 or Selma, Alabama, in 1965.[11]

Around half a dozen northern Appalachian students participated in 1964's Freedom Summer, though exact numbers are hard to determine. From Ohio University, Bonnie Guy, Jan Lipzin, and David Prince went south after receiving training at the Western College for Women in Oxford, Ohio. Bonnie Guy was a member of the Athens chapter of the Student Peace Union; it is unknown whether Lipzin or Prince were members. The dangerous nature of their work became evident for Prince when several white youths attacked him while he photographed a rally in Selma, Alabama.[12]

Over the course of the summer, Guy sent several letters to the *Post* detailing the work she was involved in and the realities of repression in Mississippi. "The summer volunteers are experiencing how intimidation impedes the freedom of Negroes in the South," Guy reported in late-July. She went on to define "freedom," saying, "Freedom here is material. It is paved streets, sewers and the end to substandard education in segregated schools. Freedom is the election of public officials who are color blind in the administration of their power and taxation. Freedom is the escape from poverty that is predetermined because of the color of one's skin." Guy's letters describe the crushing poverty faced by blacks in Mississippi and argued "This is a huge problem involving more than civil rights for the Negroes but with economic problems involving the whole country." In her final letter that summer, Guy reported on the impatience of black youths in the South regarding the slow progress toward equality and cautioned, "The unrest within them, which may explode as civil rights tensions increase this summer, should serve a warning to those who dawdle in the enforcement of justice."[13]

Guy's letters highlighted the radicalization process Doug McAdam spoke of in his work, *Freedom Summer*. McAdam argued that participation in the Mississippi Summer Project radicalized white students and fueled their later activism. However, Guy was already a member of a politically active and socially conscious group prior to her activities in Mississippi. While undoubtedly the Freedom Summer project had a dramatic effect on its participants, it may be, if Guy's experience is any guide, that those who volunteered in the first place and who made it through the screening and training processes represented a subset of activists most likely to have a predisposition toward radicalization. Thus, it may be less that Freedom Summer radicalized its participants than the summer project gave focus and direction to pre-existing inclinations. Regardless, it was not just students from elite colleges on the coasts that participated in Freedom Summer, and the skills, ideologies, and tactics developed in Mississippi's steamy summer took root in the universities of northern Appalachia.

Following Freedom Summer, the student newspapers' coverage of the civil rights movement and topics associated with the struggle for racial equality declined significantly, all but disappearing. Civil rights leaders did continue to visit northern Appalachia, but issues of civil rights became largely subsumed in discussions of the impending 1964 presidential election. Speaking to an overflowing crowd of 750 at Pitt in late-September 1964, James Farmer, Director of C.O.R.E., argued that the civil rights struggle was not limited to the American South and praised the students at Pitt for their dedication, commitment, and engagement. Farmer also stated that the election of Barry Goldwater "would be disastrous . . . [as Goldwater] is actively trying to encourage a white backlash," which would generate significant violence. In early October, the *Post* ran an article by student Morris Baines, in which he explored the impact of civil rights on the contest for the presidency and concluded, "Civil rights . . . may be the most important issue of this presidential campaign."[14]

Where only a handful of northern Appalachian students took part in Freedom Summer in 1964, over one hundred and fifty participants from the region marched in the demonstrations in Alabama after the events on Selma's Edmund Pettus Bridge in March 1965. Few of those heading south referenced Freedom Summer as a reason why they felt compelled to board buses and speed their way to Alabama; however, almost all argued some form of justification as citizens in a democracy or humanitarian duty. Where Freedom Summer, and the whole civil rights movement, had seemed to that point largely something that "others" engaged in, Selma became something to which the students of northern Appalachia saw themselves personally tied. This was perhaps due to the images of young people, like SNCC leader John Lewis, brutalized by police for engaging in a peaceful demonstration.

Several students from WVU traveled to Alabama within only a few days of the attack at the Edmund Pettus Bridge. They would remain in the state for many of the events that unfolded over the next two and a half weeks, participating in several small demonstrations and marches. Within a week of Bloody

Sunday (March 7, 1965), over 130 students, faculty, and ministers from Pitt and several of the other colleges and universities in the city boarded buses and headed to Alabama to march in protest of segregation, repression, and injustice. During their activities in Alabama, the Pitt students experienced firsthand the confusion and discomfort of tear gas as well as the fear induced by savage police attacks. A few of the students returned to Pittsburgh with broken bones as souvenirs. Traveling to Alabama was not the only way that Pittsburgh students participated in the events of mid-March; over 800 individuals came out to be part of a march through the Oakland section of Pittsburgh in honor of the life of a Unitarian Universalist minister from Boston, James Reeb, who was killed in Selma by white segregationists. Of the nearly two dozen OU students, faculty, and ministers who participated in the 25,000-person march into Montgomery on March 25, none experienced the violence or brutality of their Pittsburgh counterparts, though they did face down white intimidation as they made their way to the capital.[15]

Although less than two hundred of the several thousands of students who attended northern Appalachian universities made treks to Alabama for the marches and demonstrations in Selma and Montgomery, their efforts rippled through their respective student bodies in ways that Freedom Summer had not. Those who participated in the Alabama events came back and told their experiences to fellow students, sometimes in formal settings as a guest lecturer for a student organization function. It was an unusual experience for some to sit as the expert amongst their colleagues, occupying a role heretofore limited to professors or invited dignitaries.[16] Selma had done for them what Freedom Summer had done for individuals such as University of California at Berkeley student leader Mario Savio: it provided an authentic experience that validated their devotion to activism and change while serving as a wellspring of strength one could tap into during future demonstrations and actions. Those who participated in the events of March 1965 in Alabama became sources of inspiration for many of their classmates. As summer approached, some students announced plans to participate in civil rights and antipoverty projects and cited their fellow students' willingness to put their lives on the line in Alabama as a reason for why they were now becoming active.[17]

If Selma, not Freedom Summer, became the radicalizing experience for white northern Appalachian students, then McAdam's thesis needs some revision. Given the greater level of participation by northern Appalachian students in the Alabama protests, those who did not participate could watch the news or read the paper and see (or at least imagine) their friends in Alabama being beaten and mangled by white police officers. The much larger number of northern Appalachian students involved meant that when they returned to campuses, they would spread their stories to a significantly wider range of classmates than the few Freedom Summer participants could have reached. Though only 25,000 people participated in the Montgomery rally on March 25, that number does not count the hundreds and thousands of others who flooded into the state between March 7 and 24 but did not stay for, or were not able to make it to, the events in Montgomery. Selma, as spectacle, felt larger and more urgent, notwithstanding the violence that accompanied Freedom Summer. Further, Freedom Summer was a commitment of time and energy that many students were still unwilling or unable to make in 1964, whereas Selma was a shorter commitment that offered, seemingly, the same level of symbolic value.

Freedom Summer and the Selma marches seem to represent two different forms of citizenship activism. Freedom Summer sought to help build empowered black communities able to serve as their own advocates and claim a greater stake in the decision-making processes of the wider community. Its success derived from a willingness of participants to devote a great deal of time and energy to the process. Conversely, the Selma to Montgomery marches following Bloody Sunday were about an expression of frustration and meant to call attention to the plight of black citizens in Alabama. Their success rested in raising awareness to injustice and demonstrating to authority figures the depth of frustration through the mobilization of the largest numbers of participants possible. While marchers had to be willing to confront the potential of physical harm or arrest for their activities, as Freedom Summer workers had, the duration of this threat was significantly less. Thousands of people descended on Alabama in the two weeks after Bloody Sunday, staying a few days or possibly the full two weeks, and then returned to their daily lives content in the knowledge they had made their voice heard. The level of sustained commitment differed greatly between the community-organizing model of Freedom Summer and the mass demonstration model of Selma, and these two competing modes of citizenship engagement appeared in virtually all forms of social and political activism during the 1960s.

Embracing the community improvement model of activism, the Athens Civil Rights Action Committee (ACRAC), an organization made up of people from both the community and campus, announced in November 1965 a six-day project over Christmas break in Winstonville, Mississippi—a small town in Bolivar County and a site of Freedom Summer activism. Fifteen students participated in the project to register voters and promote community action programs. They recognized that despite the passage of both the Civil Rights and Voting Rights Acts their host families faced economic and, possibly, physical, reprisals for participating in the civil rights project. Further, the students traveled to Mississippi "to learn first hand the realities of life in our time," thereby gaining a sense of authenticity to support their developing notions of an active citizenship. In recounting their events, the participants argued that economic development was crucial to the success of civil rights activism, pointing directly to the tools made available through the Johnson administration's War on Poverty. [18]

At roughly the same time as OU students planned their "Christmas in Mississippi" civil rights project, students at WVU engaged in a heated debate over the right of a fraternal society, the Kappa Alpha Order (KA), to continue their tradition of flying the Confederate flag. The debate centered on the question of the flag's symbolism—hatred or heritage. University officials were quick to say they were not calling KA or its members racists, but that "the Confederate flag has been wrongfully used as a symbol of intolerance, intimidation, murder and almost every kind of social evil. Because of this wrongful use it is associated with these things, and as a result, some people are deeply hurt by the display of this flag." Brent Diefenbach, KA president, announced via a letter to the editor that the Order would "co-operate with any policies and regulations of the University," but argued that this stance by the University represented the first step upon a slippery slope to the full abridgment of all students' rights. Diefenbach stated, "we feel that this action may represent a precedent of far-reaching consequences tending to infringe upon the rights of students and student groups to express themselves freely in a university setting." An editorial in the *Daily Athenaeum* the following day echoed Diefenbach's concern, saying, "The biggest issue, however, is whether the University has the right suddenly to out-law long-established fraternity traditions," and concluding, "If a group is in the wrong, it should try to correct the situation, for its own welfare if for no other reason" rather than face a unilateral administration decree.[19]

The tone of the debate quickly moved from any connection to questions of race to the overstepping of the limits of legitimate power by the University and infringement on first amendment rights of expression. Reflecting the longstanding accommodationist narrative of the Civil War, as described by historian David Blight, the KA-supporting students argued the flag represented the honor and bravery of Confederate soldiers. Though one finds it oddly ironic that a fraternity with such strong Confederate ties would gain a large following in West Virginia—a state formed by pro-Unionists—this does highlight the power of post-Civil War memory construction (such as scholar Anne Marshall noted in Kentucky) as well as the constructed Appalachian identity as "Southern."[20] Ultimately, the close of the semester ended this debate over the Confederate flag at WVU.

The uproar highlights that the emerging student-citizen identity was not purely a liberal or left wing phenomenon. Kappa Alpha, a conservative fraternal organization, argued that their rights as citizens were in jeopardy and they had to an obligation to speak out against abuses of power. This idea served as the central theme in the West Virginia University Interfraternity Council's December 6, 1965, statement, which also reflected contemporary notions about respectability and responsibility:

> We, members of the Fraternity system and the University community, feel that the administration has recently acted in a manner which is detrimental to the overall relationship between the administration and the students, especially the Greeks. The administration has set a precedent in forcing one fraternity to abandon and refrain from exhibiting in public one of its traditional symbols. We believe this act and the manner in which it was handled could have been undertaken in a more suitable manner. It is our intention to strive to maintain our good relationship with the University administration. We hope that in the future, they will offer to discuss matters with the individual fraternity before an ultimatum of any kind is delivered. We also hope this isn't an indication of future University rulings concerning the fraternity system. We feel that in a University of this size, individuals and groups should be able to express their opinions and display their symbols as they see fit.[21]

By the spring of 1967, civil rights issues again gained some sustained activism on campus. In February, in Morgantown, a group of students officially announced the formation of an SDS chapter and initially set out to attack racial discrimination in the city, targeting local barbershops. Among those who announced the formation of the local chapter was a junior, history major, Harry Shaw. Shaw had answered the call the previous June to join Dr. King in Mississippi to continue the March Against Fear after the shooting of

James Meredith. He also helped form Student Action Against Poverty (SAAP) and participated in desegregation efforts in Morgantown. Shaw, who became the local SDS chapter president, represented wholly the cross-causal origins of student activism; for him, they were all part of one's role as a citizen.[22]

Not long after its official debut, WVU's SDS had found its first cause—the desegregation of Morgantown's barbershops. However, an antiwar demonstration sidetracked this effort and led to a month-long debate in the *Daily Athenaeum* about SDS, its goals, and its ideals.[23] In the end, both student government and the *Daily Athenaeum* endorsed the SDS effort to desegregate local barbershops, even if many students still held deep suspicions about the "true agenda" of SDS on WVU's campus. For Shaw and SDSers, the emphasis on civil rights represented a natural outgrowth of their visions of both citizenship, as defined by their university experiences, and the mission of SDS as an agent of socio-political change.[24]

Poverty

For some northern, white college students, their entry into social and political activism came through the Mississippi Summer Project in 1964; however, for others the War on Poverty offered a taste of community activism. Doug McAdam argued that participation in Freedom Summer was the catalyst that created the national activist network of white college students that precipitated the rise of disruptive student actions on college campuses in the North. However, for students in northern Appalachia participation in local poverty programs offered another way to integrate their campus and community activism. Recently, Thomas Kiffmeyer has explored student antipoverty activism in the 1960s, arguing that participation in the Appalachian Volunteers radicalized many members as they came to realize poverty's roots were too entrenched for the liberal reforms offered by the War on Poverty.[25] As students made citizenship claims, they also argued that all people had certain rights and standards of living that others must ensure and respect. As such, antipoverty activism became an important component of the Sixties experience for students of northern Appalachian universities.

In February 1964, the Action for Appalachian Youth (AAY) formed in Charleston, West Virginia, as part of both President Johnson's poverty initiatives and as part of the President's Committee on Juvenile Delinquency. The goal of AAY was to help at-risk youth gain the skills they needed to find gainful employment or stay in school. Despite being over 150 miles north of Charleston, the WVU Center for Appalachian Studies and Development (known colloquially as the Appalachian Center) provided a forum for the development of some AAY programs designed to reach youth in urban areas, farm communities, and the more remote regions outside of Charleston in the surrounding Kanawha County. United States Attorney General Robert F. Kennedy came to Charleston in late-April 1964 to praise the strides taken by AAY and to reiterate, "Given the ingredients of resolute community action, working in partnership with federal assistance and stimulation, we can succeed."[26]

Over the summer of 1964, while half a dozen northern Appalachian students made their way to Mississippi, four WVU students went to Kanawha County to participate in a 10-week program by the AAY. As part of their activities, Susan Dunn (junior, social work major), Bruce Jennings (sophomore, psychology major), James Sell (first year law student), and William Field (junior, political science major) participated in a lecture series that included such speakers as Harry Caudill, author of *Night Comes to the Cumberlands* (1963), and Michael Harrington, author of *The Other America* (1962). The students also worked on several AAY projects that included creation of leadership programs to empower locals as well as rebuilding dilapidated playgrounds and other community areas. The program emphasized "self-help" by providing the training and tools necessary for the poor of Kanawha County to draw themselves and their communities out of poverty. Dunn praised the program and its approach stating, "The concept of self help will have a more lasting effect than direct financial aid." While Field offered a note of caution saying the project was "expensive and time-consuming and may never be finished."[27]

Participation in AAY was relatively limited; the bulk of northern Appalachian students who became involved in poverty activism began by attending lectures and discussions or reading campus news coverage of the War on Poverty. While WVU students explored rural poverty, students at Pitt focused on urban poverty. Despite distinct and definite differences between urban and rural poverty, students throughout northern Appalachia identified a lack of good education as a key factor regardless of location. Thus, for these students the problem was largely the same and they would, in time, develop similar mechanisms for local student involvement—mostly in the form of tutoring programs for disadvantaged youths.

Campus news coverage of the War on Poverty was generally positive on all three campuses. It is not overly surprising that OU and WVU would hold such views: OU's president, Vernon R. Alden, was instrumental in writing parts of the federal government's poverty initiatives; WVU's president, Paul A. Miller, had been the driving force behind WVU's Appalachian Center, which served as a model for the later federal Appalachian Regional Commission.[28] Regardless, in all three cases, students fought the War on Poverty as words on the pages of the student newspapers in the fall of 1964, much like the rest of student engagement during this period. However, students would soon begin to move into the field and work in poverty-stricken communities and begin to advocate on campus and within their communities for the rights and dignity of the poor.

In March 1965, two Pitt students traveled to Alice Lloyd Junior College in Pippa Passes, Kentucky, as part of a conference on Appalachian poverty that drew representatives from twenty northeastern universities. One of the students on the trip, Michael Marcuse, recounted their approach to Alice Lloyd Junior College, describing a decent into a drab Dickensian nightmare of cyclical poverty and intense ignorance. According to Marcuse, "The houses were dirty grey-brown. The land was debris covered grey-brown. The faces of the children, too, were grey-brown as they played in the garbage thrown aimlessly from the windows of their shanties." The other student, Marcia McNutt, recalled, "The most predominant mood of the community is a feeling of hopelessness, which is reflected in the faces of the people, and in their way of living." These students returned to Pitt and hoped to use their experiences in Kentucky to spark greater Pitt student involvement in poverty activism.[29]

In the following weeks, Pitt hosted Judith Welles from Volunteers In Service To America (VISTA), who spoke on the "squalor and decay" caused by poverty in America. Welles was at the University to help recruit for VISTA, noting that while their efforts would not eradicate poverty, the organization served to "begin to break the cycle of poverty, and give the next generation the opportunity to learn, work, and live in decency and dignity." She argued that the current generation of college students possessed a "new social awareness" that will make the efforts of VISTA that much more effective.[30]

A few days after Welles spoke, over a dozen fraternity members from Pitt took part in a joint VISTA-YMCA urban renewal project in the Homewood-Brushton district of Pittsburgh (a region of intense poverty within the city, and also a community with a large black population). The *Pitt News'* description of the living conditions of the urban slum that the fraternity brothers worked in mirrored the earlier nightmarish images of rural penury. Its explanations were also the same—ignorance and a culture of poverty. The visions of poverty promoted by liberal reformers and engrained in the ideology of the War on Poverty put the onus for change on the poor, that they needed to adopt middle class American values to build themselves up out of deprivation.[31]

The self-help philosophy pitched by spokespersons like radio and television personality Betty Furness when trying to get students to volunteer for VISTA suggested America's overall economic system was good, right, and effective, and that pockets of poverty represented an aberration. While at Pitt on a recruitment drive, Furness reminded potential volunteers, "that they are not working for the poor and underprivileged but with them to help stem the pattern of poverty." The solution was not large systemic change but patchwork programs, supposedly meant to empower the poor. As Thomas Kiffmeyer, a scholar of Sixties student activism in Appalachia, has argued, the failures of antipoverty programs in the mid-1960s came from these faulty assumptions and resulted in a radicalization of poverty workers. In Pittsburgh in 1965, the tone was self-congratulatory, as if they had won a battle in the wider War on Poverty because they had helped to paint an apartment or distributed some flyers. However, students quickly forgot this brief flare up of antipoverty work in the rapidly shifting socio-political landscape of the mid-1960s.[32]

In 1966, OU students participated in antipoverty programs in eastern and southern Ohio. Energized by a speech from Appalachian author Harry Caudill (who came to OU in April 1966), students traveled to Youngstown, Ohio—over two hundred miles to the north and east of their campus in Athens—and then later over eighty miles south and west to Portsmouth, Ohio, to participate in community action programs. Through community organizing and education programs, the students sought to help empower the communities of Youngstown and Portsmouth to overcome the supposedly engrained culture of poverty and to become advocates for their own success. According to Lucy Puccio, a journalism major, the thirty OU students who participated in the project "were to invade the east side of Youngstown with enthusiasm and hope." Senior, English major Dennis Hefferman described "the spirit of the program" in Youngstown as one of "co-operating, ignoring differences in nationality and race," concluding that in all, they had "produced an achievement that is now evident to the residents of the East Side of Youngstown."[33]

The twenty students who traveled to Portsmouth in November 1966 shared a similar sense of hope and optimism that their action, no matter how small, would begin a ripple of change. Deena Mirrow described the actions of the OU students for the *Post* and ended by saying she "realized that people do care. And I realized how important it is that they do." A letter to the editor signed by eight fellow participants echoed Mirrow's sentiment stating, "We were turned on!" Many students emerged from the Portsmouth and Youngstown events enthusiastic about future antipoverty work. Some expressed a deep desire to return to these poverty-stricken communities and several did return over their Thanksgiving break, "because," as Bob Vanderwyst described it, "they told their Portsmouth friends that they really did care—that they were not just a bunch of college creeps on a lark or a one-shot deal—that this trip was a commitment and not a fad." Vanderwyst also noted, "Some of [the students] even wanted to drop out of school and remain in Portsmouth, because this was a real education experience."[34]

Throughout northern Appalachia, student-led antipoverty organizations formed and largely brought tutoring programs into the region's hollows and slums. In Pittsburgh, the Hill Education Project (HEP) served an urban population with the same function as OU's Southeastern Ohio Opportunities Program (SOOP) or WVU's Student Action Against Poverty (SAAP). For the most part these groups offered tutoring programs for disadvantaged youths, emphasizing acceptance of the liberal notion that education represented the path out of poverty. In all cases, students who participated in these groups also became members in other organizations, focusing on issues of campus and community concern, including civil rights and the war in Vietnam. Some even joined or formed local chapters of Students for a Democratic Society.[35] The actions of these poverty warriors were more in line with the community-centered activism of Freedom Summer than the mass demonstrations of Selma, Alabama, which were later adopted by the antiwar movement.

Conclusion

While there were sporadic episodes of activism and concern prior to 1964, that year represents a coalescing of socio-political factors on northern Appalachian campuses, such as calls for changes in women's hours, participation in civil rights efforts—including Freedom Summer, and student preparation for the presidential election that fall. However, one of the most important triggers for student political and social activism in the region stemmed from the events in and around Selma, Alabama, in March 1965. Antipoverty activism, growing from 1964 through 1967, also provided a unique entry into social and political activism for northern Appalachian students. Through the students' actions, one sees the cross-causal origins of campus activism—how the students sought to connect campus with the wider local and, in some cases, national community—and the interconnection of student identities to visions of citizenship, creating a more actively defined student-citizen identity.

Between 1964 and 1967, students at northern Appalachian universities became increasingly active in political and social movements. They moved from simply discussing the issues and listening to others lecture on various topics to actively engaging. For northern Appalachian students at Pitt, OU, and WVU, the catalyst for this change was not Freedom Summer as Doug McAdam has argued, but rather the events in Selma as well as antipoverty work, both of which gave many students their first taste of direct action.

Chapter 4

Debating the Vietnam War

Contending Visions of Patriotism and Dissent

In 1964, students seemed only marginally concerned with the question of war in Southeast Asia. Yet the war in Vietnam grew to become the dominant political concern and the lens through which students filtered virtually all other issues by 1967. Scholars continue to debate just what it was that propelled student antiwar activism. Some focus on national events, like SDS's March on Washington to End the War in Vietnam in April 1965, while others emphasize local issues such as the concern over parietals.[1] However, at northern Appalachian universities it appears that a combination of internal pushes and external pulls helped the antiwar movement develop on their campuses.

How students engaged with the issue of war changed significantly during the middle years of the 1960s. Initially, the rising concern regarding Vietnam in the fall of 1964 expressed itself through relatively passive means and through approved and sanctioned forms of political expression, such as listening to speeches made by experts (or faculty). However, announcements of changes to the selective service deferment system, late in 1965 and in 1966, began a transition towards greater levels of civil disobedience and direct action. There were many who opposed the war for a variety of political, social, and moral reasons and for whom changes in the draft laws did little to spark their concern. Regardless, the growing opposition among many college students resulted from the increasing fear of dying in military service—a reality from which their status as college students had previously insulated them. By 1967, demonstrations became more frequent, using the mass tactics of Selma to protest the war in Vietnam.

The summer of 1964 was important not just for the civil rights and antipoverty projects in Mississippi and Kanawha County, but also because of the incident(s) in the Gulf of Tonkin in August when a U.S. Navy ship came under attack. The U.S. Congress speedily passed the Gulf of Tonkin Resolution, granting President Lyndon Johnson wide powers to "protect" American servicemen stationed in Southeast Asia. The Resolution opened the door for the wider expansion of American military operations in the war in Vietnam.[2] However, for many students these events seem to have done very little to raise their awareness of the situation in Indochina. The lack of a large or vocal opposition to American involvement in Vietnam in the early fall of 1964 has much to do with the still relatively low number of advisers in place (only a few thousand), no combat troops on the ground, and largely unaltered draft calls.

In all, Vietnam did not really become an issue for many students in the fall of 1964 because it was presumably no different than many other smaller actions the United States had gotten involved in over the previous two decades. Additionally, the events of August had not yet directly affected the students' lives, so they had little reason to pay closer attention. The conflict in Vietnam was still too new, at least in the context of the fallout from the Gulf of Tonkin Incident, for activists to have mobilized in opposition. However, what is striking is that the students held no forums or debates about the issues, whether on the right of Congress to cede so much authority to the President, if American interests were at stake in the region, or on just what the United States was doing in Southeast Asia in the first place. The lack of such activities appears to have more to do with timing; the events of Tonkin Gulf occurred in early August, and by the time school was back in session it no longer carried the same urgency.[3] What coverage the student newspapers gave to Vietnam in the fall of 1964 was largely interspersed with other foreign relations stories, culled together from the various wire services. It seems that the presidential election, which had obvious war-related overtones, overshadowed specific antiwar activism at northern Appalachian universities.

Just as involvement with the black freedom struggle increased in 1965, so too did debate and demonstrations related to Vietnam. In February, a handful of members of Ohio University's Student Peace Union staged a protest march, in conjunction with a series of protests in other cities, to call for an end to the bombing of North Vietnam and, in their words, "to stimulate people across the nation to have government do what the people want and to stop senseless killing." They also circulated a petition—sponsored by the *Catholic Worker*, the Committee for Non-Violent Action, and the War Resisters League—declaring a "conscious refusal to cooperate with the United States government in the prosecution of the war in Viet Nam." The small protest drew condemnation from OU student James Lynch, who wrote in a letter to the editors of the *Post* that "National unity at a time like this cannot be over-emphasized. The situation surely is not helped by irresponsible rabble-rousers such as the Student Peace Union."[4] This event and the subsequent response demonstrate that far from being apathetic, students in northern Appalachia were engaging with their world. Further, Lynch's use of notions of "responsibility" shows how the cultural milieu of the college campus in the early 1960s tempered the debate surrounding Vietnam. Lynch rejected SPU because, in his estimation, they failed to live up to the middle-class ethos of responsibility and respectability that the University supposedly sought to inculcate amongst its students.

At Pitt, the bombing campaign and the growing likelihood of combat troops headed to Vietnam sparked a debate in the *Pitt News*. In a three-part series published prior to the landing of 3,500 American combat troops in Vietnam in early March, Irv Garfinkle blamed "myopic anticommunism" for America's initial involvement in Vietnam and advocated immediate withdrawal. Garfinkle accepted the Cold War ideas of America's global role and he believed continued involvement only weakened America's strategic position. He argued that if America's goal was to weaken the influence of Communism in the region then, "Our policy brought about exactly the opposite of our desired goal. . . . A continuation of such a policy is not, therefore, in our national interest."[5]

Garfinkle's position drew criticism, chiefly from those who believed withdrawal could only symbolize appeasement and cowardice, which would serve to embolden America's enemies. In an opinion essay meant to challenge Garfinkle's assumptions, fellow student Alex D'Ippolito launched into an anticommunist diatribe of slogans and catchphrases, including "better dead than red," and "peace without freedom is slavery." According to D'Ippolito, withdrawal meant capitulation and the acceleration of a communist conspiracy to destroy the United States and its way of life. D'Ippolito advocated all-out war in Vietnam, with the very real potential of using nuclear weapons, as the only real option; otherwise, "the ghosts of a million brave soldiers" would haunt the United States.[6]

At virtually the same time that the Garfinkle-D'Ippolito debate raged in the *Pitt News*, similar discussions appeared in the campus papers at WVU and OU. At WVU, the debate was between two professors whom the *Daily Athenaeum* declared experts.[7] Interestingly, where Pitt students engaged each other, WVU students highlighted the more passive form of politics—observing the debate of others rather than engaging in it themselves. At OU, the *Post* ran a story on a current student and Marine veteran who served in Vietnam, David Oman. Oman rejected the optimistic view of a potential American victory in Vietnam, stating, "The war in South Viet Nam is not a thing to be won." He argued American prestige "has already been damaged and our naïve diplomacy already exposed," because of the war. Negotiation represented the only alternative, according to Oman because "We're not doing the Vietnamese any favors in ravaging their country." The following week, Joe McKeefer penned a letter to the *Post* that echoed Oman's sentiments. McKeefer argued that negotiation was the only real alternative, "Our best policy is to work out some sort of neutralization of South Viet Nam, and to provide aid to other Southeast Asian nations so that they can achieve the stability to resist any future Communist infiltration."[8]

The debates at Pitt, WVU, and OU demonstrate the growing concern amongst these students for the war. Further, they reflect an effort to take up the duties of a citizen and engage the question of foreign policy, American interests, and war. Where Pitt and OU show a movement amongst the students to take on a slightly more active role in these debates, suggesting a more engaged vision of citizenship, students at WVU were still largely observers of these debates rather than participations.

While there were no rallies or demonstration on campus, in mid-April 1965, over one dozen OU students traveled to Washington, D.C., to participate in the March on Washington to End the War in Vietnam. Students for a Democratic Society (SDS) sponsored the rally in the nation's capital, which represented one of their few outright antiwar actions, preferring to focus their energies on a wider call for societal change.[9] Strikingly, the fourteen OU students who traveled to the event did not want the *Post* to print their names "for fear of University reprisals." This suggests that association with an SDS-sponsored or antiwar event could make one a marked-individual. Overall, the participants praised the event as helping to raise national awareness to the need to end the war and refocus attention domestically, saying, "funds were being channeled into the Viet Nam war when they should be directed to the War on

Poverty and that it was only humanitarian to end all the killing of civilians in Viet Nam."[10]

The war debates in the campus newspapers and participation in the national march by OU students showed the growing, if relatively small amount of, activism against the Vietnam War. Garfinkle's "antiwar" stance in the *Pitt News* in March 1965, if one could call it that, was not the attack on American militarism or imperialism that would become the left's position in the near future. Rather, his argument was "wrong war, wrong time," which still supported the underlying assumptions and justifications of the use of American military power globally. Students were beginning to engage with Vietnam as they had started to with civil rights and poverty. Further, like earlier political engagement, the argument was that students needed to listen to experts before forming their own opinions. Within a few weeks of the Garfinkle-D'Ippolito debate at Pitt on the issue of Vietnam, students in the region and the nation participated in one of the largest events to that time centered on Vietnam—a national teach-in.

Teach-Ins and Bleed-Ins

As the spring semester of 1965 drew to a close, students at Pitt engaged in their first event related to Vietnam, the national teach-in. The teach-in was broadcast simultaneously to dozens of campuses around the nation in mid-May, with speakers from the Johnson administration presenting the official view as well as experts offering dissenting opinions. Local debates and discussions followed the Washington-based portion of the teach-in; some of these sessions went well into the early morning hours. While many would come to view the teach-in as purely an antiwar protest tactic, in 1965 it still served as a means by which experts expressed and debated multiple points of view. Often, students emerged from these discussions just as supportive of the war as they had been when they entered.[11]

The teach-in, as begun at the University of Michigan in March 1965, reflected a wider, liberal notion that education was an essential component of citizenship. Many who supported the war and U.S. policy, as well as those who opposed it, believed anyone who held a different view did so out of ignorance. The entire concept of the teach-in emerged from a notion of civil debate within the prescribed political discourse. Students had long attended debate-discussions wherein two (or more) experts on a topic would engage each other in debate, with the thought that the attending students would gain a deeper insight into the topic at hand. Although the Vietnam teach-ins did represent an effort by students to become more engaged in the political wrangling of this thorny issue, it still suggested a level of passivity as students witnessed the debate and asked questions of the experts after the fact. In the years to come, students would see themselves as the experts, as the individuals who should be on the stage rather than just in the audience.

In October and November 1965, pro- and anti-war factions at Pitt held events highlighting the conflicted nature of campus, as students attempted to sort out the roles of citizens in a democracy at war. Some choosing to support, others to dissent. In October, students held teach-ins and protests in coordination with the First International Days of Protest, scheduled for October 15–16, 1965. Students for Peace (SFP) sponsored workshops and discussions on topics related to the morality of war and dissent and the proper roles of citizens in a democracy at war. They further organized events to travel to Pittsburgh area military recruiting stations to "demonstrate against the recruiting of young Americans for the undeclared war in Vietnam," and to distribute literature about the antiwar movement.[12] The picketing and leafleting events represented a limited confrontational stance but suggested a direction for future activism. By going to the recruiters' offices they were putting into practice the beliefs generated through untold hours of debates and forcing passersby to confront the picketers' concerns about the war and American militarism.

That same month of October, Pittsburgh students confronted their campus' ambivalence toward the war in Vietnam by debating the validity of draft resistance and participating in a mass rally supporting U.S. policy. The *Pitt News* published a letter from David Mitchell, a draft resister from New York, who likened acquiescence to the government's prosecution of the war in Vietnam to German submission to Adolf Hitler in the 1930s, saying, "They submitted to the call for 'law and order' which protected and executed Nazi crimes." Mitchell argued that American citizens faced a similar dilemma and "the price of immunity is a harnessed mind and a gagged mouth when our government demands that we torture, murder and subjugate other people. The price is silence and murder." Obviously, Mitchell's letter upset many and touched off a firestorm of negative responses.[13]

In many of the negative response letters, authors expressed a support for an abstract right of dissent—most often conceived of as a component of American exceptionalism. However, these same authors argued that draft resistance was not legitimate dissent nor a proper activity in which a citizen should engage. Harvey F. Dahut and William G. McGeorge's letter represented these tendencies when they stated: "There is nothing wrong with protest. In fact, protest and criticism are fundamental parts of American democracy. These parts are safety valves for dissent and the means for change. But Mr. Mitchell and those like him are . . . attempting to tear down the foundation on which American government is built. . . . I would like to ask Mr. Mitchell and his retinue of "fine American men" whether they think themselves better than the soldiers who are neck-deep in mud, blood, and death?"[14] Dahut and McGeorge's letter, like those of several others, argued that draft resistance stood inherently at odds with American values, threatened American security, and challenged America's exceptionalist heritage; thus, there was no honor nor patriotism in such actions, but simply the rejection of one's obligations as a citizen.[15]

In one of the only letters the *Pitt News* published to offer a defense of Mitchell's actions, Alex Frank argued that one must acknowledge and respect Mitchell's strength of conviction even if one disagreed with his views. Frank concluded with the lament, "In time of crisis, reason is a stranger," noting that Mitchell's opponents "cling to their shibboleths and only bar the way to intelligent study and solution of social conflict." In all, Frank saw patriotism in a citizen willing to criticize the government in time of war and in following one's convictions to force a change in policy even in the face of public denunciation. He admonished Mitchell's attackers as those who "prefer to go on witch-hunts for 'dirty, unshaven, sloppy protestors' and close their minds to the objects of protest as they judge character by appearance."[16]

While the debate over draft resistance played out in the pages of the *Pitt News*, Pittsburgh students engaged in pro-war demonstrations. Fifty local members of the conservative organization Young Americans for Freedom (YAF) staged a pro-administration picket at the federal building downtown. On Pitt's campus the Ad Hoc Committee to Express Support for Our Men in Vietnam, circulated a petition: "Acknowledging our government's commitment in Vietnam, I, the undersigned, realize that our servicemen in Vietnam are fighting and dying as they have done many times before, to preserve the rights and freedom we cherish." The group intended to send the signed petitions of support to President Johnson to challenge "the morale-defeating effects the wave of anti-war demonstrations have had on American service-men in Vietnam."[17]

In late-October, nearly 1,500 people participated in a rally to support the troops on the Pitt campus. Despite its positive mission, the tone of the speakers was aggressively negative as they attacked war opponents as un-American for engaging in dissent, calling them "loudmouths . . . doing everything possible to tear down America . . . [using] any extra legal or il-legal means to promote their course." In the *Pitt News*, the rally received a generally positive review with editorial praise for the demonstration and the "clean shaven majority" that came out "to show that not all students were draft-card burners." Borrowing the framework of responsibility used in the arguments against in loco parentis, some praised the rally for setting the ap-propriate tone of respectability and patriotic citizenship.[18]

Not all students shared in the editors' positive assessments of the rally. For example, three female students wrote to the *Pitt News* to express their disgust and embarrassment "to be part of a student body which equates patriotism with jingoism."[19] According to the University's 1966 yearbook: "It was a pep-rally presentation with gung-ho enthusiasm spurting out like cheers at a football game. . . . Those who sang along and cheered the speeches were characterized as patriots; the others they said were unpatriotic. Those who opposed the rally also sang along though. They respected their country for being a place where they could stand and protest the actions of fellow citizens."[20] The yearbook's presentation highlighted the conflicted nature of campus and the contending definitions of patriotism that adjoined the de-bates over the proper role of a student and citizen in American society.

While students at Pitt debated patriotism, held pro-war rallies, and dem-onstrated at recruiters' offices, students at OU organized a blood drive. The *Post* had reported that around the country other schools were holding blood drives to show their support for U.S. policy in Vietnam and challenge the notion that all students shared the views of the antiwar protesters at places like Berkeley. Within weeks, the OU student government had agreed to hold its own "bleed-in" in Athens just after the Thanksgiving break, to show OU's support for the troops in Vietnam and thereby support for the war.[21]

Some advised a delay and called for a poll of student opinions, to determine whether the majority did support the war and U.S. policy and if the bleed-in would thereby be representing the will of the OU student body. A group of students formed to try to convince others that if they gave blood they should do so, "to help humanity and not to support U.S. policy in Vietnam." In the end, 230 students donated blood, with more than half announcing that their donation was not in support of U.S. policy, but because they "felt that it was time they helped the Red Cross." The dissenters argued that as OU students and American citizens they saw it as appropriate to give blood so that the Red Cross could use it however they saw fit.[22]

Just prior to the winter break, OU's Student Cabinet conducted a poll of student views on Vietnam. Students took the poll after a special issue of the *Post*, dedicated to the war in Vietnam, ran on December 12. When the Student Cabinet tabulated the over 3,400 responses, the overwhelming majority supported the war on some level. However, the poll, to which roughly one-third of all OU students responded, also pointed out that over one thousand students either opposed or had misgivings about U.S. policy in Vietnam, with

Table 1.

Responses to Vietnam War Survey Conducted at Ohio University in December 1965

	MEN	WOMEN	TOTAL	PERCENT OF TOTAL
I SUPPORT U.S. POLICY—I FEEL THAT WE BELONG THERE AND ARE DOING OUR BEST.	485	267	752	21.6%
I SUPPORT U.S. POLICY, BUT ADVOCATE INCREASED MILITARY EFFORT.	981	200	1181	33.9%
I DO NOT SUPPORT U.S. POLICY, BUT CAN OFFER NO ALTERNATIVE ACTION.	43	37	80	2.3%
I DO NOT SUPPORT U.S. POLICY AND ADVOCATE IMMEDIATE WITHDRAWAL OF THE U.S.	44	31	75	2.2%
DUE TO LACK OF KNOWLEDGE OF THE PRESENT SITUATION, I DO NOT CHOOSE TO FORMULATE AN OPINION.	150	271	421	12.1%
I SUPPORT U.S. POLICY, BUT WOULD LIKE TO SEE NEGOTIATIONS BEGIN IMMEDIATELY—EITHER ON OUR OWN TERMS OR UNCONDITIONALLY.	421	266	687	19.7%
I DO NOT SUPPORT U.S. POLICY, BUT BELIEVE WE HAVE COMMITTED OURSELVES TO CONTINUE SUPPORTING SOUTH VIETNAM.	138	145	283	8.1%

*"Vietnam Poll Results Favor U.S. Policies," *The Post*, February 8, 1966.

nearly one in eight respondents having no opinion.[23] (See Figure 4.1) Just as Irv Garfinkle's articles in the *Pitt News* had done, the poll reminds historical observers that one must not confuse a lack of participation in activities with total apathy. Students may have been keenly aware of and interested in what is happening in the realm of civil rights or the Vietnam War but simply did not attend meetings or other events because such events did not exist, or because of scheduling conflicts, poor publicity, or some other factor that drove down attendance figures.

During the debates and discussions in the planning of the bleed-in, the editors of the *Post* offered a reflective editorial in which they wrangled with the meanings of citizenship and dissent, their position on the war and foreign policy, and the implications of all these things for their generation. They began by noting that the war in Vietnam was a concern "vital to college students, mainly because some of them may die in Vietnam's rice fields. And so the time has come for us to define our position on the war in Vietnam as well." The editorial went on to say the government had sold the war as part of the fight against Communism and for democracy, yet "we have seen the perversions of the War Against Communism. And we have seen the foibles of our democracy. And now, suddenly, we are called upon to perhaps risk and sacrifice the effort we have put into reaching adulthood for the sake of this 'democracy' and this 'War Against Communism.'" The editors then laid out the Johnson administration's arguments for the war and concluded that overall, the war was necessary to protect American interests and prevent the Vietnamese people from suffering under the yoke of Communist oppression. However, one would hesitate to call it a full-throated, ringing endorsement: "Optimistically speaking, we find our system of government the better system. Cynically speaking, our system is the lesser of two evils. So, with that understanding, we will support the United States effort in Vietnam. . . . We may think it a rotten war, at a rotten time in our lives, in a rotten country. And we may not like it. But we will support it. Simply because, looking at all the facts in full perspective, there is no real alternative."[24]

The bleed-in and its debates and the organization of an effort to challenge directly the stated goal of the event represented some of the first direct actions at OU on political or social issues. Here students put forward an event with an expressed political purpose and other students created their own demonstration against those purposes. There was no debate-discussion with experts in a room somewhere that students passively sat through before asking their questions of the experts. Rather, this was a direct action, like Selma. Students peacefully, yet directly, acted on their political and social beliefs. Where in Selma they attended others' rallies, in the fall of 1965 in northern Appalachia, they created their own.

Antiwar activism escalated seemingly in proportion to increased troop levels. In mid-January 1966, U.S. troop levels in Vietnam approached 190,000 and General Lewis B. Hershey, director of the Selective Service System, announced that changes would be forthcoming in the deferment structure that may allow the government to draft some college students.[25] As a result, by far the most talked about item in the campus newspapers at OU, WVU, and Pitt in February 1966, even overshadowing Greek life, was the draft. Vague statements from officials that individuals may lose deferments had many students and university administrators concerned. If one's draft status was going to be dependent on grades and class rank, then the university would inevitably function as an agent of the federal government and the American war machine.[26]

Students struggled to reconcile these new functions with their existing notions of the proper role of the university in American society. Until then, universities had limited their connections to the military-industrial complex to research funds and reserve officer training; these changes meant universities would be funneling human resources to the military, potentially for deployment in Vietnam. The changes in student deferments in 1966 did more to galvanize student activism in northern Appalachia in the mid-1960s than anything since perhaps the events in Selma, Alabama, the previous spring. However, most protesters had limited goals—end the war or end the draft— not the systemic reconstruction of American society; these limited goals provided a sufficient message for the kind of massed action learned in Alabama in the spring of 1965.

By May 1966, the changes to the draft and an escalating tide of antiwar sentiment generated a conservative response. At Pitt, students held "Fireproof Your Draft Card" events in which over 300 draft eligible men had their registration certificates laminated in plastic. Pete Janszen, local Young Republicans president, claimed the events represented a needed counter-image to "the recent draft card burnings and other unpatriotic demonstrations." Supporters of the events, including local politicians, saw them as crucial to expressing support for the troops—though how potential draftees laminating draft cards did that went unexplained.[27]

The implicit understanding was that the support for the institutions of the state (such as the selective service) carried over to a general support for the entirety of the state. The logical formation at work here stated that if one respected this manifestation of the state, whatever that manifestation was, it suggested a support for the troops. Ultimately, with "fireproofing" framed as supporting the troops, opposing the event (or non-participation) meant an attack on (or, at least, a lack of support for) the troops; thus, opposition was unpatriotic.

Challenging Campus Speakers

The Vietnam War served as the basis for a handful of debates and lectures in February 1966. While the student newspapers did not describe any of the debates as a "teach-in," their general structure and function seemed to place them within this framework: professors from the various schools sparred over U.S. policy and students watched, offered occasional questions to the professors, and hoped to learn something about the situation from what they witnessed.[28] Late in the month, OU hosted General Maxwell Taylor, former ambassador to South Vietnam and former Chairman of the Joint Chiefs of Staff, who told his audience that the debate regarding Vietnam "was over" and that the U.S. had to fight to win there. While Taylor spoke, a small group of protesters sat silently outside to symbolize how the University administration had silenced opposing views on Vietnam.[29] This action represented one of the first student anti-Vietnam demonstrations at OU, and in its wake discussions began about the organizing of an SDS chapter in Athens.[30]

In September 1966, Vice President Hubert H. Humphrey came to WVU to speak, and his lecture became the occasion for a limited attempt at student dissent against the war in Vietnam. A group of students solicited signatures on a petition expressing opposition to the war. One day after the antiwar student petition emerged, a pro-war group organized and counter-demonstrated, circulating its own petition supporting the current U.S. policy in Vietnam. The pro-war folks advertised their petition with a giant sign reading, "Register Your Patriotism Now."[31]

In the ensuing debate in the *Daily Athenaeum*, some took issue with the pro-war group's assumption that opposing the war was unpatriotic. Psychology major Robert E. Rankin said the pro-war slogans seemed "to equate the situation with a football game." Rankin went on to state, "Surely the complexity of the Viet Nam situation can be appreciated on all sides by now . . . but the effect of cries such as these is to polarize the issue and make peace more unlikely and discussion difficult." Adding his support to the antiwar folks, Craig T. Rainey argued that "at the very heart of a democratic process [is] a process which is supposed to encourage full and free debate." However, Rainey argued, "Instead of enlightened dissent, what would the 'Patriotism' group have—an unquestioning consensus?"

Ultimately, Rainey would not have to look far for his answer. A letter from fellow student Buzz Wagner published the same day stated emphatically, "These [antiwar] students should be hung by their thumbs on the tree in front of Woodburn Circle." Wagner concluded, "I say let's keep this kind of trash off our campus. Don't give Hubert Humphrey the idea that we are all another group of those long-haired fanatical students."[32] Overall, while the antiwar group suffered mocking and verbal assaults and only garnered about 75 petition signers, compared to the over 1,200 who signed the pro-policy statement, their actions revealed that WVU's campus was neither apathetic nor disinterested. Their petition had afforded an opportunity for some debate on American policy—a part of their stated goals.[33] Further, this limited action encouraged larger events in the future. The Vice President's visit to WVU revealed a conflicted campus trying to come to terms with the dual roles of students and citizens.

In November, WVU student Jim Gilkerson wrote an impassioned call for students to exercise their freedom of speech and directly linked the campus with the wider community. Gilkerson's call to action struck similar chords as the March 1964 editorial at OU that called on students to engage more fully with their community. As students and citizens, Gilkerson argued, young people could not be afraid to tackle difficult issues because of the "fear of what our peers will think . . . we are wasting our time on too many trivial things for FEAR of facing serious problems." In Gilkerson's estimation, it was not apathy that kept his classmates silent but timidity, and their silence bordered on the immoral.[34]

At roughly the same time as Gilkerson was calling on WVU students to find their voice and engage with difficult issues, students in Pittsburgh were participating in a "speak-out," drawing nearly 2,000 participants and representing the largest peace action so far in Pittsburgh of the Vietnam War era. The speak-out, entitled "The War Nobody Wants," brought together members of the various college campuses and the community-at-large. The event was part of several activities planned in the fall of 1966 to coincide with the National Days of Mobilization. Although called a "speak-out," students, who made up the bulk of the attendance, did not actually have an opportunity to speak but rather sat and listened to local congressional candidates and religious leaders express support for calls to halt the bombing campaign against North Vietnam and defend dissent as a central component of the first amendment right to free speech. Faculty members from the local universities also participated in the forum, discussing a range of topics from the legitimacy of dissent to economic repercussions of an escalated war. The three-hour event drew a counter-demonstration from members of YAF and a small contingent of veterans who marched carrying American flags as symbols of their patriotism and as an explicit attempt to portray the event happening inside as unpatriotic.[35]

In early December 1966, students at OU organized a silent peace vigil as an exercise of free speech; through the sound of their silence, protesters hoped to demonstrate to visiting lecturer Secretary of State Dean Rusk and to their fellow students the deep convictions held against America's war effort in Vietnam. The thought was that by standing silently in opposition, protesters would force passersby to confront their own silence in the face of the war. This protest was similar to the way WVU students had silently protested Vice President Humphrey a few months earlier. Some of the OU students holding the vigil in opposition to Secretary Rusk had participated in the anti-poverty campaign in Portsmouth in early November, suggesting the growing cross-causal relationship of activism on campus. Using the language of respectability found in the debates over the University's parietal policies, the editors of the *Post* praised the vigil as a responsible form of protest and called on Secretary Rusk to address several difficult questions regarding the administration's war policy. In the end, Rusk faced no interruptions as he delivered his speech, but the editors of the *Post* found Rusk's arguments stale and unconvincing. Like WVU at the beginning of the semester, OU became a site where students peacefully protested the Johnson administration's policies by directly targeting members of the president's administration.[36]

The peace vigil at OU, first initiated as a form of direct protest during the visit of Secretary Rusk, took on new life in 1967. Early in January, student Elaine Herald announced her intention to hold a weekly peace vigil on campus. Each Wednesday from noon to 1 p.m., Herald and whatever students chose to join her would sit on the College Green by the campus gate and provide a witness for peace. In a letter to the editor, Herald argued that "we cannot push our responsibility to this concept, this ideal, this problem aside," rather one must devote one's life to the meaning of peace and the noon demonstration would serve as an affirmation of this dedication. This same phenomenon, Wednesday noontime peace vigils, also appeared at Pitt. Here a group of Quakers—students and faculty of the surrounding universities—stood in front of Stephen Foster Memorial Hall, near the corner of Forbes Avenue and Bigelow Boulevard (adjacent to the Cathedral of Learning), standing through all forms of inclement weather. Herald, a sophomore at OU, from the city of Pittsburgh, may have brought the idea with her to Athens from Pittsburgh, as she noted in her letter that her proposal was "not original" but "being done on other campuses in other communities," suggesting a connection between southeastern Ohio and western Pennsylvania.[37]

Regardless of where it originated, a Wednesday noon silent peace vigil made a good deal of symbolic sense. The action asked people to take one hour in the middle of the day, in the middle of the week, in the middle of everything to reflect silently on the situation in Vietnam. The vigil was nonviolently confrontational and encouraged the observer to become a participant and evaluate her or his own individual connection to war and peace. Further, it represented a version of protest that ran counter to the mass rallies that were increasing in frequency and differed in orientation and goals from the community organizing that was also under way. This was a singular act by an individual meant to reach other individuals on an intimate and personal basis.

The peace vigils raised the question of appropriate forms of dissent, a topic often discussed on campus as students attempted to negotiate their roles as citizens in a democracy. They also highlighted a concept at the heart of 1960s protests: the centrality of the individual. An editorial in the *Post* argued that antiwar sentiment was not limited to "the SDSers, beats, and Communists" but shared by the "silent majority" of respectable students. The editors went on to praise several dozen student leaders around the nation who wrote a letter to President Johnson in which they challenged the war and U.S. policy in a responsible and measured fashion. The editorial optimistically concluded, "The Government cannot disregard this latest dissent because the critics represent America's future."[38] Like the peace vigil, affixing a signature to a letter was an individual statement of support for the sentiments of the protest and like the vigil it was non-violent, respectful, and nonthreatening to the established political framework.

The vigil was an individual act, a single person attempting to change their world and forcing others to confront them as individuals. It reflected the sense of dehumanizing conformity of the early Cold War years, but it was not an act of civil disobedience or a challenge to legitimate authority or political processes. Even when large groups gathered in protest, one could best describe the occurrence as massed individual action. In a letter to the *Post*, Ronald Meltzer stated:

> Contrary to popular conceptions, constructive protest is highly patriotic, it is protected by the First Amendment and often acts as a prerequisite to change and reform. Protest reflects the solemn beliefs of an individual, not an infamous plot to foster unrest. Many of our accepted institutions today were once inspired through protest. But people tend to become reluctant, and somewhat apprehensive, in accepting change—they cling to the status quo. Longevity and complacency lead to stagnancy and corruption. People scorn ideas which they do not understand or perhaps approve. We must respect an individual's beliefs even though they may not be our own.[39]

At the heart of the community organizing of anti-poverty and civil rights programs was the power of the individual, just as the central notion of participatory democracy was the value placed on the individual within the group. Thus, in this simple act of protest, Herald and her Quaker counterparts in Pittsburgh provided an essential component of Sixties activism.[40] However, as this nonviolent, respectable activism seemingly proved incapable of altering policy over time, individuals began to move toward civil disobedience and similar threats to the legitimate political process.

Until mid-February 1967, OU students had only demonstrated against lecturers who had come to campus to speak in favor of the war. However, a staged demonstration against Dow Chemical Co. represented students' first foray into a wider field of protest. Here several dozen students were protesting both the company's production of napalm, because of its brutal effects on the human body, and the right of such a company to recruit students on campus. Serving as spokesperson for the anti-Dow students, Joel Forrester stated, "We want students who might go to work for the company which supplies a weapon like napalm to know precisely what its use in Vietnam means." Similarly, an editorial in the *Post* supporting the anti-Dow action stated, "We urge all Ohio students to consider not just the salary and security which goes along with a particular job but also what will be accomplished by doing that job."[41]

Dow had come to OU before and students had not reacted this way, suggesting a marked shift in the student as activist. The anti-Dow protest, which drew condemnations from fellow students in the form of letters to the editor, was the first time a protest related to the war at OU did not target a political figure who had come to speak.[42] It was not an effort to present another opinion administrators had failed to present, rather it represented an effort to define the actions of the university. Here students were saying they had a right to determine who could and could not have access to the physical space of the university. It was an exercise in empowerment and ownership; it suggested the melding of a student-citizen identity.

Protest and the Arts

In March 1967, the newly formed chapter of SDS at WVU entangled themselves in a month-long debate after picketing a student-created variety show organized to present student support for U.S. troops in Vietnam—not necessarily for the administration's war policy. The University's News and Information Services promoted the event as a display of the WVU campus' support for the American war effort, much as some had attempted to present the bleed-in at OU in 1965 as a statement of campus-wide support for the war. Though the organizers and participants in the Twin Towers Variety Show did not intend for viewers to see their performances as a pro-war stance, nor did they seek to claim to speak for all WVU students, they refused to offer an official statement to that effect—upsetting members of SDS.[43]

The members of SDS decided that in the absence of an official statement saying that not all WVU students support the war, SDS would protest the war at the performances. Harry Shaw, WVU's chapter president for SDS, was adamant, and members of the variety show stated they understood that the protest was against the war not the show. Shaw rejected the University's implication "that anyone opposed to the war is opposed to the servicemen"; one could oppose the war but support the troops in his estimation.[44] However, the negative responses to the actions of SDS were swift and ferocious, and the nuances of the SDS protests were lost almost immediately.

While most who assailed SDS mouthed some generic statement of support for dissent, they went on to attack the picketers for daring to use that right, as if exercising the American right to dissent was un-American. A *Daily Athenaeum* editorial in one sentence defended the right of dissent and in the following asked, "Who does SDS think it is that it can intimidate students into accepting its terms or else subject them to a demonstration?"[45] The letter-writers who challenged the stance SDS took on the war did so in breathless, emotionally charged calls for strident anticommunism or face the eradication of America. One letter writer argued, "SDS do not seek a democratic dialogue any more than does Ho Chi Minh," attempting to invalidate SDS's right to dissent because of their supposed Communist inclinations. Another student argued that a seething hatred of America existed in Asia, which, if not stopped in Vietnam, would result in war in Main Street, U.S.A. He further argued that if SDS members could not see this they were blind. The author concluded with a disturbing image: "I only wish he [an SDS member] could be transplanted to any street in Peking during a Red Guard rally. There for a brief moment he might see this hate before an Oriental sword sliced through his neck. And then, in the ultimate demonstration, his head would be paraded through crowded alleys held high on a bloody stick."[46] In this image the author captured the fears of domino theory, yellow peril, American exceptionalism, and Orientalism and argued that by picketing a talent show in Morgantown the members of WVU's SDS would cause all of America to collapse.

Nearly a full month after the initial protest the anti-SDS sentiment had not abated but had caused some, in their eagerness to join in the denunciation of SDS, to tie themselves into intellectual knots. For example, a duo of authors argued that the right to dissent "was bought by every drop of blood that was ever spilled by the American fighting man anywhere at any time," but anyone who exercises or condones the use of this hard-fought right "is unfit to call himself or be called an American." The authors saw no inconsistency in arguing the right to dissent was patriotic but to actually dissent was un-American. Ultimately, because of the anti-SDS fervor, conservative students laid plans for the creation of a Young Americans for Freedom (YAF) chapter at WVU.[47]

In the month-long fracas, opponents regularly attacked SDS president Harry Shaw, claiming he was a power-hungry demagogue. In the single letter of response published by the *Daily Athenaeum*, Shaw offered no invective against those who personally maligned him, only a concern for correcting "inaccurate statements" made about the organization and its efforts. Shaw confirmed, "SDS members have been threatened with physical violence by some individuals" because of their protest and maintained "SDS was not trying to impose its views on anyone by the demonstrations." Ultimately, Shaw's letter suggested that SDS had acted in a responsible and respectable manner both to raise awareness of the war and to counter an image of university-wide support for the war effort. Through the spring of 1967, Shaw seemed to suffer willingly personal abuse if it meant getting the message out—that there were deep-seated problems in America and that students must be the ones to lead the way to new solutions.[48]

On April 15, 1967, as a culmination to the national Vietnam Week events, New York City and San Francisco hosted major rallies. Organizers of the Spring Mobilization hoped these protests would be so large that the Johnson administration could not continue to ignore or dismiss the antiwar movement. The event did draw government attention; the U.S. House of Representatives' Committee on Un-American Activities issued a report supposedly detailing the Communist plot underpinning the movement.[49] Regardless, nearly one hundred students from throughout northern Appalachia travelled to New York City to participate in the rally. In the week prior to the April 15 rally, students and faculty in northern Appalachia, and around the nation, participated in a series of locally organized and targeted activities. The Ohio Valley Region Peace Conference distributed handbooks that advised local antiwar groups how to construct campus organizations and raise funds for such events.[50] In Pittsburgh, local organizers created an event entitled "Angry Arts Against the War."

The Angry Arts festival drew participants from throughout the city and the region. The Pittsburgh Area Students for Peace sponsored the event and ran a full-page advertisement in the *Pittsburgh Press*—which students and faculty from twenty local Pittsburgh colleges, universities, and high schools signed—calling the war illegal and demanding an end to Operation Rolling Thunder, the bombing campaign against North Vietnam that was already in its second year. The program featured poetry, art, music, and photograph displays on a theme drawn from the paraphrasing of ancient Roman historian Tacitus' appraisal of the *Pax Romana*, "They Made a Desert and Called It Peace." Speaking to the nearly 1,500 participants who filled the Pitt Field House, history professor David Montgomery (Pitt) and sociology professor Sidney Peck (Western Reserve University, Cleveland) analyzed America's Vietnam policy and praised dissent as a means to counter the dehumanizing effect of war. Several hundred individuals undertook a candlelit march following the reading of an emotional letter from a currently serving GI to his parents in which he described the chaos and brutality of war and stated he was "not proud of myself, my friends or my country." The marchers travelled through the Oakland neighborhood (home to Pitt) as a peaceful witness to the patriotic duty of citizens to dissent.[51]

Vietnam Week and the Spring Mobilization stand at the end of a long transition in student activism beginning in 1964. Students moved from passive observation to direct action and crossed a threshold to a new chapter of student activism in which demonstrations would grow larger and claims to citizenship and patriotism would be made more forcefully. The years between 1964 and 1967 represent the first step in the evolution of student political and social activism during the Sixties.

Conclusion

The period 1964 to 1967 saw significant changes in the way students at northern Appalachian universities engaged with social and political issues. They saw the concerns of the day as interconnected and requiring them to challenge existing, passive visions of citizenship by substituting increasingly active definitions and questioning not only the status quo of the university but also of American society. Together these impulses helped to forge a dual identity as students and citizens.

Initially during this period, students at northern Appalachian universities did not hold events or activities related to larger socio-political issues. Instead, they often simply discussed national trends or participated in accepted modes of political expression, such as attending lectures or writing about their opinions in letters to the editor (with no sense of a plan of action that they or other students could engage in). However, over time, discussion (or raising awareness) led to direct action protests, marches, and attendance of national rallies, all of which resulted from envisioning the role of student and citizen as one who is actively engaged. The conflicted nature of what it meant to be a student, questions about the role of the university in American society, and an increasing dissatisfaction over the restraint of individuality within mass education and mass society helped propel students into greater levels of engagement.

The presumed quiet and conservative campuses of northern Appalachia faced similar challenges as did other college communities around the country, and exploring how their populations engaged with these questions explains why these campuses did not have large, disruptive protests and that lack of such events did not make them isolated from the impulses of the Sixties.

The Sixties experience of protest did not skip over Appalachia, nor was the region so hopelessly lost in its own isolation or poverty that it was incapable or unable to share in these national trends—contrary to the image generated by the near silence of existing scholarship. The debates over patriotism and citizenship, war and dissent that emerged on college campuses during the Sixties reflected the fractures within both campus and American society.

Part 2

1967–1968

Scholars have written much about the period from August 1967 to December 1968, claiming that it was the turning point, the high-water mark, the very definition of "the Sixties."[1] This section accepts a limited version of this thesis. Important changes happened on the campuses of northern Appalachian universities during these months. Between 1964 and 1967, student activism characterized by cross-causal foundations increased, transitioned in style from community-building to mass rallies, and continued the formation of the student-citizen identity of the Sixties. However, the 18 months from the end of the summer of 1967 to the end of December 1968 witnessed a series of events that, for many, defined the Sixties experience.

In this period, much of the cross-causal framework of student activism became somewhat obscured, with notable exceptions of sporadic civil rights flare-ups and challenges to in loco parentis. This was a time almost exclusively devoted to the issues surrounding the Vietnam War, from the draft to militarism in American society. Community-building projects in civil rights and poverty activism seemed to disappear from the headlines, replaced by the near-constant drumbeat of war coverage. However, despite the dramatic shift in emphasis to a central issue of the war, the student-citizen identity and the conceptions of the proper role of the university in American society continued to define the context of the debate. Declarations of the rights of university citizenship served as the means through which students attempted to exert influence and control over the larger political process that they had little say in—especially, since most students were too young to vote in statewide or national elections.

In many ways, the events of 1967–1968 were a natural outgrowth of the previous three years of activism and tactical developments. The teach-in movement gave way to the mass demonstrations. The desire to discuss and debate issues turned into disruption and demands. The antiwar movement militarized, seeing its actions as a confrontation, a war against war (or, at least, a war against the Vietnam War). The changes in the draft laws, which removed enrollment in a university as a bulwark against conscription, turned the war that had been distant and a largely academic abstraction for most college men into an immediate and personal concern. This immediacy, combined with a growing sense of frustration over their liminal space as not quite adults within the university context and as not full citizens of the nation because they lacked the vote, resulted in outbursts of demonstrations. Increasingly, students argued that they had a right to participate in the decision-making processes—within both the nation and their campus communities.

Demonstrations, confrontations, and individual acts of resistance represented efforts to stake a claim to the decision-making process. They became the mechanism through which the disenfranchised made their voice heard within a political system that granted them no voice. For many, the role of the student merged with a more active conception of citizenship and the tactical shift toward the airing of grievances through the issuing of demands. These individuals increasingly saw the identity of "student" as another example of a disenfranchised subset of Americans yearning for recognition as equals in the power structures of both the university and the nation. Further, they argued that as citizens of both the nation and the university community, they had a right, guaranteed under the U.S. Constitution, to participate in the decisions that effected their daily lives.

If the university was going to act as an agent of the state and the enforcer of morality, as it claimed the right to do through in loco parentis policies, then as citizens of the university and the state, the students had a vested interest in participating in the decisions made by the university. The logic of the argument rested wholly on an abstract assumption that the university operated under the same rules—the same concept of consent of the governed—as civil society. While one may potentially have argued that an 18-year-old is not a stakeholder in the larger American society and therefore not deserving of the right to vote, students declared there could be no similar objection to their stakeholder status within the university. Further, once they had gained greater control over university decision-making they could use this to justify expanding the right to vote to 18-year-olds, thereby enhancing their ability to participate in the decision-making of the nation at large. However, administrators and trustees did not generally share the assumption of the university as a microcosm of American society, with parallel structures of government. Despite whether it was an accurate vision of the relationship of students to the university, many students accepted this vision and it became an integral part of the student-citizen identity that helped to sustain and promote student political and social activism.

Student activists never quite gave up the hope that their actions could end the war in Vietnam and end racial discrimination, but they realized that by attacking campus-specific issues they could affect local change that could ripple out into a wider societal change. Students continued to challenge in loco parentis policies as well as the issues of racial discrimination and poverty, all out of a belief that individuals should have a greater control over their daily lives and that the American ideals of liberty and equality dictated these changes. As much as ROTC represented the most obvious and direct connection to the American military apparatus on campus, student attacks on the program had to do with questioning its fit within the wider educational mission of the university in American society and with the idea of academic freedom. Similarly, reactions against military and defense-industry recruitment on campus had more to do with whether the university served as a conduit for the militarization of American society, or whether it had a higher purpose to generate individuals who would challenge this militarization. The spread of draft resistance on campus was another manifestation of this rejection of militarization. In all these cases, from campus issues to the draft, the concern was with the expansion and elevation of the student voice in decision-making processes; these students believed they were an equal part (if not the most important part) of the university and should have their views heard. Further, some recognized that if they could get a foothold of power within the university, giving them the ability to exert control over certain aspects of their world, they could use that as leverage to gain a greater voice over issues within the wider American society.

Student activists adopted a confrontational footing, called for disruption, and issued demands regarding the workings of the university by claiming a status as citizens of the university community. All of this served an allegorical function because of their liminal space within American society, which resulted from their lack of a political voice in the decision-making process.

Thus, the arguments for student power derived from the student-citizen identity were about a larger effort to empower young people and represented a political ideal that individuals should have a say in the policies that directly affected their daily lives. If they could exert power and influence over the campus community, they believed they could establish a pattern that would lead to wider political participation.

Chapter 5

Campus Citizenship

Responsibilities, Rights, and ROTC

In 1967 and 1968, the calls for greater student voice in the decisions of the university came within the national context of student takeover events at places like Berkeley and Columbia, making some wary that student unrest could lead to similar events in northern Appalachia. In an interview with writers for *The Owl*, the University of Pittsburgh's yearbook, Chancellor Wesley W. Posvar responded that Columbia- or Berkeley-style takeover events occur only when there was a "sense of frustration and loss of identity." He went on to recognize peaceful dissent as "a normal part of the scene in a free and open University"; however, the chancellor was quick to add he would not accept obstructionist tactics.[1]

Chancellor Posvar's statements suggested that dissent against the government and its policies did not inherently make one unpatriotic, but when the expression of one's dissent prevented others from pursuing their academic interests then one crossed the line of acceptable behavior. Thus, Posvar acknowledged and supported the student-citizen identity while rejecting obstructionist tactics as counterproductive to the full functioning of student citizenship. Protests were part of the free expression of citizens in a democracy, and as long as they acknowledged the existing power relations of state and citizen, administrators should not only tolerate but also encourage such actions. However, disruptive actions served to challenge the power structure and as such represented a threat that administrators must stop.

By late 1967, the war in Vietnam had become the central focus of student activism. Civil rights and antipoverty activism largely faded as students retooled and filtered their understandings through their connection to the university, the war, and notions of citizenship. Increasing calls for student power represented an effort to claim whatever levers of power were available so students could feel as if they had some control in a tumultuous moment of upheaval. For many, the Reserve Officer Training Corps (ROTC) on campus became the focus of their rage; realizing they may not be able to end the war, many students thought ending ROTC was a more tangible and seemingly realistic goal. Students' efforts to expand their influence over the decisions made at the university rested on an increasingly potent notion of student-citizenship.

Campus Policies

In academic year 1967–1968 and into the fall of 1968, universities' campus housing and visitation policies (often referred to as parietals) and in loco parentis policies served as points of tension throughout northern Appalachia. Though concerns over women's hours and housing issues had dwindled some from previous years, they occasionally popped up in conjunction with student calls for a greater voice in the decision-making processes of campus life. Student demands for greater power over their own lives manifested in various ways during these years. At OU, the student government passed bills calling for increased student voice in the priorities of the campus and in selecting the next president of the University. There was also a riot, driven initially by a possible labor strike and the breakdown of the legitimate channels of grievance redress. At WVU, students constructed and voted on a Code of Conduct, using its creation as a means for expressing their vision of student rights, one that saw a direct link between citizenship of the University and that of the nation. Additionally, the Code connected seemingly disparate forms of civic engagement through a shared vision of empowered and engaged citizenship. These events highlight the continuing development of a cross-causally defined student-citizen identity. They demonstrate that even as other issues, such as the draft, crowded out attention and activism on some fronts, the call for change and for a greater voice in campus affairs retained its intimate link to student conceptions of citizenship.

Concerns persisted over where students could live and the hours they kept. Students had made a great deal of progress in the previous few years and the trajectory continued toward liberalizing women's hours and opening housing to black students. Experiments in "no hours" halls for segments of the female student population proved successful and students took efforts to expand these to encompass more women. An editorial in West Virginia University's *Daily Athenaeum* put it bluntly, "College-age coeds have their own sense of responsibility, and they are not going to let the University be their conscience for them." Interestingly, few argued for total abolition of restricted hours, suggesting that freshmen women should have greater limitations imposed upon them than any other class. The editors of the *Daily Athenaeum* also argued that, "women's hours are a necessary evil. . . . Because of in loco parentis doctrine, under which University students are governed, University officials must keep a close surveillance [*sic*] on its coeds."[2]

In terms of access to adequate housing, students and administrators at Ohio University attempted to create new off-campus housing standards that ensured black students did not face discrimination. These efforts included not only new university policies but also advocating for open housing laws in the local community; unfortunately, these laws often failed to materialize. For example, a May 1968 referendum at OU to support calls for an open housing law in Athens drew a great deal of student attention briefly to the subject as students wrangled over whether such laws and policies were effective.

In late April 1968, the OU Student Congress passed a statement calling on the city of Athens to pass a fair housing ordinance. The statement passed with near-universal support. Norman Brague, the only Student Congressman to oppose the action, explained his vote stating, "open housing laws infringe on the personal rights of property owners." Brague's dissent demonstrated his wrangling with the difficult question of how to ensure the rights of citizens when their interests are at odds with each other.

Student Congress later passed legislation stating all students "must live in University-sanctioned housing," which would guarantee that housing not only conformed to health and safety regulations but also to non-discrimination policies. Student Congress put the legislation to a student referendum and students ultimately rejected it by a 2-to-1 margin. Student government president David Stivison described the vote saying, "It is not that the students are for racism, but rather they are against the University getting actively involved in this area." From Stivison's perspective, students voted based on their interpretation of the proper role of the university in society. Opponents to the referendum had argued that it was poorly constructed, ambiguous, and represented an overreach of the University's power. Robert Jemess argued that students living off-campus "are legally adults and . . . capable of directing their lives. This includes deciding where to live." He went on to say if a landlord discriminated, existing laws allowed for a remedy. In the end, those who defeated the open housing referendum at OU did so by framing it as a question of students' rights and how best to ensure the University upheld those rights. An editorial in the *Post* summed up why the student body had to act on these issues saying, "An academic community, committed to human rights, cannot permit rights to be denied in its midst."[3]

In the spring of 1968, students at OU faced the possibility of another campus-wide strike, like the one that rocked the campus in March 1967, and again the threat of University closure. At the end of March 1968, Student Congress issued an ultimatum to OU President Vernon Alden demanding greater student input in University decision-making or risk a student strike. The impetus for this demand was an increase in student fees that some members of Student Congress felt was unfair. Student Body President Rob Christie, who authored the ultimatum bill that was passed by Student Congress fifty to three, called the fee hike "one more glaring example of the lack of community participation in the decision-making at Ohio University." Christie went further to say: "Until our right to have a say in the decisions which affect us is recognized, we do not feel that we can continue to support this institution. . . . Moreover, if we are to accept an increase in the cost of receiving an education, it is only fair that we should assume greater responsibility for the allocation of our money." The bill further proposed establishing "watchdog" committees of students, faculty, and administrators to ensure decisions made by the University were in the best interests of the students. Christie validated Student Congress' actions saying, "I don't think a student is a second class citizen. I think we have a right to participate in decision-making processes of this University community."[4] In the end, the administration paid only lip service to the student concerns and no student strike emerged. However, tensions remained high.

Within a month, the recently formed non-academic employees' union, Local 1699 of the American Federation of State, County, and Municipal Employees (AFSCME), announced a potential strike. On May 8, Local 1699 announced their objection to University restructuring efforts because of the new regulations created for staffing supervisory positions. For over a week, the *Post* reported on the sparring of Local 1699 and University spokespersons, making a strike and possible closure seemingly inevitable. However, on the night of May 18, at the eleventh hour, negotiations began, averting a strike.[5]

Given the ultimatum of March and the build-up of later tensions in the first half of May, many students had seen a strike as inevitable. Some students had planned on a possible closure and were upset that they had to finish the last few weeks of the quarter; many of them took to the College Green to voice their frustrations at being left out of crucial decisions that directly affected them. The following night, May 19, over two thousand students flooded onto the College Green and marched on the President's house. They chanted slogans—mostly calling for the University to close so they could go home—and moved en masse causing minor damage to University property as they went. The National Guard stood in reserve at the Athens fairgrounds, about a mile away, as University security, local police, and the state highway patrol moved to gain control of the situation.[6]

Though the May 1968 disturbances seemingly emerged out of frustrations over the University not closing, deeper underlying concerns bubbled up in successive nights of protest. On May 21, over three thousand students attended a meeting in Memorial Auditorium and laid out their grievances. From these concerns, students constructed a list of approximately one hundred demands that they later presented to the administration. Concerns ranged from issues of fees, housing, and grades to demands for greater student control and input, an end to women's hours and dress codes, and a call for expanded black studies curriculum. Students vowed to continue their protest until the administration listened to them, forcing the University to close if necessary.[7]

The administration had threatened closure in 1967 and had sent the students for an early Spring Break; it would surely not be a stretch to assume continued pressure could result in an early end to the current academic session. In the end, the University remained open though President Alden asked, "Those persons who cannot make this commitment to Ohio University are requested to leave."[8] In this way, Alden was making an appeal to the student sense of university citizenship by asking them to affirm their allegiance to the University and questioning the citizenship of those who challenged the University.

These events highlight the existence of a student-citizen identity. The student protesters argued that they had a right to speak out and for the administration to bring them into the decision-making process. They resented that both the union and the University used them as pawns in their negotiations. While the initial disruption served as a manifestation for the growing frustration of students, the mass meeting and construction of a list of grievances showed an effort by students to give a rational voice to their sentiments. The chants of "close it down" during the protests were as much from short-sighted desires to escape the quarter without taking exams as they were from a desire to see the University as it currently functioned cease and become more responsive to the students' needs. As some student leaders of the protest noted, "We are presenting the University with the chance to deal with us rationally. If they turn us down, they will have to face us as part of the mob."[9] In the minds of the students, their demands were meant to level the playing field, to exert their influence over aspects of their daily lives and futures, to have a degree of control that they generally felt was lacking from their lives as citizens of the University and of the United States. Their actions represented a reaction to the fractures generated in the University by the growing multiversity concept of higher education.

West Virginia University President James G. Harlow commented on the fractured nature of the university community at a student government conference in September 1968. Harlow argued that the role of the university in American society had expanded beyond purely instruction. His arguments that "students are important but not the only responsibility of the University," reflected the recognition of the multiple constituencies of the modern university within the military-industrial-academic complex of the Cold War. Further, Harlow argued "research and consultation" determined the position of the university in American society and as such, WVU could not be an agent of social or political change without threatening those ties.[10] In this way, Harlow became the very embodiment of the multiversity president Clark Kerr described in *The Uses of the University*.[11] It seems that Harlow was willing to focus greater attention on the less fractured research and consulting wings of university activities in part because these public and private contractors and constituencies provided greater revenue, prestige, and stability to the University than students.

The fractures in the student body at WVU became evident in the fall of 1968 when students voted on a new Code of Conduct. Drafted over two years, the Code sought to outline the expectations of student involvement in their own governance and provide a new judicial procedure. Opponents of the Code, led by the Committee for Student Rights, criticized the limitations on student power in the proposal, though they did not advocate radical revolution. The Committee for Student Rights argued the Code, despite "recognizing that students are citizens of the U.S., sets out to make certain they are second-class citizens." Further, they encouraged students to write a disclaimer next to their signature during registration when they signed indicating they had receive the new Code of Conduct. The suggested language rested on a vision of the student-university relationship as that of civil society dictated by the consent of the governed, "Signing this receipt does not imply acceptance of the regulations in this code as part of any contract between the University and myself." They argued that students should have a larger seat at the table and on equal terms with administrators.[12]

However, supporters of the Code argued that while students should have a seat at the table and a voice in decisions, the constant turnover of the student population prevented a coherent leadership from forming and therefore called for limiting student control to specific areas. David Zinn, Rick Becker, and John Nutter, drafters of the Code, argued that, "When we speak of student power it is foolish to isolate student power to mean students only. In the University community as defined in the preamble of the Code, student power means responsible student interaction with the other two segments of the community which are the faculty and the administration." Thus, while Code supporters accepted the notion of student-citizenship, their vision of its exercise was significantly more constrained than those opposing the Code.[13]

The debate over the Code suggested an agreement on the importance of the student as an individual to whom the administration should not dictate. Additionally, the Code dispute also highlighted a deep divide over the goal of student empowerment. Students who opposed the Code envisioned larger, long-range goals that would ultimately result in students—seen as an identity akin to ethnic, religious, or gender identity—gaining equality. Bob Rothman from the Committee for Student Rights argued that the Code would "abrogate our Constitutional rights" and that "the issue is, where does the power lie?" Ultimately, Rothman argued that true power at the University rested with those governed by the University, the students.[14]

Those who supported the Code argued students should aim for short-term and more easily attainable goals. Far from establishing new mores and redefining the relationship between students and administrators, the Code served as "guidelines for establishing a system of involvement. . . . It is not up to the Code to legislate such things as hours for women, what committees students will sit on, or in general what constitutes student involvement." Where code supporters argued that students should play some, limited role in disciplinary measures, opponents of the Code argued for the liberation of the entire student judicial system from administration control. When the Code

Committee brought their proposal to a referendum vote, students rejected it by a three percent margin.[15] The Code fight generated no threats of violence, obstruction, take-over, or riots; in part, this was due to the Code's opponents winning but also, and perhaps more importantly, because there was no contingent on campus calling for revolution in 1968.

The possibility for disruptive actions emerged at OU in the fall of 1968 when President Vernon Alden announced he would soon step down and the Board of Trustees would organize a search for his replacement. For Student Body President Dave Stivison this represented an excellent example of when the administration should hear the student voice, because "we [the students] have a more intimate knowledge of the needs of the University" then the members of the Board of Trustees. "If the students are not involved in choosing the next president of Ohio University," Stivison declared, it will be further proof that "the University belongs to the Trustees and not the students." Unfortunately, when the Board of Trustees established the five-member search committee it offered students no input into the decision-making.[16]

Over the next few weeks Stivison made student representation in the decision-making process for the next president a major priority. He even threatened civil disobedience and campus disruptions, evoking the images of the previous May's riots. In time, the Board of Trustees offered concessions and eventually granted students a limited role in the presidential selection process. Many students, as well as faculty and even some alumni, attacked Stivison as power-hungry and self-aggrandizing. However, in a campus-wide referendum that drew the largest student voter turnout in OU history, an overwhelming majority voiced their support for his actions. When finally able to appoint student representatives, Stivison confounded his critics by not naming himself as a delegate. He argued that he had fought for the students' voice not his own and that they should have a say in who leads their University. According to Stivison, "It is the duty of the educational institution to develop in students the ability to make well-thought-out decisions and develop the faculty of free inquiry. . . . For us, one of the best ways to do this is to become involved with the decision-making process of the University." In this way, Stivison was giving greater credence to the actions of May by reiterating the importance of student voices.[17]

After securing a student voice in the presidential selection process at OU, another issue emerged on campus prior to the Thanksgiving recess—the arming of campus security officers. The newly reformed Students for a Dem-

CAMPUS CITIZENSHIP

ocratic Society (SDS) chapter at OU issued a demand to the administration calling for the disarming of campus security forces—because "no piece of University property is worth the life of a single student."[18] Predictably, the administration refused to disarm campus security, sparking a peaceful sit-in by approximately twenty SDS members at the campus security office. When the students failed to disperse, the Athens police arrested them and charged them with trespassing. While their sit-in failed to end the arming of campus police, their actions led to wider campus newspaper coverage and initiated a debate amongst the student body.[19]

While many rejected SDS tactics, some showed a willingness to consider their arguments just as others argued that police were within their right to fire on someone to protect the University. John Felton, columnist for the *Post*, noted that trying to mobilize the campus around any issue in the days before the Thanksgiving recess was a flawed strategy. Felton stated, "If students cannot be mobilized to protest a $90 per year fee increase (which certainly hits most students where it hurts), they will obviously react with intense disinterest when told 24 seemingly harmless campus cops should be stripped of their unused weaponry." In a letter to the editor, student O.E. Frank offered a law and order critique of the SDS position and took issue with SDS statements that the standard service revolver was "meant only to kill or maim a human being." He went on to argue: "It is really only meant to stop lawbreakers. . . . They said at his [the Security Officer's] whim he can shoot and kill you. I think that if you get shot by University Police, it will be by your whim, not theirs. They said no piece of University property is worth losing a life. I say leave University property alone and you've got nothing to worry about."[20] It seemed that Frank supported the use of deadly force against suspected criminals and that anyone arrested was obviously guilty, and therefore deserving of whatever pain and suffering she or he received.

The debate over arming campus police highlighted a wider national conversation on gun control in 1968, following the assassinations of Dr. Martin Luther King Jr. and Robert F. Kennedy and the increasing incidents of fatal gun violence nationwide.[21] In a letter to the editors of the *Post*, SDS members Pat Dorner, Marty Denlinger, and Eric Fralick stated that, "SDS has as its primary objective a total and complete restructuring of the University (and the society in which the University exists)."[22] Thus, OU's SDS claimed a right as concerned citizens of their University community, as well as of American society, in their disarmament efforts.

For much of the period from August 1967 to December 1968, the growing concerns over the draft and the war in Vietnam pushed issues of poverty and civil rights out of the student newspapers. In recent years, scholars of the civil rights movement have challenged the narrative that the death of Martin Luther King Jr. during this period brought on the transition from the nonviolent, direct action civil rights movement to the aggressive, militaristic Black Power movement. They have also noted an increased disinterest in the civil rights movement amongst white liberals who had supported the King-brand of nonviolent activism as these activists shifted their attention to radical causes and revolutionary violence.[23]

Northern Appalachian universities saw a degree of radicalization on civil rights issues, though black populations on these campuses were always small. Organizations such as the Black Student Action Coordinating Committee at OU, the Black Action Society at Pitt, and the Black Unity Organization at WVU, formed to promote black consciousness, advocate for black educational and cultural opportunities, and demand redress of grievances. At the same time, administrators formed committees and organizations to investigate discriminatory hiring and housing standards, as well as to promote black enrollment and address issues of discrimination within the wider community in which the university resided.[24] Further, while these issues and concerns received sporadic coverage in the campus papers, one of the largest single events connected to civil rights in this period was the assassination of Martin Luther King Jr., and this tragedy sparked several campus tributes and memorials in April 1968. Moreover, if civil rights failed to register with students, poverty activism seemingly dissolved entirely as a campus concern.

In April 1968, campuses around the nation reeled in horror at the assassination of Martin Luther King Jr., and northern Appalachian campuses felt the same shockwaves. The campus newspapers afforded a great deal of column space, editorials, and even dedicated special issues to the assassination of King and to discuss the ramifications of his death. Students and administrators, as well as local community members, participated in memorial services or engaged in acts of peaceful civil disobedience in honor of King's legacy. However, in Pittsburgh, the city's black community, like so many others around the nation, erupted into violence, forcing the governor to declare a state of emergency and to send 1,500 National Guard troops and several thousand additional law enforcement personnel to the city. The rioting did not reach Pitt's campus and it is difficult to know with certainty whether any Pitt students participated in events during these chaotic days. Despite the outburst of grief and unrest caused by King's death, little in the way of civil rights activism seemed to change on campus.[25]

In 1968, black students at northern Appalachian universities issued various "demands" or generated lists of concerns and presented these declarations to university administrators in hopes of redressing their grievances. A one-page petition circulated at WVU in mid-April, in the aftermath of the King assassination, called for an end to discrimination in housing and employment at the University and in Morgantown. The petition echoed the message of Dr. King as it pledged signers "to work for an end to discrimination in Morgantown through use of all legal and non-violent means at our disposal."[26]

At Pitt, the Black Action Society, a recently formed organization that claimed to speak for the campus' black community (roughly 200 students on a campus of several thousands), issued a statement in late-June 1968 denouncing the failures of the University "to meet and understand the fundamental needs of Black people." The statement contained a list of demands that they declared required immediate attention, including increased recruitment and retention efforts directed at black students, the construction of black residence halls, the creation of a black-centered curriculum, expanded black faculty, and increased power for black students in the decision-making process of the University.[27] In early December, an ad hoc group of a dozen or so black students delivered a list of demands to OU president Vernon Alden and called for immediate action, much as BAS had six-months earlier at Pitt.[28]

At both OU and Pitt, black students claimed the right to issue such demands as citizens of the University and of the United States. As part of their founding document, BAS announced, "A people, until it uses its own talent, takes pride in its own history, expresses its own cultures, and affirms its own self-hood, can never fulfill itself."[29] At OU, the black students issued a blunt and straightforward statement justifying their actions, saying, "We the black students of Ohio University, have found that no difference exists between the campus and community. Both treat us as Niggers."[30] Thus, both claimed that for too long black students had existed as second-class citizens within both communities and improving their condition in the University would serve to enhance their position within American society.

The campus reaction to these demands varied, with many claiming the efforts would serve only to further fracture the campus community. Many white students responded with a degree of hesitancy to the demands issued by black students, seeing the declarations as unnecessarily divisive. One letter to the editor of the *Pitt News* argued "You cannot fight white racism with black racism," and went on to state that the BAS demands only perpetuated the emphasis on race, as if people simply stopped talking about race the issues of discrimination would evaporate.[31] Even the white student editors of the campus newspapers drew the ire of black students when they balked at the demands as unfeasible despite having supported various radical positions during the 1968 presidential campaign. The editors of the *Post* stated, "For the most part the demands are too vague, and explanation and discussion are needed before any of them can be instituted."[32]

While black demands generated push back from their fellow students, they elicited at least lukewarm responses from administrators. At both OU and Pitt, university officials expressed a degree of caution on most demands but fully rejected segregated black residence halls as not only unrealistic but a violation of non-discrimination policies of the University as well as state law.[33] In the end, at both Pitt and OU most of the demands of black students went unanswered as 1968 faded into 1969 and would serve as fodder for later civil rights activism on campuses over the next few years.

In contrast to the on-going debates and discussions about race and discrimination, coverage of poverty issues shrank significantly after the fall of 1967. Only infrequently did the campus papers refer to the student antipoverty organizations, such as the Associated Student Volunteers (ASV), the Southeastern Ohio Opportunity Program (SOOP), the Student Action for Appalachian Progress (SAAP), or the Hill Education Project (HEP). Whereas in previous years the newspapers covered in detail the projects the students engaged in and called on students to join the poverty struggle, the irregular coverage of these groups and their issues now largely came by way of reminding students that these groups existed and that their community-based organizing and activism was continuing.[34]

Students continued to work to build empowered communities. However, where there had been debates and forums in previous years about the nature of poverty, especially in the Appalachian region, now there was largely silence. Dozens of students continued to participate in projects sponsored by these groups, mostly in the form of tutoring and mentoring programs, but there appears to have been little of the radicalization amongst these antipoverty students that Thomas Kiffmeyer noted happening with the Appalachian Volunteers in his 2008 *Reformers to Radicals*.[35] Given the cross-causal nature of student activism, one may expect to see such radicalization expressed in areas beyond poverty activism, such as antiwar or students' rights positions. While student activism in these areas persisted, the rhetoric used was largely still more liberal than radical.

By-and-large, the issues of civil rights and poverty did not become less urgent during the period of late 1967 to the end of 1968, but newspaper coverage of and student engagement with these issues changed. The ascendancy of the war in Vietnam as the chief political, social, and economic issue left less room for activist labor and consciousness on other issues, at least, as presented in the campus newspapers. The demands made by black students represented a way to cut through the cacophony of noise created by the war. It seemed that anti-poverty activism could not take the sort of actions black students had taken because of a lack of a shared poverty identity and sense that the university had an obligation to act. Students found it difficult to mobilize individuals around a constructed identity of poverty, something most considered a transitory condition or a social negative that one could find little pride in or use as a basis for a personal and empowering identity.

ROTC

For many students, especially antiwar protesters, ROTC was the most immediate physical representation of the American military establishment on campus. As such, it became the target of demonstrations and activism on several occasions. Northern Appalachian student efforts to disrupt ROTC classes or challenge its accredited status represented, in some cases, proxy fights for larger issues, specifically the war in Vietnam. They attacked ROTC in an attempt to impede the government's pipeline for creating officers but did so by claiming the mission of ROTC did not conform to that of the university that housed the program. They objected to the curriculum as "courses in death" and for denying the spirit of academic free inquiry essential for the university.

In so doing, students were laying the foundations for wider political engagement. If they, as concerned citizens of the university community, could affect change on this policy, a policy both local and national in origins, then in the future they could claim greater legitimacy to confront other policies with which they disagreed. Thus, the debates and protests surrounding ROTC were simultaneously local and national in perspective. Claiming ROTC was inconsistent with the nature of the university provided a framework for challenging national issues that students felt were out of step with the mission of the nation.

Students, faculty, administrators, and the public at large had debated the question of military training and education within public universities for nearly a century by the 1960s. By the 1830s and 1840s, officer training beyond the official American service academy at West Point had begun at several private military institutes and was beginning to take form at public universities. The passage of the Morrill Land Grant Act of 1862 expressly made military training a component of any college created by its provisions. However, it was not until 1911 that the Reserve Officers Training Corps (ROTC) came into existence. After a rocky start during World War I, the program blossomed over the next three decades, eventually expanding to over 350 ROTC units by 1950. The primary mission of ROTC was the creation of reserve officers for national defense in a time of crisis. In 1951, however, the program transitioned into one that created mostly active duty officers because of the needs generated by the Korean Conflict. Between 1951 and 1964, enrollments in ROTC fell, the result, in part, of changes to the Selective Service deferment system. In 1964, the ROTC Vitalization Act attempted to stop the downward trajectory of enrollments. Though initially conceived prior to the Gulf of Tonkin Incident(s), the effort to strengthen ROTC came alongside the growing American war effort in Vietnam; as draft calls increased, so too did ROTC enrollments.[36]

The Vietnam War brought ROTC into a brighter light of scrutiny than it had been since the end of World War II. However, the Sixties' criticisms of ROTC built on earlier opposition, especially that of the 1930s when thousands of American men swore a modified version of England's Oxford Oath to refuse military service unless an enemy invaded the nation.[37] In the decade prior to World War II, ROTC programs came under fire by students who argued against what they saw as the militarization of the civilian academy. While prewar objections to ROTC faded because of American's entry into World War II and the birth of the Cold War, there remained some who questioned whether ROTC should continue to hold a place on campus. By-and-large, the movement to shift ROTC from compulsory to voluntary in the Sixties was not simply a rejection of ROTC's place on campus but also an attempt to normalize ROTC, which prior to World War II had mostly been voluntary.[38] An example of this normalization exists in West Virginia, where legislators and administrators began efforts in 1965 to transition West Virginia University's compulsory ROTC program to voluntary, which eventually occurred in 1968. However, in all these efforts the proponents argued that military education had a role at the University suggesting its heritage as a land grant university made such training part of its educational mission.[39]

As the war in Vietnam grew a dualistic movement occurred on campuses around the nation: students attacked ROTC as the most immediate example and embodiment of American militarism while simultaneously flocking into the ranks of ROTC as a way to avoid the draft or, at the very least, to exert some level of influence over their potential military assignment.[40] While anti-militarism and antiwar sentiment served to heighten criticism of ROTC, at the heart of Vietnam War era debates over ROTC were questions surrounding the nature and purpose of higher education in American society and whether ROTC conformed to that educational mission.

In the wake of the Gulf of Tonkin Incident(s) and the ROTC Vitalization Act of 1964, little student activism existed to challenge ROTC's position on college campuses. In the nearly two decades since the end of World War II, most Americans had simply taken for granted that ROTC was a component of college life, and that colleges would compel (or, highly encourage) their male students to take two years of military training at minimum. However, as the American war effort in Vietnam expanded, as draft calls grew, and as deferments shrank or ended, ROTC became a focal point for antiwar activism. Students recognized they may never be able to end the war or the draft and that they could exert only indirect influence over elected officials. Yet ROTC represented a symbol of American militarism, a key cog in the war machine, and something they could directly affect. A spokesperson for Pitt's Students for Peace argued, "If some people want to become officers in organizations which serve to promote wars, we cannot force them to change their minds. But, we can, and will object to the twice-weekly display of weapons and uniforms on campus; the University is not a military base and should not become one."[41]

Faculty and administrators had validated ROTC's presence at the university by arguing that through this process they were helping to inculcate civilian values within the officer corps and thereby blunting the effects of military doctrine. Student defenders of ROTC argued that the themes and lessons taught in ROTC—such as leadership and logic—were transferrable skills to civilian life. As *Daily Athenaeum* columnist Jim Jordan put it, "Even if the majority should consent to the complete removal of ROTC from the University campus, do they have the right to limit the professional aspirations of the minority? Of course not." In this way, he argued that the military was consistent with other civilian career pursuits.[42] However, some students who defended ROTC made arguments that the program was bringing civilian ideals into the military rather than suggesting a compatibility between military and civil military training. For example, *Pitt News* columnist Dan Booker, in November 1967, stated, "The overriding factor is that ROTC helps maintain societal values in the military establishment."[43]

However, this liberalizing mission of ROTC does not seem to be supported by evidence from the time period. In a study conducted in 1970, in the wake of the controversy surrounding the My Lai massacre, scholars found that while some differences existed between officers who had entered the military through the service academies or Officers Candidate Schools (OCS) and those who gained their commission via ROTC, all groups shared more values in common than those who earned bachelor's degrees without participating in military training. The study ultimately determined that students who voluntarily joined ROTC held preexisting attitudes favorable to aggression and authoritarianism as well as being more inclined to accept immoral orders or military control over civilian affairs than non-ROTC students.[44]

Further, the research determined that efforts to shift ROTC to a purely volunteer basis served to weed out students who possessed the liberal, humanistic values that supposedly validated the ROTC program. The researchers argued that only by ensuring that individuals with strong support for humanist, civilian values made their way into the officer corps could the university have a liberalizing effect on the military. They argued:

> Those who indicated that they were humanities majors were *less* willing to obey immoral orders than were social science, natural science, or engineering majors. They were the *least* willing to use nuclear weapons; they were the *least* likely to respond physically to insult; they were the *least* capable of imagining a situation in which a military takeover of the U.S. government would be justified; they were the *least* interested in endorsing "My country, right or wrong"; and they were the *most* critical of the size of the military budget. The trouble is that humanities majors do not seem very enthusiastic about joining the military . . . [they] are less interested than any of the other majors in joining ROTC, and

more insistent than others on "the right of the soldier to criticize his superior officer and/or government policies without facing sanctions for his dissent."[45]

Ironically then, while antiwar activists—many of whom were humanities majors—were busy trying to dismantle the compulsory ROTC programs that they saw as an overbearing militaristic hand of the federal government, they were creating conditions in which the military would be less connected to civilian values and, according to the researchers' findings, more accepting of immoral, aggressive behavior.

Students often made the antiwar arguments against ROTC in conjunction with, or as auxiliary to, arguments about the proper role of the university in American society. In making these arguments, students raised two important, if contested, points about the nature of the university and its mission in society. First, students argued that the educational mission of the university rested on the principle of academic freedom—the free and open inquiry into often-controversial issues, which may or may not lead directly to career preparation. Students noted that the federal government, and not the university, controlled ROTC and asked whether its emphasis on protocol allowed for the free inquiry and questioning that were key components of the educational mission of the university. The *Pitt News* columnist David Rosenblum argued, "In order for this institution to maintain a position of complete academic freedom it should have no part of a course over which it has no control."[46]

Second, students argued that as citizens within the university community they had a right to participate in the decision-making processes of the university. In an editorial regarding the growing ROTC controversy at the University in November 1968, the *Pitt News* argued that students should be engaged and concerned as well as voice their opinions, stating, "We feel the issues are paramount, for they reflect the very integrity of this institution. . . . It is a matter of academic principle." The following week, Pitt's Student Government passed a resolution supporting the removal of ROTC's credit toward graduation in part because they felt it right and proper that the elected representatives, as a "group with any jurisdiction on the campus," should weigh in on such an important topic. The resolution stated that ROTC's "present structure and operation makes it fundamentally inconsistent with the notion of an academic field of study, academic freedom, and the aims and philosophy of a liberal arts education."[47]

In the end, the editors of the *Pitt News* hailed the decision to end ROTC accreditation as a triumph of the power of student engagement in the decision-making process. However, the editors argued the success occurred only because students eschewed "violent confrontation or legitimate civil disobedience" and worked within "established channels." The editors concluded that "If an issue does not have legitimate gripes and is aired in a highly irrational manner, it can not [sic] be accepted. And we hope that the students of this University learn the value of this lesson in the future."[48] Thus, the editors saw the ROTC confrontation as establishing a framework for other student grievances, one that did not embrace civil disobedience or disruption but did prize the importance of the student voice. Students connected their activism on the question of ROTC to wider issues of their roles as students and citizens, and as such demonstrated the cross-causal connections of student activism during the Vietnam War era.

In the ROTC debate, students confronted the question of whether the university needed to remain neutral to controversial issues of society for it to achieve effectively its educational mission, as faculty and administrators claimed. What students saw, however, was the university not maintaining neutrality but rather supporting one political position by accepting, promoting, and accrediting ROTC programs within the campus. Students argued that to accept ROTC and to defend its presence on campus by claiming it had a liberalizing influence on the military (with no evidence), was to put the university on one side of the political debate over the role of the military in American (civilian) society. This side accepted the status quo militarization of American society, which represented a specific political orientation and not neutrality. However, faculty and administrators hesitated in eliminating ROTC, claiming that to do so would serve the interests of the antiwar factions and as such would be unacceptably politicizing the university.

Robert L. Holmes, scholar of social and political philosophy, noted in a 1973 article on neutrality and ROTC that virtually all decisions favor one political side or another, what mattered was the reasoning. Holmes argued that the elimination of compulsory ROTC—in fact, the abolition of ROTC entirely from a university—although supported by one political side, could and did represent a movement toward neutrality, just as maintaining the status quo often was not a mechanism for neutrality. Though Holmes never made the connection, the simplest analogy is to civil rights in the South, where maintaining the status quo of legal racial discrimination was not a neutral act. One side of this issue advocated the removal of inherently biased laws that hindered social and legal neutrality. Ensuring that the law treated everyone equally, therefore, was not a loss of but a gain for neutrality. In this same way, student activists pointed out that ROTC was a threat to the university's neutrality. However, many of the more radical students argued that since the university had leaned in one direction for so long, they should now swing the bias in a different direction; they attempted to use the weight of the university to affect change on several socio-political issues. It was this desire to shift the university from one biased stance to another that created some of the strongest opposition to student activism on campus, especially since faculty and administrators generally did not accept the premise that the status quo was biased.[49]

During the series of ROTC protests at Pitt in 1967–1968, students advocated for "intellectualism, not militarism" in higher education and questioned whether allowing ROTC on campus put the University on one side of the political debates that were taking place in America at the time. Students for Peace argued that the University was offering tacit support for "the study of warfare and death" by permitting ROTC on campus. The student group rejected administration arguments that ROTC had a place at the University because of the universal military obligation for American men. Students for Peace argued that not all men did, in fact, serve in the military. Rather, they noted that as citizens of the United States, they (as many non-college men had) could petition for conscientious objector status if drafted and receive non-combatant service; yet they could not achieve a similar status vis-à-vis ROTC. Thus, as citizens, they had the right, the obligation even, to object. The students argued that other paths to an officer's commission existed and that their goal was not to end the American military. Instead they aimed to remove military training from the University because it failed to meet, and indeed flew in the face of, the educational mission of open inquiry that was at the core of the University. An SFP spokesperson stated emphatically, "We believe that teaching people to kill other people should not be a part of the curriculum of an institution dedicated to the development of thinking minds."[50]

Conversely, students who supported the status quo of ROTC used the same themes of academic freedom and the right of students to participate in decision-making to argue their positions. In a letter to the editor of the *Pitt News*, a student argued, "Clearly ROTC does not violate the concept of academic freedom—a foreign language or physical science course is equally as regimented."[51] Implicit in this line of reasoning was the assumption that a military career was no different from any other profession for which students were preparing, and thus the instruction in combat was no different from any other course in skill set development. An OU student argued that if one did not believe in ROTC one "does not have to eat from its table." The student argued that it would be wrong to deny others this opportunity to decide for themselves.[52] For this student, as with many others throughout northern Appalachia, academic freedom meant the right of the student to choose the career path they so desired and to pursue coursework to that end, including military careers.[53]

At Pitt in the fall of 1968, during a debate over whether to retain ROTC accreditation, several ROTC supporters formed pro-ROTC accreditation organizations and argued that administrators should hear their voices before they reached any final decision. Dave Ehrenworth, a cadet sergeant in Pitt's Army ROTC, noted that a petition to retain ROTC accreditation received over 2,300 signatures, which "is over one third of the student body at Pitt. I think the faculty should take this into consideration when they make their decision."[54] In this way, the forces for the status quo argued for the vocalization of the student voice, while at the same time highlighting the reality that there was not a single student voice.

Conclusion

For students, the ability to affect change in curriculum represented an affirmation of their rights as citizens within the university community. Thus, the debates over demands issued by black students or the accreditation of ROTC highlight how these various movements intersect—through the sense of citizenship. Students had the right to dissent, the right to participate in decision-making, the right to challenge and change their world. There was often a direct connection drawn between debates over issues such as women's hours, arming security officers, creating black studies programs, and the war in Vietnam; a direct line connected them all as the purview of the adult American citizen. Thus, it seems to make sense that one of the strongest nexus points for the convergence of campus and community issues would surround the question of civilian military obligation.

It is not surprising that students infused antiwar arguments into the ROTC debate, but the debate over ROTC was so much more than just a question of militarism in American society or a question of the academic mission of the university. The debates over ROTC get to the heart of a question about what it means to be an American and to the very central theme of Sixties activism: What limitations and powers, what rights and obligations, what privileges and penalties does one have as an individual in American society? These questions find voice in student antiwar activism and efforts to define who had legitimate rights to the university space.

Chapter 6

Challenging the War

Antiwar Activism and Draft Resistance on Campus

By the fall of 1967, Vietnam had taken over as the chief issue of concern on campuses in northern Appalachia. Escalating American involvement in Vietnam and the widening credibility gap between what the Johnson administration stated publicly about the war and what the public saw for themselves in nightly news reports, made students more concerned with the war and their connection to it. However, aside from the October Mobilization for the Confrontation against the Warmakers in Washington, D.C., there did not appear to be a great deal of general antiwar activism. While this period saw a great deal of student activism that drew inspiration from the antiwar cause, the various national and local events often targeted individual components of the war machine rather than the war itself. An International Student Strike in April 1968 represented one of the few antiwar events on campuses during this period; organizers at this event issued a general call to "stop the war," not a list of several demands to dismantle the mechanisms of war. They simply demanded: end the war.

Much of the activism of these months in 1967–1968 that was connected to issues of the war focused on specific targets, such as ROTC, military or defense-industry recruitment on campus, or the draft. Occasional, infrequent, and small antiwar protests and pickets at northern Appalachian universities occurred, including ones directed at Dow Chemical or against secret research undertaken by the university. However, for as much as the campus papers covered the war through wire service stories, their reporting suggests that activism calling for an end to the war was limited.

Activism was growing in some areas, like draft resistance, demonstrating a more focused approach to student opposition of the war. Where from 1964 to 1967 they called for a general halt to hostilities, by 1967–68 they were emphasizing specific points they deemed crucial for ending the war. Debates about the origins of American intervention and continued presence faded from campus. Though the war played a key role in how students viewed candidates in the 1968 presidential election, the campus papers presented the issue as only one of many concerns students should use to evaluate a potential leader.

The October Mobilization

In October 1967, Washington, D.C., hosted one of the largest protests against the war in Vietnam. The event, billed as a confrontation with the warmakers, represented the shifting emphasis in antiwar activism toward large mass rallies and away from the smaller teach-in style actions that sought to build knowledge as well as raise consciousness. The planners hoped to attract a few hundred thousand protesters to the events of October 21, and the expansive range of possible messages and actions allowed a wider cross-section of antiwar activists to participate. Organizers divided the event between an antiwar rally that drew over 100,000 to the Lincoln Memorial and a march that led to the Pentagon where radical protesters attempted to levitate the building. The daylong event, which included the iconic moment of protesters placing flowers in the barrels of the rifles trained on them by soldiers at the Pentagon, culminated in the arrests of over 700 protesters.[1]

In the week prior to the Washington events, local demonstrations occurred that were meant to either encourage people to travel to D.C. or were held separately because local organizations knew they could not all travel to the capital. Ohio University, the University of Pittsburgh, and West Virginia University all held rallies or staged events in mid-October and students from all three schools went to the national protest. In total numbers, the representation of these schools in Washington in October 1967 significantly outnumbered those who traveled to Selma in March 1965, where nearly 200 northern Appalachian students had participated in various events.[2] Unlike student attendance of SDS's March on Washington in 1965, when OU students asked the *Post* not to identify them, the campus newspapers openly covered the exploits of the peace demonstrators in 1967. However, in both cases, northern Appalachian students felt compelled to act based on a moral sense of duty as citizens of the nation.

Local Pittsburgh participation in the October Mobilization drew together students from throughout the city and centered on the arrival of the "peace torch." Students from Duquesne University, Carnegie-Mellon University, Chatham College, and Mount Mercy College joined Pitt students in a series of rallies in support of the October Mobilization. On the evening of October 16, 1967, the peace torch—a torch ignited in Hiroshima, Japan, and containing fragments from an anti-personal mine used in Vietnam—passed through Pittsburgh on its way to Washington, D.C., for the national antiwar demonstration. When the torch stopped at Bellefield Presbyterian Church near Pitt's campus, several hundred spectators came out to see the torch and hear a brief message from Rev. Edward Biegert of the United Oakland Ministry. Biegert reaffirmed the demonstrators' commitment to peace and their desire to end the war in Vietnam saying, "We will not cop-out or drop-out. . . . We would rather have a hard peace than an easy war." A few dozen members of the local Young Americans for Freedom (YAF) chapters counter-demonstrated and passed out flyers calling into question the patriotism of those supporting the October Mobilization. The peace demonstrators generally ignored the YAF leaflets and the peace torch march resumed; however, the potential for physical conflict existed.[3]

The brief set of ceremonies that took place in Pittsburgh culminated in a rally on Carnegie-Mellon's campus a few blocks up Forbes Avenue from Pitt. Even though events earlier in the day passed without incident, the University's administration decided to lock down the campus prior to the rally for fear that the peace demonstrators would turn into rioters. However, the only threat of violence came when a uniformed soldier roughly made his way through the crowd, resulting in some pushing, shoving, and name-calling. In the week after the rally, students wondered aloud why the administration had equated peace demonstrators with "vandals."[4]

In the week prior to the confrontation in D.C., WVU's chapter of SDS set up a table on campus to distribute anti-draft literature and to get signatures on a national draft and war survey. The two dozen WVU students who traveled to Washington, all SDS members, joined with students from other West Virginia colleges and universities to march as a state unit. The WVU chapter of SDS announced they would not participate as an organization in the Pentagon civil disobedience, so as not to force any of its members to take an action their conscience did not support. Rather, they argued that civil disobedience was a personal decision and that they would support any of their number who wanted to participate. In the end, three WVU students did engage in the actions at the Pentagon and police arrested them for their activities.[5]

Seven of the 150 OU students and faculty protesters who traveled to D.C. also engaged in civil disobedience at the Pentagon, though none went to jail. The Athens Committee to End the War in Vietnam, chaired by Elaine Herald (the Quaker student who helped initiate weekly silent peace vigils on campus), held a sympathy march on campus at the same time as the Washington protest. In an editorial, the *Post* noted that while neither the rally in Athens nor in Washington would change President Johnson's mind that was not the goal. Rather, the editors argued the intention was to "encourage other political aspirants to think more seriously of the peace movement—its support and its determination."[6] Editors of the *Pitt News* echoed this sentiment when they issued their own editorial on the same day in which they stated, "What does matter is that opposition to the war does not center around a fringe element any more. . . . We can no longer point to an organization such as Students for Peace as an isolated example of people opposed to the war."[7]

Antiwar Activism and Campus Recruiting

If opposition to the war had become more mainstream within American society by late 1967, it had not necessarily become more frequent on campus. The campus newspapers show few general antiwar activities on campus, most war-related activities targeted specific components of the government's war effort. The lack of news coverage of general antiwar sentiment may be a function of the mundane not being newsworthy; in other words, students may not have seen an antiwar picket on campus as as much of an oddity as it had been in previous years, and thus it elicited little or no interest from the campus papers. However, this does not appear to be the case.

In the previous three years, with increasing regularity, campuses in northern Appalachia had witnessed Vietnam War debates and educational programs. Often, faculty experts at these events would square off against each other, and campus newspaper coverage of the events remained relatively consistent or increased somewhat. It appears that by late-1967 these events halted almost universally. As students promoted new conceptions of their rights and power, they became less likely to listen to faculty debates and more likely to engage directly themselves. One of the few exceptions to this transition to a demonstration model from a teaching model of antiwar activism was a "Vietnam Dialogue Week." Held at OU in February 1968, this event featured speeches by politicians and a handful of faculty-centered debates.[8] Despite this exception, the shift was away from a general antiwar focus to specific, actionable foci—ROTC, campus recruiters, or the draft. Students no longer needed to debate and discuss how the United States got in or whether it should get out of Vietnam, rather they now sought to challenge things that had a tangible or symbolic link to the war and the nation's capacity to fight it.

In April 1968, still reeling from the assassination of Martin Luther King Jr., OU students participated in the International Student Strike and Boycott, holding a series of events on the College Green. The goal was to get the bulk of the student body to boycott classes on April 26 in order to draw media attention to student concerns about the war, the draft, and racism in America. The event demonstrated the cross-causal nature of student activism: they rallied against the Vietnam War and racial discrimination at home, arguing that they were both part of a larger problem with American society. An editorial in the *Post* declared, "The United States is not the perfect place that those in power try to tell us it is. It's time we realize this and commit ourselves to trying to change things. Particularly in this election year, a massive display of opposition to current policies could have effect." However, the events at OU, including speeches and folk singing, only drew about 200 students and only limited attention from one of the local Athens newspapers. Though the effort played out across the nation at various campuses, there was no real sense of a national, much less international, event in northern Appalachia. Neither Pitt nor WVU observed this day of protest and boycott.[9] The strategy of decentralized mass protest would prove to be an important tactical shift in future antiwar efforts—especially the October 1969 Moratorium. However, in the spring of 1968 its time had not yet come.

Activists still relied on the mass rally tactic as the chief mode of expression of student frustrations. While large rallies functioned as communal expressions, they also served as massed individual actions of dissent and thereby as mechanisms for giving voice to the frustrations of the disenfranchised, if not necessarily serving to build sustainable communities of engaged citizens. The New Left prioritized the idea of a community of individuals capable of participating in the democratic process. Yet while mass rallies demonstrated the size and extent of the disaffected population, they did not draw these individuals into the decision-making process or help to generate workable solutions. However, they did on occasion create lists of demands that infrequently resulted in changes. Mass rallies were transitory and temporary events meant to energize individuals, especially those whose dedication to the cause was situational or minimal. It was through smaller actions of dedicated individuals attempting to exert control over the decision-making process that solutions to the problems expressed at mass protests developed. It was also at this smaller, more personal scale where community empowerment grew and achieved sustainability. However, in 1967–1968, even these smaller actions took on a greater oppositional tone. Campus protests against military and defense-industry recruiters demonstrate this clearly.

In challenging the right of the military or defense-industries to recruit on campus, students were claiming a right to control the university based on their citizenship within the university. Students argued they could deny access to the physical space of the university to any people or group that they believed conflicted with their interpretation of the university's mission. In November 1967, students throughout northern Appalachia protested recruitment efforts by Dow Chemical, the producers of the napalm used by U.S. forces in Vietnam. Nearly 100 students at both OU and Pitt participated in the anti-Dow marches over two days in mid-November.[10]

Protesters reasoned that failure to oppose publicly Dow's use of campus space would send a message that students—and by extension their universities—endorsed the war and the mechanisms of war-making in the United States. In a letter to the *Pitt News* editor, Ivan Abrams and Joshua Chasan argued that Dow had a right to recruit employees, just not at the University. They noted that Dow was free to speak at the University if it chose, like the Communist Party was, but, just as the administration prevented the Communist Party from recruiting on campus, so too should Dow be restricted. They argued:

> Ultimately it is a question of the nature of the University. Should the University exist within and become a part of the moral vacuum outside its halls, or should it sit in continuous and urgent judgment and criticism of the society in which it exists? Should it, with the companies with which it cooperates so directly, abdicate the moral responsibility which is so lacking in our society? Are we in this University merely part of a fact exchange, or are we involved in an experience for which the transition of values is an integral process? And has not the University abdicated any sense of its role in shaping, debating and

exchanging concepts so basic as right and wrong? Dow Chemical Company's presence on campus is merely one manifestation of the perversions of the nature of our University.[11]

Abrams and Chasan believed that corporations should not use the University space to recruit students into enterprises that perpetuated the corrupt status quo.

Similar rationale underpinned efforts by WVU's SDS chapter to deny Marine recruiters' access to the Student Union in October 1968. In a letter to WVU president James G. Harlow, SDS denied the legitimacy of military recruitment on campus and denounced the growing connection between the University and the military-industrial complex. As SDS local chapter president Louis Horacek put it, "We're interested in the aspects of the University tied to the war machine." Horacek went further to indicate, "SDS decided to take action against the Marines because it was a direct action against the agencies supporting the war in Vietnam."[12] In this way, the WVU chapter of SDS was going beyond the proxy fight OU and Pitt students were having with Dow and attempting to affect directly US policy. In all cases, northern Appalachian students rallied against Dow or the military expressing their frustrations with the nation and the university.

Draft Resistance

Beginning in 1967, the selective service system underwent several important transitions, raising greater amounts of resistance amongst college-aged young men. Steadily, college enrollment eroded as a bulwark against conscription and as deferment options dwindled the once distant conflict in Southeast Asia became an uncomfortably closer reality for many students. As Michael Foley has noted in *Confronting the War Machine*, there were distinct differences between those who sought to avoid the draft—dodgers—and those who challenged it—resisters.[13] Those who disagreed with draft dodgers and resisters lumped the two groups together, and scholars have often overlooked these distinctions as they speak in generalities about the draft and its opponents. However, the distinctions are important since incidents of resistance rose locally and nationally almost exponentially during the eighteen months from August 1967 to December 1968.

Draft resisters in the Sixties drew on earlier episodes of non-compliance, including those during World War II. During the 1930s, college students throughout the United States signed statements refusing military service if conscripted and denouncing the futility of war.[14] Thousands rejected, evaded, or resisted the 1940 Burke-Wadsworth Selective Training and Service Act: some formed families, others sought deferments or exemptions from military service, and a small minority actively refused to participate with conscription at all. In total, authorities arrested and jailed roughly six thousand men for draft noncompliance during World War II. While the number represents a small proportion of draft age men during the war, the fact that these men felt such a strong conviction against conscription during World War II—the last "good war"—suggests a need to reevaluate both the popular and academic understanding of the war and draft resistance.[15] The political opposition to World War II seems counter to the popular image and memory of Americans during the war and suggests a connection to a much longer tradition of political dissent for resisters of the Vietnam War era.

While draft resistance became more frequent from late 1967 to late 1968, the phenomenon in northern Appalachia did not begin with draft resistance ceremonies in late 1967, but rather in the spring of 1964. A young man from the city of Pittsburgh, Thomas Rodd—the son of William Rodd, an official in the Johnson administration—announced that he would refuse induction into the military in late-March 1964. Rodd staged a one-man sit-in at the federal building downtown demanding police arrest him for his refusal; he also announced his intentions in the Carnegie Tech student newspaper, the *Tartan*. Rodd's arguments against the draft and in defense of his actions were representative of the statements made by later resisters in northern Appalachia—the war was immoral, conscription was illegal, and accepting deferments rather than resisting the system was complicity with murder. Further, he hoped his small act of rebellion would serve to inspire others saying, "I seek to generate power in this witness, power to help end the war in Vietnam." Rodd believed that individuals could change their world one small act at a time and that with each effort the power to change grew—a message consistent with student calls for greater control over their lives within the university. Rodd received probation, though he would eventually go to prison for his participation in antiwar demonstrations in violation of his probation.[16]

Debates over the duty of citizens in a time of war flourished in fall 1967. In September, General Lewis Hershey, director of the Selective Service System, came to Pitt to discuss conscription and the military obligation of young

American men. Members of the Pitt Students for Peace (SFP) handed out pro-resistance literature and chocolate Hershey's kisses (as a symbol of peace) in the lobby prior to the general's speech. During the question and answer session following his speech, Hershey often came back to the theme that citizens have a duty to their country stating, "Congress never gave the right to the citizen to choose his war."[17] Hershey saw no patriotism in resistance to the draft and equated citizenship with military service (and, apparently, being a man).

In stark contrast to the pro-war rally at Pitt in 1965 that reinforced the image of patriotism as the public expression of unconditional support for America *qua* the state, a late-1967 anti-draft demonstration on the same campus focused on patriotic expression as reasoned opposition to policies perceived to run counter to America *qua* the ideal. In December 1967, students gathered at a draft resistance rally at a church just off Pitt's campus. At least five men engaged in acts of individual resistance when they turned in their draft cards, and several dozen others signed statements of support. Graduate history student Joshua Chasan spoke during the event and argued that the war was inconsistent with American beliefs and values and went on to lay out the resisters' argument against the war and the draft, suggesting, "the Resistance . . . is above all a quest and a stand for human dignity." Again, the proper role of a citizen and patriot came to the forefront as Chasan argued that a moral imperative, a sacred duty, compelled citizens to stand against injustice.[18]

The seriousness of the night's activities hung in the air, mixed with the acrid stench and smoke from an arsonist's failed attempt to disrupt the peaceful event. Following a brief delay caused by a chair and some rags being set ablaze, with varying degrees of militancy speakers expressed their personal disdain for the war and the draft as well as their belief that citizenship required active participation. Former graduate student and current substitute teacher in the Pittsburgh school system, Ted Marsh, challenged the constitutionality of selective service. At the same time, Carnegie-Mellon University computer science graduate student, Ed Fuller, called the war in Vietnam "bloody madness." The service ended with Monsignor Charles Owen Rice, an activist Catholic priest from the Holy Rosary parish in the Homewood section of Pittsburgh, calling forward those who were willing to resist the draft by turning in their registration certificates and those who were willing to sign statements of support. Mgsr. Rice closed the event by reaffirming the strength of the resisters' convictions, saying, "We are stronger than the violent. . . . We will not stop."[19]

Chasan's roommate and fellow resister, David Morrison, also spoke during the event. Morrison's speech represented a call to action when he stated, "the draft and the military are not to be fled or dodged; they are to be opposed and resisted." The following day, Morrison drove three hundred miles to appear before his local draft board in Lansdowne, Pennsylvania, and to inform them of his act of resistance the previous night. The board members present for Morrison's personal appearance struggled to understand why he would not accept a deferment or civilian work as an alternative to military service. Morrison was 24-years-old at the time, married, and working as a research chemist at Pittsburgh Plate Glass, as well as a graduate student at Pitt. Due to his job and studies he was entitled to deferments (which he refused), and as a Quaker he could opt for civilian service rather than serve in the military as a medic. However, Morrison argued that accepting alternative service or deferment represented a tacit support for the system as legitimate, which he simply could not do. For Morrison, resistance represented an "internally derived" principle that one must uphold even (or, perhaps, especially) when it challenged the position of the government.[20] When called for induction in the summer of 1968, Morrison refused stating, "Every individual has a fundamental right to determine his own destiny; no governmental authority such as the Selective Service has the right, legal or moral, to tell someone what to do with his life."[21]

In 1968, the incidents of draft resistance in Pittsburgh increased. Ted Marsh, the pacifist schoolteacher, refused induction in January while a crowd of nearly two hundred stood vigil outside the federal building downtown in sub-freezing temperatures. Marsh argued that he chose to resist rather than flee the country because he "likes the American way of life too much to throw it away"; only through resisting the draft could Marsh exercise his simultaneous love for country and his right to dissent. A reporter for the Duquesne University campus newspaper, the *Duquesne Duke*, called Marsh's resistance an act of courage.[22]

Also refusing induction in early 1968 was Francis Shor, a Pittsburgh native, who attended Pitt between 1963 and 1967, the years Dr. Kurtzman identified as so full of "unreal" changes. Individuals like Shor highlight the cross-casual nature of student political and social activism. Shor was heavily involved in the civil rights and antiwar movements as well as anti-poverty work and local community organizing. He was an active member in a wide variety of organizations and activities including SDS, Friends of SNCC, Student Peace Union, and programs aimed at tutoring black children from impoverished areas of the city. Shor, self-identifying himself as a New Left scholar and activist during his years at Pitt, had at one point in 1965 considered applying for a conscientious objector's deferment from the draft, but by 1966 he had "decided the draft was also oppressive and signed [a] 'We Won't Go' statement, refusing my student deferment." After graduating from Pitt, Shor participated in Vietnam Summer as a draft counselor and, as a graduate student in history at the University of Minnesota in October 1967, engaged in active resistance by turning in his draft card. He would later face legal action due to his 1968 refusal of induction. Shor saw social and political activism, especially those rooted in non-violence and based on moral witness, as providing effective means to change society.[23]

In April 1968, as Pittsburgh and the rest of the nation struggled to come to terms with the assassination of Rev. Martin Luther King Jr., a full-page ad appeared in the *Pitt News* signed by over forty faculty members who expressed their support for a second draft resistance ceremony at the United Oakland Ministry and for those students who chose to resist the draft or sign statements of non-compliance. That same month, David Worstell, a University of Chicago student from the North Hills region of Pittsburgh and an active member of the Pittsburgh Resistance, refused induction. He previously considered conscientious objector status but recanted saying, "I refuse to admit that any individual must ask his government for an exemption so that he won't have to kill." Carnegie Mellon's *Tartan* ran Worstell's story with a companion piece by resister David Morrison about how one could seek draft reclassification and "maximize [their] civil rights under the law."[24]

During the first week of April 1968, as part of a national draft resistance campaign, Pitt graduate student and member of the Pittsburgh Draft Information Center, David Morrison, went to WVU to hold a two-day workshop on draft counseling and conscientious objection. Meanwhile, two WVU students, both members of SDS, held a press conference at which they read statements of resistance and packaged their draft cards for return to General Hershey at the Selective Service. From the steps of Wesley Methodist Church on the edge of campus, Harry Shaw, former president of the WVU chapter of SDS, and Louis Horacek, serving president, stated that their consciences had driven them to conclude that they could no longer continue to comply with "a system that is totally undemocratic and totalitarian," in Horacek's words. Meanwhile, Shaw stated: "I can not [sic] reconcile my belief in democracy and the dignity of the individual with a totalitarian system which denies the natural rights of man. . . . We in the United States are living a lie. We talk about democracy and human dignity, yet we put ourselves against the poor and oppressed peoples of the world. This system of oppression can not [sic] continue. Change is demanded, and for this change society needs free men, free from prejudice and agression [sic]."[25]

Unfortunately, for Horacek and Shaw, the outcry of grief from the assassination of Martin Luther King Jr. in Memphis that same day largely drowned out their statements of resistance. One week later, freshman forestry major Joe Hinson wrote to the *Daily Athenaeum* to express his displeasure with the acts of resistance of Horacek and Shaw. Hinson attacked the two as "pseudointellectuals" existing in "self-made protective wombs" and that they needed some "common patriotism . . . driven in to their long-haired heads."[26]

Two days later, a junior education major, Sam Hoye, came to the defense of two resisters. He argued their actions represented the deepest love for their country and highest form of patriotism, concluding: "America needs more of those people, people who can stand up for the things they believe are right at a time when standing on the issues may be contrary to traditional ideas of patriotism."[27] The two responses highlighted the contours of student debate over the proper role of a citizen, with Hinson representing a traditionalist conservative view and Hoye a more liberal perspective. Should citizens follow where their nation's leaders direct them and accept these leaders' definition of the nation's interests, or should citizens actively challenge leaders when they believe the direction set is counter to the best interests of the nation?

The question of how a citizen should respond to the actions of their government directly linked to student perceptions of their role within the university. For traditionalists such as Hinson, student-citizens must conform to a perceived normality subsuming their own interests to the will of the majority and dutifully fulfill their obligations regardless of if they agreed with them or not. Student-citizens must not challenge the authority of their administrator-leaders, who defined the parameters of acceptable behavior; one must conform and oblige because dissent was disloyalty. However, for Hoye (and by extension, Horacek and Shaw), the role of a student-citizen was to seek to improve the campus-national community. Their efforts echoed the words of Henry David Thoreau: "There will never be a really free and enlightened

State until the State comes to recognize the individual as a higher and in-dependent power, from which all its own power and authority are derived, and treats him accordingly."[28] For students like Hoye, Horacek, and Shaw, the university functioned as a conglomeration of citizens that could serve as a tool for refashioning the state to meet the needs of citizens.

In May 1968, OU student Peter Fromm refused induction into the Army, and the *Post* offered brief coverage of his experiences. Fromm admitted he was not a member of any organized resistance organization but drew inspira-tion from the same rejection of systematized killing that motivated resisters throughout the region, stating he disagreed "with the de-humanizing effect of the military system on the lives of individual citizens." However, as the prospect of jail time became a more distinct reality, Fromm sought ways to prevent a prison term. Though he claimed "his anti-draft beliefs were based on 'the totalitarian structure of army life' and not any particular political be-lief," according to the *Post*, it appeared that Fromm was never as committed to draft non-compliance as other resisters. His willingness to accept a defer-ment stood in direct opposition to the resisters' argument that the draft was itself inherently immoral. The Fromm experience highlighted the difficulty in classifying and understanding resistance to conscription as he appeared to reject the idea of military service and its corrupting influence on humanity just as resisters did, but, unlike resisters, he seemed to have not accepted the idea that he should suffer to end the system.[29]

Joshua Chasan, the Pitt graduate student who had spoken eloquently on the meaning of the war, the draft, and resistance in December 1967, himself became a draft non-compliant in early October 1968. His act of disobedi-ence became part of a larger rally calling for "non-violent, radical change" to end the "bloodbath" in Vietnam. Students marched on the home of Pitt's Chancellor Wesley W. Posvar to demand the end of the University's support for conscription and rallied downtown outside the federal building as Chasan refused induction.[30]

For the resisters and their supporters these actions represented the duty of patriots. The ridicule and scorn they faced for their decision reaffirmed their sense of martyrdom rather than discouraged or dissuaded them. Some saw their actions as part of a long tradition of anti-militarism associated with the nation's founding generation. Though their actions were public, and often collective, they were still instances of private, individual witness. The Pitts-burgh Draft Information Center's counselors advised potential conscientious objectors or resisters that pursuing this course required a "willingness to go to prison for his convictions." Echoing Thoreau's sentiment, David Morrison described the centrality of the individual's conviction saying, "Instead of the people always being brought to the bidding of their leaders, why can't the leaders be brought to the bidding of the people."[31] To those who refused to comply with the draft, their actions represented the obligations of all citizens to force their government to live up to its ideals. As students made greater claims to participation in the decision-making of their campus community, draft resistance represented a parallel call for greater personal control and a hope for reform in their community.

Conclusion

In April 1968, at the same time that draft resisters such as David Worstell, Louis Horacek, Harry Shaw, and Peter Fromm were making their intentions known, a couple hundred OU students participated in the International Student Strike and Boycott, and several hundred more prepared to engage in a quadrennial mock Republican convention. The mock convention at OU drew national attention as the National Broadcasting Company came to Athens in mid-April to do some pre-convention interviews and film a parade of convention participants. Campus newspapers throughout the region offered biographies and general interpretations of the various contenders for the presidency in 1968, and many of these individuals or their surrogates traveled to the region. The students and their newspapers debated the merits of the candidates, as previous students had in 1964, and offered endorsements and critiques. Hundreds, perhaps thousands, of students in the region participated in the 1968 presidential campaign by going "Clean for Gene" or working for some other candidate in canvassing, handing out leaflets, and stuffing envelopes. Statistically speaking, at least several hundred of these young people did vote in the election. However, there seemed some distance between the election and other issues students directly engaged with, perhaps a result of still not having the vote.[32]

Northern Appalachian students participated in Choice '68, a national mock election sponsored by *TIME* magazine that drew in over one million student votes nationwide. While the OU mock Republican convention named New York Governor Nelson Rockefeller the winner of the party's nomination (with Illinois Senator Charles Percy as VP), Choice '68 declared Senator Eugene

McCarthy the overall winner of the student vote, with a majority of students also supporting the call for a "phased reduction of U.S. military activity" in Vietnam. The strong showings for both McCarthy and Robert Kennedy in the mock election (accounting for nearly half the ballots cast combined) demonstrates how mainstream antiwar sentiment had become amongst young people.[33]

As the war became a more important part of college students' lives, the way students engaged with it changed. Students no longer felt the need to discuss Vietnam but felt compelled to act. Through attacking smaller, more tangible targets, they sought to affect larger change. Unlike the ROTC debates at the time in northern Appalachia, which almost universally focused on the general issue of the militarization of American society and the role of the program and its consistency with the mission of the university, antiwar activism during these months sought to dislodge the idea of university complicity with the war. Attempting to prevent Dow Chemical or the Marines from recruiting was an effort by students to claim greater control over the operations of the university, the same way that OU students demanded the right to participate in selecting their next president or WVU students chose to reject the proposed Code of Conduct.

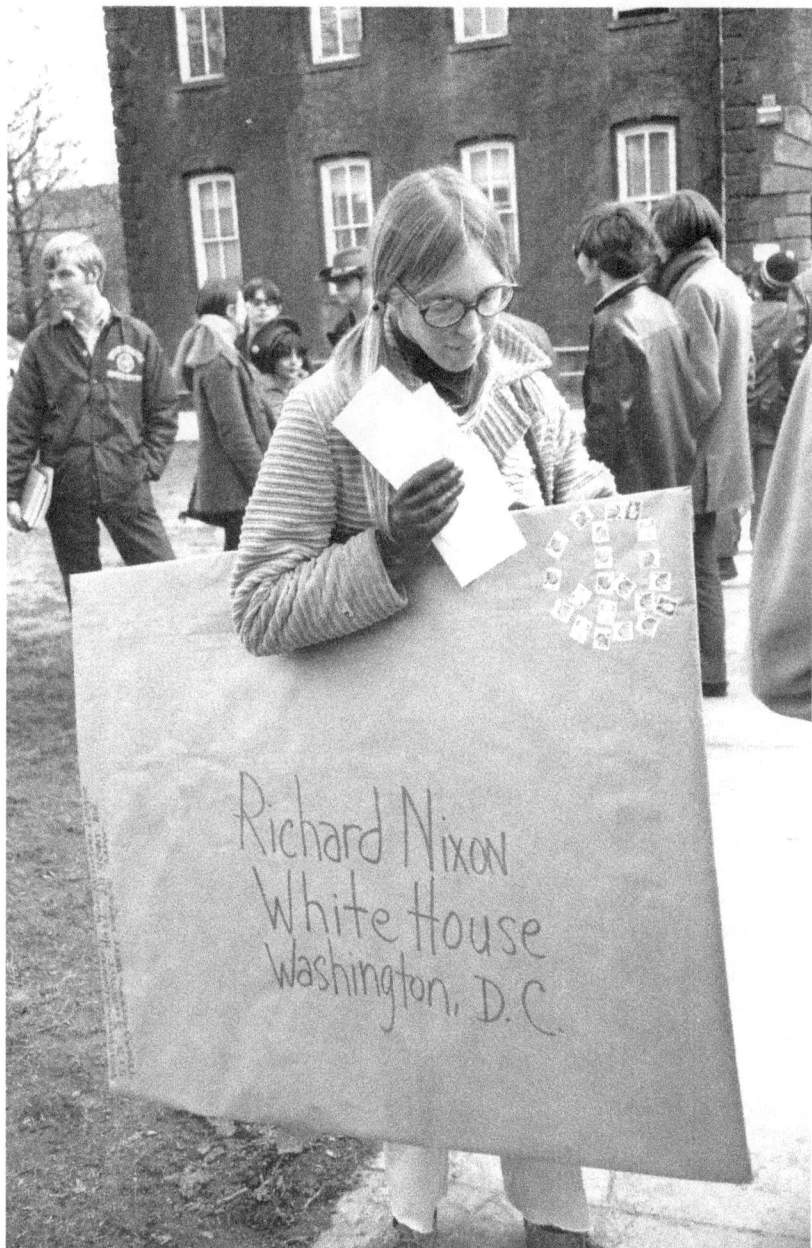

Peace Movement Member with Large Letter to Richard Nixon, West Virginia University (1970). West Virginia and Regional History Center, WVU Libraries.

War Resisters League Marches against Death and the Vietnam War, West Virginia University (Winter 1969–1970). West Virginia and Regional History Center, WVU Libraries.

Students Protest the State Road Commission and Arch Moore, West Virginia University (1969) [the person clapping is Pat Samargo, and on the left with the mustache is Harry Shaw, an anti-war activist]. West Virginia and Regional History Center, WVU Libraries.

Students Urge Participation in Vietnam Moratorium Day, West Virginia University (1970).
West Virginia and Regional History Center, WVU Libraries.

Vietnam Moratorium Day Protest in Courthouse Square, West Virginia University
(October 15, 1969). West Virginia and Regional History Center, WVU Libraries.

State Police Attempt to Break up Anti-War Demonstration on University Avenue, West Virginia University (May 7, 1970). West Virginia and Regional History Center, WVU Libraries.

Freedom March protester hold "OU Local Student Peace Union" sign at Ohio University, 1963.
Ohio University Digital Archives Collection.

Crowd at Ohio University Mock Republican Convention, 1964.
Ohio University Digital Archives Collection.

Bird's-eye-view of Ohio University's Mock Republican Convention speaker, 1964.
Ohio University Digital Archives Collection.

Jim Steele speaks from the center of Martin Luther King Jr. Memorial ceremony blocking intersection, April 7, 1968. Ohio University Digital Archives Collection.

Students protest against fee increase in Cutler Hall, 1970.
Ohio University Digital Archives Collection.

National Vietnam Moratorium Day, October 15, 1969, Athena Yearbook (p. 191).
Ohio University Digital Archives Collection.

Grover Center student rally, May 1970, Athena Yearbook (p. 282).
Ohio University Digital Archives Collection.

Grover Center student rally, May 1970, Athena Yearbook (p. 282).
Ohio University Digital Archives Collection.

National Guardsman in front of Baker Center (old), students looking on, May 1970.
Ohio University Digital Archives Collection.

Class Gateway (new) in early spring, 1960s early. Ohio University Digital Archives Collection.

U.S. President Lyndon B. Johnson speaks
from the West Portico of Memorial
Auditorium, May 7, 1964. Ohio University
Digital Archives Collection.

U.S. President Lyndon B. Johnson speaks at Ohio University, May 1964.
Ohio University Digital Archives Collection.

Part 3

1969–1972

While 1968 gets a great deal of attention as the turning point year of the Sixties—the transitional moment or high-water mark from which everything begins to decline—the events of 1969 to 1972 suggest that this assessment may be overstated. The largest national protest against the war in Vietnam, the Moratorium, occurred in October 1969. The tragedy at Kent State University, for many the defining moment of the Sixties, occurred in May 1970, and the national reverberations extend for months in places like northern Appalachia. However, in the wake of the failure of the Moratorium to end the war immediately and the tragic deaths in Kent, student activism did not completely end. However, as the Seventies wore on, the large mass demonstrations against the war declined in frequency. One of the many factors in this transition appears to be the combination of fatigue and frustration that arose from the seemingly limited successes from a half-decade of mass-protest activism. Additionally, students came to recognize that defining success by numbers at rallies was an ineffective metric, as large crowd size did not translate into tangible policy change.

In 1967 and 1968, student participation in massed demonstrations had grown significantly. Changes to the draft made many male students more susceptible to conscription; however, the institution of a draft lottery by 1969 removed a degree of uncertainty that had plagued draft-eligible men in previous years. Prior to the lottery, young men spent every day anxious that they may receive an induction notice. As such, the size of antiwar demonstrations grew during these years as enrollment in college became a less certain guarantee of avoiding military service. The steady decline in draft inductions, to where the Selective Service conscripted only one-third as many men in 1971 as in 1969, helped to reduce some anxieties over the draft.[1]

While the draft lottery instituted in 1969 continued to have flaws, it provided a degree of control for individuals. Knowing one's draft number meant that one could calculate his potential risk and the extent to which he may need to concern himself with the issues of the war. For example, men whose draft number was 100 had a greater likelihood of being drafted and thus had a greater incentive to care about the nature of the war, whereas an individual with a draft number of 325 could be fairly well assured that he would not be called and no longer had to live with the same fear of a seemingly inevitable induction notice.[2] The earlier changes to deferment structures had made many young men face uncertainty about being drafted, which propelled large numbers of them to participate in antiwar activities as a way to exert some control over their situation. The draft lottery removed a degree of uncertainty and made fair-weather protesters less likely to participate in the large rallies.

After peaking in 1969–1970, large mass demonstrations began to wane as it became more and more obvious that they were not affecting significant policy change despite their vast numbers. No matter how many people they mobilized, no matter how forceful their demonstrations, no matter how pithy, provocative, or erudite their rhetoric and slogans, the massed actions achieved seemingly little tangible change in national policy on the war or the draft. Although some advances in terms of civil rights at the universities or alterations in campus policies did emerge from these types of demonstrations, by-and-large the changes that did occur came because of means other than larger protests. People began to wonder aloud how much longer they would have to protest, how many more thousands they must mobilize, how loud they had to chant their slogans before the nation heard their message. They noted with dejection that they had been marching against the war and discrimination at the university for the better part of the decade, and seemingly little had truly changed.

In his work on the Moratorium in 1969, journalist Paul Hoffman noted that the massive protests had made the Nixon administration confront the possibility of changing some short-term war policies. However, Hoffman also stated that national leaders in the peace movement had begun to wonder if mass demonstrations could have the intended effect of ending the war. Moreover, the students of northern Appalachia were reflecting national trends, as discussed by Simon Hall in *Rethinking the American Anti-War Movement*.

Hall argued that the peace movement did have some tangible effects on the American political process, though indicated it was difficult to know the extent to which the peace movement shortened or prolonged the war.[3]

In his participant narrative history of the Sixties, former national SDS leader Todd Gitlin argued, "the post-Cambodia uprising was the student movement's last hurrah." Gitlin went on to note the shrinking size and frequency of protests in the academic years 1970–71 and 1971–72, though some events did draw a half-million participations, "Demonstrations declined at the old centers of protest and press coverage declined precipitously."[4] While Gitlin was right that activism had shifted from national to local in focus, that change did not begin after May 1970 but rather with the Moratorium in October 1969. As Hoffman noted "the day of the mammoth rally is over. In October, more than a million turned out in city after city, community after community, campus after campus to protest the war. In November, hundreds of thousands massed on the Mall or gathered at the Golden Gate. It's doubtful we shall see their like again."[5] The idea of decentralizing national protest meant local groups had a greater say in the tone of the events, it could potentially increase the number of participants, but it also created too many points of interest for the media to effectively cover or frame within a narrative.

In part, the inability to affect immediate and thorough change through massed demonstration was an intrinsic failing of the form of protest students engaged in: rallies and marches called on individuals to devote little time to the deeper cause and represented transient outbursts of expression. As it became increasingly apparent what level of dedication was necessary to achieve substantive change in the face of institutional inertia, many people disengaged or turned away from the massed actions that seemed, at best, to elicit only limited tangible results. There was a shift for some to smaller direct actions and occupations as a means of achieving change. These rested not on the mobilization of as many bodies as possible but on a small, dedicated cadre of individuals deeply committed to the cause at hand. Frustrated by the limited change created and worn out from the near-Sisyphusian nature of the struggle, individuals began to turn away from the large demonstrations, channeling their energies into more immediate matters within which they felt they were more able to achieve definite results.

As the type and focus of protest changed, so, too did the student-citizen identity forged over the previous decade. The students' emphasis on massed actions represented attempts to utilize the language of a student-citizen identity. However, they had failed to offer ways to nurture and grow that identity, seemingly turning it into a student-protester identity. The rhetorical calls to citizenship rights continued, but student activists made little effort to create and sustain a community of engaged student-citizens. The turnover in student population facilitated this transition as well. Older students, imbued with a sense of student empowerment, left campus and the new generation of student activists emphasized demonstrations over community building.

Chapter 7

We the People

Campus Issues and Civil Rights

By the end of 1968, at all three northern Appalachian campuses, the Vietnam War became the central focus of concern for many student activists. Additionally, attention shifted away from poverty issues as students focused on other concerns, mostly the war. It is not clear why antipoverty efforts faded, although it may have been due in part to the Johnson and Nixon administrations' shift in priorities away from the War on Poverty.[1] Civil rights activism on campus continued to emphasize curriculum changes and the need for dedicated spaces for black students, though student tactics became significantly more confrontational. Women's hours, ROTC, and the need to expand or alter student relations to university decision-making continued to serve as rallying points for activism.

The wider national context of these local events was always present. Frustrations over the limited achievements and fatigue caused by the constant state of tension put students and administrators on edge, and fears of riots like those reported in the national media, such as the Columbia takeover in 1968, played into decision-making. Some students continued to view the university as an instrument for positive social change while others saw it as an obstacle of the entrenched establishment perpetuating a flawed system.

Rights on Campus

On January 15, 1969, Martin Luther King Jr.'s birthday, over two dozen black students at the University of Pittsburgh entered the University Computer Center on the eighth floor of the Cathedral of Learning and staged a sit-in.

The students refused to leave until administrators addressed their demands for expanded black studies curriculum, increased efforts at black student recruitment and retention, a special section in the library dedicated to the interests of the black community on campus, and the creation of school holidays honoring black national icons like Dr. King and Malcom X, among other concerns. The sit-in lasted into the early morning hours and ended without bloodshed or arrests. Pitt's Chancellor, Wesley W. Posvar, met with the students and agreed to implement changes and work with them on several of their issues. The standoff came, in part, as a response to perceived lack of administrative concern for black students and the demands the Black Action Society (BAS) had issued the previous year.[2]

The January standoff at Pitt demonstrated that one did not need massive crowds to achieve change. Further, the occupation was not violent or actively threatening to University property as the Columbia takeover had been the previous year; rather, the students peacefully, yet forcefully, occupied an important University center and through nonviolent confrontation forced the administration to take their concerns seriously and address them in earnest. Black students at OU had issued demands the previous December using similar tactics and found the administration willing to work with them to achieve positive results.[3] However, at WVU, black students coupled their demands with not-too-subtle threats of violence saying administrative inaction may result in more "drastic measures," ensuring that administrators would be reluctant to initiate reforms.[4]

The mid-January 1969 occupation of the computer center stirred a great deal of debate in the *Pitt News*; many students argued that it was never acceptable to occupy University property, while others stressed the righteousness of black indignation. Seniors Sam Liscook and Ken Huber wrote a letter to the editor in which they warned that "if every minority group used force to attain ends which they believed just, chaos would result." Other authors and campus speakers worried about a drift toward separatism that threatened King's vision of integration, blaming the Black Power movement for corrupting the vision of civil rights reform. The University Committee on the Racial Crisis (UCRC), an organization made up predominantly of faculty with some student representation, argued, "When legitimate grievances are met with indifference or persistent and self-defeating hostility," there is a potential for violent confrontation.[5]

At the end of January, UCRC ran a full-page advertisement in the *Pitt News* stating that the computer center incident provided an opportunity for the administration and the University community to take up the mantle and reaffirm their commitments to racial justice. Over 240 faculty and staff from various departments and schools within the University (including in the humanities, social sciences, medicine, and engineering) signed the statement. In the end, Chancellor Posvar concluded, "All of us in this nation have a duty as citizens to support that progress; as members of an academic community, we ought to welcome the special opportunity we have to speed it," reinforcing the sense of special position student-citizens occupied.[6]

A perennial question for the better part of the previous half-decade, the issue of women's hours came back to the foreground in 1969. Throughout northern Appalachia, women became more insistent on the need to abolish these vestiges of in loco parentis. Activists attempted to end the curfews through legitimate channels such as student governments, petitions to administrators and boards of trustees, as well as writing campaigns to get parents to sign broader permissions. Interestingly, there were some in this movement who argued that the abolition should not be universal, and that freshmen women should continue to have restrictive hours imposed upon them. Others, fed up with the slow process and the endless debates over who should receive privileges, moved beyond established channels and demanded immediate and universal abolition.

At OU, women staged protests against the curfew system, marching around campus and holding peaceful rallies after their curfews. In May 1969, they used the opportunity of the dedication of the new library, in honor of outgoing President Vernon R. Alden, to make their call for an end to the University's in loco parentis policies. Nearly 1,200 students participated in a rally outside the newly named Alden Library and demanded an end to what they saw as a breach of democracy when it came to social issues like women's hours. They issued a statement declaring, "In any issue affecting individuals directly, those individuals, being responsible, have a democratic right to decide for themselves what action they will take in dealing with that issue."[7] In the end, the OU women did not secure an immediate end to hours (though phased endings to women's hours had begun at both Pitt and WVU), but they moved the debate far enough that total abolition, inconceivable five years earlier, seemed realistically within their grasp.[8] In this way, OU students had achieved a success, over the long-term, even if they had not achieved their short-term goals.

The status of ROTC, an issue of continuing concern, again became an important debate in early 1969. Faculty at Pitt had begun to move toward ending the accreditation of ROTC, a move supported by the student government. In January, the American Legion issued a demand to have the state discontinue funding Pitt if the University ended ROTC accreditation. Top administrators moved to reverse unilaterally the faculty decision, shifting the tenor of the debate on campus squarely to a question of the power of constituent members of the University, in this case students and faculty, to affect control over the decision-making processes of the University. When peace advocates raised the question of ROTC's privileged position at Pitt's freshman orientation and asked for equal time to present other options, administrators either ignored or rebuffed them.[9]

At OU and WVU, the question of ROTC accreditation arose, following a similar pattern as events at Pitt the previous year. One key difference from the Pitt movement was the explicit argument that attacks on ROTC were aimed at the American war effort in Vietnam. Pitt ROTC protests had revolved around issues of academic freedom and whether ROTC adhered to the overall mission of the University.

Ultimately, the issue of ROTC led to greater amounts of student and faculty actions. At OU in April 1970, eight female students participated in a sit-in during an ROTC class as a silent protest against the program and its place on campus. When Major Stanley L. White, the instructor of the disrupted ROTC course, asked the women to leave, they "insisted that they, as University students, had the right to attend any class at any time, anywhere in the University," according to White. When the women refused to obey a request that they leave the classroom, campus security arrested the women, as well as a male bystander. Over the next few days, students held a handful of protests attended by, at most, several hundred students. University President Claude Sowle made himself available to the disgruntled students largely to express administration disapproval of student actions. Despite student claims that the issue was the status of ROTC on campus, Sowle argued the issue at hand was the students' behavior and that such disruptions were not productive.[10]

Radicals on Campus

The campus debates over ROTC and the general level of student unrest drew the attention of state lawmakers in Ohio, Pennsylvania, and West Virginia.

Many of these legislators believed the university administrations were failing to rein in student radicals. The media image of radicals run amok on college campuses nationally hardened positions against things such as the removal of ROTC credits. Further, an existing "law and order" impulse also gave rise to many state bills to enforce harsh punishments against student radicals (and their faculty enablers).

Lawmakers asserted control over state institutions, based in part on the faulty assumption that administrators lacked the will to prosecute agitators. A 1969 Ohio bill, sponsored by OU alum and recently elected member of the Ohio House of Representatives George Voinovich, would automatically dismiss any student who engaged in ambiguously defined "disruptive activities." In a letter to Voinovich, James J. Whalen, the Executive Vice President of OU, expressed concern over the ambiguity of the language of Voinovich's bill and stated that he and the state schools of Ohio already had the statutory powers necessary to deal with campus disturbances. "I fear that the degree of autonomy for institutions of higher education . . . could be diminished," Whalen wrote to Voinovich, concluding the proposed bill "could be interpreted as a direct infringement upon academic freedom." He argued that all Voinovich's legislation would do would be to prevent state university administrators from dealing with situations on a case-by-case basis and apply an unnecessarily harsh unilateral policy, from Whalen's perspective.[11]

Voinovich's bill did not become law, though in the wake of the Kent State tragedy the following year Ohio legislators proposed a flurry of such bills. In Pennsylvania and West Virginia legislators introduced or enacted bills that sought to withdraw state aid from state-controlled or state-related universities if administrators did not implement draconian repression against potential student radicals, as well as fining and jailing students who participated in disturbances. Pitt's Chancellor Posvar echoed Whalen's objections to Voinovich's bill when he called such legislation unnecessary, a threat to university autonomy, and the product of legislators misreading national events, like the takeover of Columbia in spring 1968, as potentially happening on campuses like Pitt's.[12]

Not surprisingly, students decried these pieces of legislation as undue restraints on free expression. However, more surprisingly, they also denounced the state efforts for threatening the autonomy of the universities. The editors of the *Pitt News* said the legislation, "represents a serious infringement of constitutional rights. It reveals a profound lack of confidence . . . in the

University and its Student Affairs staff. It represents a central authority setting up regulations to govern conduct at institutions encouraging free thought
and expression. It represents a central authority telling a great institution
how to operate."[13] They argued that the university was a unique space within
the American community, a place where free expression was necessary, especially the ability to dissent. In this way, the student response to the actions of the state legislatures was to claim a special or privileged status as
student-citizens, which afforded them greater leeway in the expression of
unpopular positions.

Students based their argument on the concept that the university was a
unique space governed by rules that encouraged free thought and dissent. In
an opinion editorial for a special edition of the *Pitt News* sent to Pennsylvania
legislators as part of a coordinated response to State Senator Robert Fleming's
proposed "anti-riot" bill in February 1969, journalism student Dave Kuhns
stated that not only did the University encourage dissent as part of the educational process but that such expressions were necessary because students
lacked any actual voice in the political process. He stated emphatically:

> The University community is a living, dynamic, changing entity—we are not
> a bunch of degenerate zombies who wallow in the hypocritical paternalism of
> so-called leaders that refuse to listen to us, or even make an attempt to under-
> stand where we're at—in short, who don't give a damn about us. I hope . . .
> I really hope that somebody in Harrisburg is still human enough to stop for a
> moment and think and feel . . . if they and their counterparts across the nation
> will only listen to us, talk with us, feel with us as human beings . . . if not . . .
> that's cool . . . Legislate, Man, Legislate, 'Til You're Blue in the Face . . . Then
> Send Your Billy Clubs and Tear Gas and Bayonettes [*sic*] . . . hatred, violence,
> tears, blood . . . all of these will nourish the monster . . . it will grow and wax
> strong . . . and one day, devour us all.[14]

Unfortunately, despite the vigorous opposition of students, faculty, and administrators to state laws that would punish students (and faculty) for participation in disturbances on campus, state legislators regularly proposed and
occasionally passed these types of laws to ensure to the wider public that law
and order would reign on college campuses.[15]

The public's concern for student radicals came precisely at the time the
most widely known New Left and radical student organization, Students for
a Democratic Society (SDS), faced internal implosion. At the national level,

SDS had confronted growing internal divisions over the goals and tactics of the organization. The Progressive Labor (PL) faction with its strong socialist precepts clashed with a growing faction, the Revolutionary Youth Movement (RYM), made up of individuals enamored by revolutionary violence in the wake of the Columbia take-over in 1968. During their annual conference in the summer of 1969, the two factions as well as other coalitions within the organization, like the Rank and File Caucus, reached a point where they could no longer exist together under the umbrella of the same organization. The RYM moved to expel the PL and the entire convention fell apart; SDS broke into different groups.[16] However, local chapters like those in northern Appalachia had long been essentially autonomous, so that the breakup of the national organization was not necessarily representative of their own decline. Yet, some of the divisions that existed at the national level existed even in the northern Appalachian chapters.

In January 1969, when the national organization of SDS declined to endorse the "Counter-Inaugural" in Washington, D.C., an action meant to put pressure on the new administration from day one, the OU chapter sponsored buses to take students, arguing such an event was consistent with the spirit of SDS.[17] Following the Counter-Inaugural, OU's SDS embarked on a series of workshops to raise the political discourse of its members and OU students in general. In February, SDS at OU sponsored an Anti-Military Ball, part dance and part teach-in, to coincide with the ROTC Military Ball, obviously harkening back to the previous month's demonstrations against President Nixon's inauguration.[18] That summer, however, as the national SDS tore itself apart and their presence in the campus media evaporated, it appears that OU's chapter chose to fold and New Left students sought other undetermined outlets.[19]

At Pitt, while an independent SDS chapter existed, New Lefters participated in a range of radical groups beyond SDS, including the "Resistance" and an ad hoc group known as "Concerned Students and Faculty." Concerned Students and Faculty emerged in February 1969 and provided the nexus for activism for several months, coordinating a series of events, including issuing demands, holding teach-ins, and staging vigils, fasts, and occupations. In February, 500 students and faculty issued a series of demands to Chancellor Posvar, who was still recovering from the fallout of the brief occupation of the University's Computer Center by black student activists.[20]

These demands revolved around students and faculty having a greater voice in University decision-making. History teaching fellow Wolf Swoboda asked the assembled protesters, "Is the University a corporation or an institution for the search for truth? If it is a corporation, let's unionize. If we are searching for the truth, then it's not their [administrators and the Board of Trustees] university but ours." Swoboda's comments show how students were struggling with defining their position within the University community and thereby how best to exert power to achieve change. However, the individual who emerged from the February action with the greatest influence was fellow history graduate student Joshua Chasan—who had made headlines the previous semester by refusing induction. Chasan became the voice of the concerned students, raising questions about the role of the university in American society and how students could and should influence that role.[21]

The following month, nearly one thousand students and faculty at Pitt participated in a teach-in as part of the Free University established by several dozen radical students and professors. The teach-in became an occupation of the Common Facilities Building. Upset by the lack of student input in University decision-making and state efforts to punish student activists, protesting students meant for the peaceful teach-in to demonstrate the flaws in the sweeping legislation that equated virtually all activism with a threat to law and order. As the night wore on and over successive days, Joshua Chasan emerged as the spokesperson, though he adamantly denied the label and expressed the New Left's rejection of hierarchy, stating emphatically, "There is no leader. The beauty of this group is that decisions can be made in the form of open democracy."[22]

While nationally, the Revolutionary Youth Movement, a wing of SDS that would morph into the Weathermen, called for revolutionary violence, New Left students at Pitt were embracing the nonviolent stance of the *Port Huron Statement*. As Chasan put it, "We're trying to create a non-violent context, and we're being very reasonable and tolerant. If the administration rejects our proposals, they will be denying the spirit of the University that we've been trying to create." Chasan and the Pitt New Left were countering the popular media image of radical student violence while projecting a nonviolent and active conception of a student-citizen identity.[23]

When SDS collapsed that summer, the Pitt SDS chapter responded by debating their future, including which, if any, faction to follow. It appears that the Pitt chapter, with its 17 members, rejected both the PL and RYM factions, choosing to disassociate with the national organization, while professing a closer connection with the Rank and File Caucus, if they had to choose a national faction with which to affiliate. However, Geoffrey Bauman, local secretary, suggested the Pitt chapter would retain the autonomy it had cultivated over the previous years. Bauman stressed the growing coalition between the local SDS chapter and the Black Action Society—both calling for radical change at the University and in society-at-large. In testimony to a State Senate hearing on campus unrest held over the summer, Pitt SDS outlined their philosophy and why they believed campus disturbances were happening: "We believe the growth of campus unrest is a part of a larger problem, an increasing anger and discontent among more and more people throughout the country. . . . We believe that, to a large extent, these problems are rooted in the lack of real democracy in the United States." Over the next year or so, Pitt's SDS attempted to promote their vision of democracy on campus and continued to eschew violence.[24]

At WVU, following the failure to receive recognition from the administration in 1968, members of the campus SDS chapter formed two other organizations to continue their efforts, and in doing so reflected, to some degree, the rifts found at the national level. In early 1969, former SDS members founded the Mountaineer Freedom Party (MFP), a student political party to run candidates in the upcoming campus elections. At its core, MFP believed in "the ideal of participation in those decisions directly affecting us is the essence of true democracy." They argued, "The university is a microcosm, a cross-section of the society at large," and that the goal of the university is to "teach people how to learn; educate them to think independently. Rather than the molding of students into obliging technocrats, the students must be free to mold their own character as individuals." Though MFP embodied many of the same ideas as the WVU chapter of SDS had, it gained official recognition from the University and was able to participate in student elections.[25]

The creation of this party seems to have been a calculated effort by some WVU radicals. They would play within the system as a means by which to change the system. As MFP co-founder Scott Bills put it, "The MFP was organized to go through this system of political parties and try to get students involved in the system." The long-term goals of MFP, however, did not change significantly from their initial iteration as SDS, which led the *Daily Athenaeum* to brand them as too idealistic and pursuing goals that were simply not attainable within a single academic year.[26]

Bills ran for student body president as the MFP candidate and argued that of course their goals were wider ranging than a single academic year, because that was the only way to achieve true change at the University. The party stated, "Our most important undertaking [is] to break student apathy on campus, but this is a long term effort and cannot be accomplished in one campaign." As Bills put it, "Sometimes you've got to commit yourself, ideologically, to work toward a really big thing." MFP had declared in their announcement of formation: "We recognize our responsibilities as members of the university community to leave the university better than we found it." Not surprisingly, MFP did not win many seats in the student elections, but the fact that they won any at all suggests that when radicals presented their ideas to students in less confrontational terms, some students were willing to accept them.[27]

The other organization formed after the failure of SDS to achieve recognition at WVU was the Student Activist League (SAL). This group carried on the "outside-the-system" approach of SDS, rejecting MFP for being too limiting and for watering down radical ideas. Oddly enough, some members of MFP were also members of SAL, including Scott Bills, the MFP candidate for student body president. Student Activist League sought to confront students, faculty, and administrators with radical solutions to campus and social issues. While never as radical or accepting of revolutionary violence as the Weathermen, SAL did represent a similar rupture in WVU's chapter of SDS as those in the larger national divisions.

While SAL seemed to embody the more confrontational wing of the former SDS, their lack of deep, radical ideology reaffirms the reality that radicalism on the WVU campus differed significantly from that in the national movement, such as in the Weathermen. In January 1970, SAL issued thirteen demands, which among other things called into question the practices of WVU's student union, the Mountainlair, and the campus bookstore. While it did ask the administration to exert its influence to reorganize the Board of Regents to represent better the people of West Virginia, SAL did not declare a revolutionary principle behind any of these demands. They issued no manifesto of radical ideology, no calls for revolution to overthrow the system (at either a collegiate or a national level). In the end, their demands were fairly limited and seemed to echo changes happening at Pitt and OU, changes that were occurring without the use of revolutionary violence. Aside from calling for the University to recognize the rights of workers to unionize, the most radical proposal over which the administration had direct control was "an immediate end to all academic credit for ROTC programs on campus and an unconditional end to all war-oriented research."[28] The point of a university, for SAL, was not to sustain the war machine but to promote peace.

The administration's response to SAL was dismissal and derision. Joseph Gluck, Dean of Students, wrote two letters to Scott Bills as the supposed, or at least *de facto*, president of SAL. The first reminded him that the administration had not recognized SAL and threatened him with disciplinary action should the group attempt to use University space without proper authorization. In the second letter, Gluck informed Bills, in a less than veiled threat, of the University policy against actions that disrupt or prevent normal University business. The *Daily Athenaeum* and local Morgantown papers feared an imminent showdown between the administration and SAL that could boil over into larger civil disobedience and demonstrations, possibly riots. However, when Bills and President Harlow met on January 28, 1970, the meeting was cordial and productive (according to both parties).[29]

The official line for many of the problems highlighted by the demands of SAL was that the administration had begun work on some issues or that there was nothing they could do. Harlow referred Bills to student government to address some of the demands and suggested "SAL was laboring under two misconceptions when it brought him the demands"; (1) "that all the problems were 'simple and under University control,'" and (2) that the president "has the authority to move unilaterally in all areas." Just like with black students' demands, Harlow dismissed both the request as misguided and SAL as too small a faction on the campus for him to take seriously—suggesting that their 100 student supporters was far too small a number to carry any real weight on a campus of over 13,500. Harlow went further to state, "a student referendum or petition, would not influence him in anyway," suggesting a decidedly one-sided understanding of dialogue between the administration and students, that of polite listening on his part and then the total evisceration of their ideas with no room for further negotiation.[30]

Bills emerged from the meeting with Harlow determined to continue to organize in support of the causes he believed justified. He argued that the administration's unwillingness to support change meant that only through student activism and the exertion of student power would any meaningful progress occur. He cited changes in women's hours in the recent past as an example of how students organized and fought until the administration relented. While changes in curfew hours was admittedly a rather limited change, the erosion of the University's claim to in loco parentis was a necessary step for any larger changes to occur. Bills argued that if students wanted to see the thirteen points implemented, they would have to do the heavy lifting, saying, "Students are going to have to organize and push and take things. . . . We can expect no help from the administration, but I hope we don't have any hinderance." Bills refused to rule out the need for civil disobedience as a tactic in achieving change but stated that Harlow had made his position on demonstrations clear—he would "deal with disruptions severely with expulsions and arrests."[31]

At virtually the same time as SAL was issuing demands at WVU, students at OU took to the College Green to protest a tuition fee increase. This was not the first fee hike many of these students faced, rather it seemed to be a regular occurrence. Students were frustrated that they paid more and more and felt they received nothing substantively better in return, no quantifiable or qualitative shift in student-administration relations. On January 29, 1970, nearly 100 students staged a protest on the College Green outside the administration offices in Cutler Hall, before entering the lobby and demanding to speak with President Claude R. Sowle. Recognizing he was outnumbered and that in this current state of agitation the students would be disinclined to demonstrate the patience necessary for productive dialogue, Sowle sent them away with a promise to meet with five of their leaders the following day. Initially the students rejected this offer stating they had no leaders and that Sowle should meet with all of them. However, Sowle's refusal combined with a promise of further meetings seemed enough to placate the students who eventually dispersed.[32]

The following day, protests devolved and seemed on the verge of a riot, yet this did not fully manifest. At 10:00 a.m., the appointed time at which Sowle said he would meet with the leaders of the student protesters, there were a few dozen students milling around Cutler Hall, but none agreed to serve as spokespersons for the assembled students. With the students seemingly unwilling to talk, Sowle left the group and proceeded to a press conference with local and campus media to answer questions about the fee increase. However, after he left for the press conference, more students arrived at Cutler Hall and were quite upset that Sowle had refused to meet with all of them on their terms. The students began marching around the College Green, hemmed in by local and campus police. Officers read a court-ordered injunction to the gathered students and ordered them to disperse but the students did not leave. Over the next few hours police moved in and arrested forty-six people—generally the noisiest and most likely to start violence. However, in their sweeps, they nabbed a few students who had attempted to cut through the Green on their way to classes.[33] The events in January suggest the degree of frustration mounting at OU as students felt they had no alternatives and as the student-protester model of engagement superseded other forms of citizenship expression. Ohio University was already a powder keg looking for a spark when the tragedy at Kent State happened barely three months later.

Conclusion

In the wake of the Kent State tragedy, students continued to make claims of student-citizenship. By the fall of 1970, students from across the state of West Virginia met and forged an inter-campus student organization, the West Virginia Union of Students (WVUS). What drew these students together was their shared interest in improving both the colleges they attended and the society they inhabited. The constitution of this organization embodied an active interpretation of the rights and liberties of students and citizens and called for recognition of this dual identity. Their call to action stated emphatically: "As students we will dedicate ourselves to the highest level of intellectual accomplishment of which we are capable and pledge that our efforts will be directed to solving problems which will improve the conditions of the people and humanize our society. As citizens we will actively participate in political and social movements dedicated to the elimination of exploitation."[34]

The WVUS' expression of the dual identity of student-citizen was the most direct encapsulation of a sentiment floating around northern Appalachian college campuses for at least the last few years of the 1960s. Accompanying this statement was a call for greater student engagement to counter exploitation and degradation at multiple levels of society. However, WVUS did not embrace revolutionary violence, or even massed disruptive action, as a means by which to achieve these goals. They viewed the university as a tool to achieve change, if wielded by active students who recognized their multifaceted identity. Students must be part of the decision-making process of universities because they were a vital constituency that deserved representation if the university was to retain any semblance of being a partner in American democracy.

As the decade came to a close, campus issues and civil rights activism continued to play important roles, though often connected to the larger issue of the war in Vietnam. Issues related to poverty had all but fallen off the radar for students because of the war in Vietnam. Following the transitions of 1967–1968, activism on campus became more and more about issuing demands and holding disruptive demonstrations. The use of radical rhetoric existed, but aside from the small cadre of dedicated student activists who planned and organized rallies and demonstrations, most students did not seem overly committed to a revolutionary transformation of society, at any level.

Chapter 8

The War Comes Home

*Protest, Demonstration, and Activism from
the Moratorium to Kent State*

By 1969, the most important issue drawing student activism was the war in Vietnam. The war had become the filter through which students understood virtually all other issues. As the decade ended, students would participate in some of the largest demonstrations and events of the period. The year that saw over 400,000 young people gather at a farm in upstate New York for a three-day music festival dedicated to peace and love would also experience the biggest antiwar demonstration in the nation's history. The two largest events of student activism in 1969–1970—the Moratorium and the post-Kent State riots—were not efforts to create and sustain communities of student activists. Rather, they depended on these communities already existing to make the events effective.

In many ways, the Moratorium and post-Kent State riots represent the height of the student-protester model of engagement. They gave voice to years of frustrations felt by the participants. Further, while they held cathartic power, after releasing these pent-up frustrations most students returned to their regular lives. As it became apparent that despite mobilizing millions of young people little had changed, the demonstration model of protest that had arisen after Selma in 1965 began to fade.

Moratorium

In the fall of 1969, despite the dismissive views of some in the general public and even of some administrators of the role of the university to engage with local and national issues, students and community members began to organize local events for the Moratorium and sought the assistance and approval of the local university administrations. The Moratorium, a national movement to focus attention on the horrors of the war in Vietnam and to motivate individuals to demand its end, found expression in hundreds of cities and on college campuses around the nation. For colleges in northern Appalachia, the Moratorium generally represented the largest war-related event to occur on campus. Unlike earlier major peace demonstrations, which called on antiwar activists to descend on a particular city (such as Washington, D.C., New York City, or San Francisco), the Moratorium asked activists to protest where they were.

The point of the Moratorium was to take a one-day break from one's ordinary routine, to spend it in quiet or directed meditation on the war, its horrors, its costs, its purposes, and its need to end. The limited goals of the Moratorium reflect what journalist Paul Hoffman described as the liberal philosophy behind the event, in his 1970 book about the Moratorium. The hope was to bring out those who had not protested before and to emphasize the "respectable" nature of war opposition. However, these liberal goals did not stop the Vietnam Moratorium Committee from circulating an anti-draft pledge under the heading, "They Can't Jail a Generation," asking people to pledge to resist the draft in a statement reminiscent of the Oxford Oath of the 1930s. Despite this blip of radicalism, organizers focused on the argument that if the entire nation took just a single day and said they would not work or go about business as usual it would show the Nixon administration how much the American people wanted the war to end. Through its decentralized yet national nature, President Nixon and other leaders could not dismiss the protesters as the usual suspects of rabble-rousers and outside agitators.[1]

Working together, WVU students and Morgantown citizens created a full day of activities, discussions, and vigils. A national CBS television report featured the WVU-Morgantown Moratorium planning as part of "an effort to focus on a representative campus involved in the Moratorium," challenging popular conceptions of northern Appalachia's distance from the rest of America. In a letter to faculty, James Buchanan of the Morgantown Moratorium Committee asked for donations of support and that they cancel classes for the day. Student organizers met with President James G. Harlow to ask that the University close for the day to allow students to participate or, at the very least, to instruct professors to excuse those students wishing to join in the scheduled events.[2]

Harlow refused to close the campus, not a surprising position given that most college presidents, when faced with similar requests, declined. He argued that as a state institution, WVU represented all constituencies, both those who opposed the war and those who supported it, and to close campus would suggest an alignment of the University with one faction over the other. The administration would not prevent Moratorium activities, but it would not advocate them either. This position remained consistent with Harlow's previous decisions that the University did not exist to serve as an agent of change and that in its service to constituencies beyond the student body it could not take a stand on the war without jeopardizing some of its potential research and consulting contracts.[3]

The daylong events in Morgantown went off with little threat of violence or confrontation. Over one thousand people participated in activities that included the screening of several antiwar films and a twenty-four-hour sit-in at the Commons. During the day, following a prayer vigil, students processed peacefully from campus to the county courthouse a few blocks down High Street where they assembled for a series of speeches and some folk music. As congregants gathered to hear a message of peace and hope, they were also assaulted by heckles and jeers. One woman, hanging out of her window overlooking the courthouse plaza, shouted obscenities at the gathered crowd. In another instance, a carful of college co-eds cruised past the courthouse several times streaming an American flag behind their sports car and chanting pro-war slogans. According to various newspaper reports, these were the only significant confrontations that day.[4]

The Moratorium in Athens was not nearly as detailed and intricate as events in Morgantown, though there were some important similarities. Events on the OU campus were part of a community-wide effort coordinated by the Athens Peace Committee, much like the Morgantown Moratorium Committee. There was a march that took participants through town and campus, and a rally with the reading of names of soldiers lost in Vietnam.[5] Both schools' events encapsulated the sense of the Moratorium nationwide as "demonstration, teach-in, and memorial service," according to student activism scholar Charles DeBenedetti.[6] New to his position as President of Ohio University in the fall of 1969, Claude Sowle's actions displayed a great deal of skill and echoed the actions of WVU President James G. Harlow.

Moratorium organizers in Athens, as in Morgantown, asked the University to cancel classes for the day, a request denied by Sowle. He stated that while the University would hold classes, "all efforts should be made to provide on that day facilities and equipment for those who wish to discuss the Vietnam War." Sowle went on to state that his decision derived from his vision of "the nature of institutions, especially educational institutions." Continuing, he said: "I can only reiterate my faith in the principle of the open university—open to carry out its primary, educational responsibilities and open to provide a ready forum for debate on crucial issues of the day. I, for one, profoundly believe that only individuals can take stands on moral issues . . . neither I nor anyone can assume the responsibility for speaking for the thousands of persons who make up Ohio University."[7] Conversely, advocates for class cancellation argued the University had a "responsibility to indicate to the leaders of the country that it does not support the war," which closing the campus for one day would symbolize.[8]

The argument that the University could speak with a singular voice highlights the lack of institutional memory at places like universities where there is high turnover in personnel. In 1965, only four years earlier, antiwar students balked at the idea that the pro-war "Bleed-In" held by organizations at the University stood as a statement of the entire student body's support of the war effort. The bulk of blood donors expressly rejected this premise even as they gave blood. Now, in 1969, antiwar activists claimed to speak with the unified voice of the student body that they had previously denied to the pro-war faction. Regardless, like his counterpart at WVU, Sowle argued the University could not take a side on the Moratorium, that the University was home to a wide range of political views, and that individuals must make the decision whether to "participate or not in accordance with his own conscience," as an article in the *Post* put it.[9] The decision not to cancel classes at OU, as it did at WVU, served only to strengthen the meaning of the Moratorium and the message of its participants.

By not cancelling classes, Sowle and Harlow forced students to make a conscience choice to protest. It seems likely that numbers of participants would have increased if the University did not hold classes; Moratorium events would have had little competition for student attention. However, the point of the Moratorium was to stop "business as usual," for a single day and devote that time instead to trying to stop the war in Vietnam. No classes would mean it was not business as usual and the students' efforts would lack the note of sacrifice, limited though that sacrifice may be, that provided symbolic power to the event. If students were not willing to face the limited consequences of a missed day of class, it would be fair to question their dedication to the cause. By ensuring the University held classes, Sowle and Harlow forced the students to make a harder choice and by participating, they were saying for at least that moment that stopping the war was more important than getting an education. Thus, what some organizers may have decried as a lack of courage on the presidents' part, in retrospect served to strengthen the symbolic power of the event.

The Moratorium in Pittsburgh came as a culmination of increasingly vocal rallies throughout the year. Members of the Black Action Society had briefly occupied the computer center in January, and large numbers of students and faculty demonstrated for many days in various lecture halls in February and March to protest conscription or to express opposition to new state legislation that would punish student protesters.[10] In October, thousands of Pittsburgh students and faculty members participated in Moratorium events at Carnegie Mellon University, Duquesne University, and Pitt. In all these cases, students made the conscious decision to walk out of class as these institutions did not suspend classes for the day's activities. Michael Kosloff, a member of the Pittsburgh Resistance and sociology major at Pitt, described the events in Pittsburgh as less than radical and geared more towards breaking down the myth of the "bad youth" by saying that the tone of the event was "to impress the Nixon administration that we are good, clean, white, middle class, non-violent Americans."[11] It is interesting to note the intersection of race in Kosloff's construction of the "good" young American. In this way, the events in Pittsburgh reflect the description of the Moratorium by scholars Nancy Zaroulis and Gerald Sullivan, who stated, "For some, long kept in silent restraint by radical usurpation of the ground they might have taken, [the Moratorium] was, at last, a chance to be safely heard."[12]

In all, nearly 15,000 demonstrators marched through the city, converging at and briefly occupying Point State Park in downtown Pittsburgh for the culminating events of the daylong protest. The 15,000 represented only a portion of the thousands who participated at events on campuses throughout the city that day. At Point State Park, speakers addressed the questions of the morality of war and the patriotic duty of citizens to dissent. Many left downtown that evening with the feeling they had accomplished something, though the war would continue to drag on. Others expressed disappointment that the demonstration seemed geared more towards talking about change rather than taking action. In describing the result of the Moratorium,

Kosloff expressed frustration that at the end of the scheduled events everyone dispersed and returned to their daily lives as if nothing had happened.[13]

In part, Kosloff's disappointment may have stemmed from expectations generated by knowing the radicals who had initiated and organized the effort in Pittsburgh. Graduate students and members of the Pittsburgh Resistance and the Peace and Freedom Center, including David Morrison and Joshua Chasan, were important coordinators and voices in the planning of the Pittsburgh Moratorium events. Morrison adamantly insisted on a daytime march, initially hoping to get 1,000 participants rather than a suggested candlelight vigil. Ed Fuller, David Worstell, and Joshua Chasan, all draft resisters like Morrison, insisted that the Moratorium had to be a springboard for radical activism; in particular, according to Morrison's record of these conversations, "Chasan said that what was needed was the building of a radical college community." Morrison had initially called for "a march to Mellon Square [downtown] with a draft card burning and flag washing." However, Msgr. Charles Owen Rice, the local Catholic priest who had served as officiant at several local draft resistance ceremonies, suggested a less radical and confrontational approach, which seemed to coincide with the desires of students beginning to coordinate Moratorium activities on the various Pittsburgh campuses. Obviously exasperated by the "liberal" nature taking over the events he was planning, Morrison left for Chicago in early October to participate in the Days of Rage in order to immerse himself in radical activism.[14] In the end, what Morrison and other radicals had hoped to use as a means of energizing and mobilizing a radicalized city and student population became an expression of liberal opposition to the war.

The Moratorium in northern Appalachia helped to signal a shift in student activism, bringing the national back to the local. By decentralizing resistance, and empowering local groups to stage large events, the Moratorium reinforced the idea of a fading national structure to protest. Further, the Moratorium highlighted the limits of activism centered on large protests. Hoffman noted in his book on the Moratorium that afterward national leaders questioned the influence of mass protests: "If these outpourings couldn't get the message across to the administration—and all the evidence indicates they didn't—than no amount of mass action will."[15] Many emerged feeling as if they had accomplished something with limited sacrifice; however, only minimal, if any, change actually occurred. Six months later, when the Nixon administration announced the Cambodian invasion, the explosion of student response was locally focused and a visceral reaction to years of pent up frustrations not addressed by events like the Moratorium.

Kent State Tragedy

The month of May 1970 began with Americans reacting to President Nixon's announcement of military involvement in Cambodia. A shockwave of protest surged through the nation, especially on college campuses. After several days of escalating conflict at Kent State University, Governor James A. Rhodes called in the National Guard, which had recently been involved in altercations at Ohio State University in Columbus, to help defuse the situation in Kent. The Guard attempted to disperse a demonstration of several hundred students on May 4, 1970; a combination of various factors led to the Guard firing on the students and to the tragic death of four individuals and the wounding of nine others.[16] The events shook the nation and inspired Crosby, Stills, Nash, and Young's "Ohio"—an ode to the dead, the refrain of which, "four dead in Ohio," hangs hauntingly in the air.[17]

In the wake of the Kent State tragedy, as hundreds of campuses around the nation suffered major disturbances, the scene in Pittsburgh was comparatively subdued. Several hundred students from six of the city's colleges and universities (Pitt, Carnegie Mellon University, Chatham College, Duquesne University, Carlow College, and Point Park College) gathered at events in the week after Kent State, but they never achieved the riotous standards of events at OU or WVU. Students at CMU broke windows and threw ROTC manuals into the courtyard, only to then go out and pick up what they had just thrown out in one of the most polite riots on a college campus.[18]

Pitt had already ended its spring term, graduating nearly 4,800 students on Sunday, April 26, and during the summer session, which was already underway, there were significantly fewer students on campus. Pitt student body president Lenny Klavonic and the president of the University Senate Council, Dr. Jack Matthews, sped to Washington, D.C., to meet with members of the Pennsylvania congressional delegation. As formal representatives of the University, they explained the situation on campus and called for an end to the war in Vietnam. Meanwhile, back on campus, students, faculty, and even Chancellor Wesley W. Posvar (a retired Air Force brigadier general and former political science professor at the Air Force Academy), called for an end to the war, renewed efforts at addressing America's domestic ails, and the recognition of student voices within the political process. In an emotional editorial in the *Pitt News*, the editors asked, "Is it wrong to want America and Democracy to be synonymous with the word PEACE?" The editors went on to argue that student protesters were fighting for the soul of their nation in much the same way as their parents had during World War II: "The parallel is fairly obvious. Those Kent Staters were no different than your parents would have been and others were. They were protecting their America and the freedoms entailed; or rather, striving to gather again the freedoms entailed, or rather still, striving to gather for the first time the promised freedoms." In the end, the editorial suggested it took great courage to face "a fully equipped and well-armed squadron of soldiers, with only bricks and tin cans, and sticks."[19]

During the evening of Sunday, May 3, students at OU gathered on the College Green to protest President Nixon's expansion of the war into Cambodia. When word reached OU the next day of the killings at Kent State, between two and three thousand students gathered again on the College Green that evening and voted in favor of a two-day peace strike against "business as usual" in a not-too-subtle recall of the October Moratorium a few months earlier. A May 5 editorial in the *Post* described the disturbing reality that, "The war came home yesterday." In an effort to direct student outrage toward peaceful outlets, the United Campus Ministry initiated a three-day fast to reflect on the killings in Kent. [20] Over the next few days, hundreds and thousands of students continued to meet to denounce the war, the killings, and, increasingly, the administration of Ohio University.

The question OU students and administrators confronted was whether the violence of Kent State would travel to Athens, a legitimate fear as unrest swept across the nation engulfing several million young people at hundreds of colleges and universities throughout the nation.[21] On May 5, several thousand students gathered on the College Green throughout the day, moving as if in a fog and still trying to comprehend what had happened. President Sowle addressed students saying the University would remain open and while he understood the need of some students not to attend classes, they had to respect "the rights of those students who wish to attend classes."[22]

Between 2,500 and 3,000 participants marched from campus, through town, past the Selective Service office, and back again to campus on Wednesday, May 6. The "March against Death" was an hour-long procession before which protesters wrangled over the need for radical violence as the only acceptable response to what had happened in Kent. This lead Rev. Thomas Jackson of the United Campus Ministry to tell the assembled marchers, "I'm beginning to think it's more radical to call for non-violence." The day ended with a disorganized rally of several thousand students outside Memorial Auditorium. In his diary, Rev. Jackson described these days as pregnant with the anticipation of violence, "Everyone merely milled around, as if waiting for some catalyst to act, but nothing violent happened."[23]

President Sowle appeared on a national ABC television special on campus unrest on May 8, where he noted that by-and-large students at OU and around the nation wanted to keep their schools open, they were just frustrated at feeling as if no one could hear their voices. Sowle called on President Nixon to "seriously listen in the days ahead. . . . It is very important that we feel we (the university communities) are being listened to." Over the next few days, Sowle would have several opportunities to put into practice his message of listening to students. However, when students asked him to reverse his decision banning controversial speakers from campus, he demurred, causing tensions to flare up again. [24]

By May 10, the worst of the protests at OU seemed to have passed. Unfortunately, an administrative decision not to allow Skip Taube and Benson Wolman, whom the *Post* described as members of the White Panther Party (a radical anti-racist group of politicized hippies from Ann Arbor, Michigan), to hold their scheduled talk rekindled the embers of unrest. In response to the administration's decisions, thousands of students gathered on May 11 for rallies throughout the afternoon and evening, issuing statements and demands reminiscent of those made during the riots two years earlier. Naming themselves the "People's Institute for Radical Studies," the students called for, "The removal of the war machine from campus: ROTC, Defense Department projects . . . the presence of the acceleration lab, etc., . . . Student self-determination . . . City police, Nat'l. Guard, etc. not be allowed on campus . . . [and] That profs. not be denied tenure due to political activity," among other demands. After midnight, a group of one hundred students moved to occupy the old Chubb Library that had stood empty since the opening of the new Alden Library the previous February. Students saw this effort as a way to help force the University to close. Additionally, the action stood as a symbol for the students' sense of limited control over their own lives at OU—that they could only control an abandoned building in the middle of the night.[25]

While several dozen students occupied Chubb Library, others, presumably student protesters, set fire to the cafeteria across campus in Nelson Commons on the South Green. The blaze resulted in tens of thousands of dollars-worth of damage and brought the University to the brink of closure. In an editorial following the occupation and arson, the *Post* expressed deep reservations about the violence on display, though not with the nonviolent occupation of Chubb Library: "We do not condemn those occupying students. However, we do condemn those acts of violence that imperil the safety of all members of the University community. . . . The present trend of violence will not end in revolution. It will end, instead, in unbearable repression from the right. It will end in an irretrievable loss of academic freedom, closing not only the universities but also the minds of millions of people."[26] The following two nights brought more demonstrations, denunciations, and destruction, as students and security forces clashed. Reluctantly, the administration decided that for the safety of their students, staff, and community, the University would close.[27]

The decision to close OU was a difficult one, made only after lengthy debate amongst administrators and the failure to prevent additional disturbances. President Sowle hoped to find other solutions to the crisis short of closure. Assuming that a handful of radical students were instigating the crisis, Sowle moved to suspend seven students on May 12. Sowle also encouraged a counter-movement amongst the University community to challenge calls for closure, saying in a statement on May 12, "It will take the active participation of the overwhelming majority of students, faculty, and staff to keep this University open in the face of a tiny minority bent on disruption and destruction." However, the tide of activism against the administration and for closure was too great to withstand.[28]

Like so many other campuses around the nation, May 1970 at OU proved to be an amazingly contentious time; a time when lingering frustrations over students' rights and deep passions surrounding the questions of war, dissent, and patriotism intertwined in the aftermath of the Kent State shootings. The outrage and indignation at OU was representative of the frustrations and disillusionment endemic to America's youth in the opening years of the 1970s. Ohio University was only one of dozens of campuses across the nation that closed in the weeks that followed the tragedy.[29]

Protests at WVU in the wake of the Kent State shootings began on May 5 and lasted for only a few days. Over one thousand students participated in a relatively peaceful demonstration on May 6 in what organizers called an effort to "Support our brothers and sisters at Kent State and across the country."

Protesters occupied Oglebay Plaza, an area of campus in front the student union, the Mountainlair, milling about, offering slogans, and expressing a wide-ranging disgust and anger at events in Kent, the war, and the University. A smaller protest on May 7 called on "all citizens to assume responsibility for peacefully expressing their opposition to the extended war." This protest began with a march that started at the Morgantown courthouse before moving to campus and resulted in the destruction of a bulletin board used by the ROTC and a few windows in various campus buildings and the use of tear gas to disperse demonstrators.[30] The students at WVU, like their counterparts around the nation targeted ROTC as a focal point of their outrage after Kent State, though their destruction of a bulletin board pales in comparison to the torching of ROTC buildings that happened at dozens of other campuses.[31]

The largest threat of violence and injury in all the protests at WVU came on May 7 when conservative counterdemonstrators surged into the peaceful, if minimally destructive, marchers who had trekked from the courthouse up to campus. Newspaper reports described the conservative crowd as "a large and vocal group violently opposed to the demonstrators." This group of pro-war students and townsfolk launched into the peace protesters, threatening to physically remove them from campus if the police were too afraid to do it themselves. Luckily, the altercation did not devolve into full-on melee, and the police restored order before blood was shed. The peace demonstrators called on President Harlow to denounce both the Cambodian invasion and the KSU shootings, which he refused to do. The only statement he offered said the events of May 7, 1970, were unfortunate but that "the cleavages among University groups revealed by the circumstances of the last few days are shallow enough and narrow enough that the University community will be able to heal them quickly."[32] On the whole, the incidents at WVU lacked any sense of violent revolution and, while disruptive, were largely harmless.

Nearly one month after the demonstrations, and with the University seemingly moving on without lingering effects, the administration brought indictments against six individuals they claimed had led the disturbances on May 7, 1970. The administration claimed these six students engaged in or incited others to the destruction of University property, yet local and college officials did not charge any of the conservative counterdemonstrators for their actions that day. Six men received summons signed by Dean of Students Joseph C. Gluck to appear before the Committee on Student Discipline. This action by the administration to bring charges against Scott Bills, Scott King,

Steve Stepto, Mike Weber, Dan Bucca, and Pete Cowan set the campus along a path toward more demonstrations and threatened the public image of WVU.

The "Morgantown Six" retained legal counsel and fought back against the accusations—charges that they argued the administration simply did not have any evidence to support. It seems that the indictments served as a ploy by the administration to exert their power over the students, not because they thought they should act to straighten out the students but to placate other constituencies who may have wanted to see a firm hand used in dealing with disruptive students. President Harlow had previously threatened expulsion and arrests during the SAL demand fight in January, which may have hemmed him into taking these actions. His attempts to pawn off the indicated students on federal, state, and local authorities to prosecute (all of whom declined for a lack of evidence) suggested the administration had little desire to see the legal proceedings through to their logical conclusion and that he may have acted under pressure from one of the other University constituencies, such as the general public.[33]

Perhaps the administration thought the six would simply roll over and accept punishment as others had done over the previous few years; what the administration did not count on was a coordinated and impassioned defense. Among the six indicted, Cowan was a freshman and the only one that the administration thought may re-apply for the following school year. As for the other five: by the time of the indictment King had graduated and entered the Peace Corps, Bucca and Weber had dropped out of school, and Stepto and Bills were set to graduate. The administration, recognizing the weakness of its evidence and position, initiated its standard delay tactic, postponing any hearing indefinitely. However, the students were unwilling to let the matter drop quietly and leave the University without further incident. Rather, they wanted their day before the Disciplinary Committee.[34]

Fellow students and sympathetic faculty held rallies and spoke out on behalf of the indicted students, creating further headaches for the administration and making it harder for them to back down without losing face. Bills and Stepto both applied to the Graduate School, expecting (and receiving) denials, so they could increase pressure on the University to either dismiss their case and issue a public apology or bring the case to the committee. The Morgantown Six drama effectively ended only when a court order compelled action. An appeals committee finally sat to review the admissions denials of

Bills and Stepto and found no evidence of the students engaging in inappropriate behavior.[35]

The Morgantown Six debacle highlighted the difficulties of universities serving multiple and contradictory constituencies. Without perceived pressure from outside groups, the administration might never have brought such flimsy charges against the six students. By choosing to fight both the indictment and the delay tactics, the students suggested that the University did not exist as an undemocratic, authoritarian regime, which obligated administrators to respect students' rights. They saw themselves as equal partners with the governance in the University community, and that the administration must adhere to due process of law or else the students would become second-class citizens. The fight of the Morgantown Six was consistent with the existing tradition at WVU of students viewing themselves with the dual identity of citizen and student, one informing the other.

The response in northern Appalachia to the Kent State shootings in many ways mirrored the national reaction. Nearly four million students participated in myriad demonstrations, some violent, yet overwhelmingly they rejected full-scale revolutionary violence. Regardless, the numbers involved, the nationwide nature of the student strike that followed the Kent State shootings, and a fear that this could become something more dangerous forced President Nixon to seek refuge temporarily at Camp David.[36] For the students, seeing members of their generation—and quite possibly high school classmates— shot and killed was simultaneously sobering and terrifying, and this duality carried into the demonstrations at the schools in northern Appalachia. Some levels of violence occurred, but as radical students at most of these schools had eschew the more violent path of the Weatherman following the national disintegration of SDS in the summer of 1969, it is perhaps not surprising that these campuses did not see wider violent outbursts. The seemingly leaderless, large protests in May 1970 demonstrated what the Moratorium had made clear the previous year: the era of the student-protester model of engagement was waning. Student activism going forward would need a new model.

Election of 1972

While the story of student activism in northern Appalachia does not end with the presidential election of 1972, this episode helps demonstrate just how much had changed in the previous eight years. This election represented the first presidential contest most students on campus could participate in, since it was the first held after the ratification of the Twenty-Sixth Amendment, which lowered the voting age to 18. Students now had a legal voice and could participate in the established political channels of American governance. In many ways, this represented the culmination of the student-citizen struggle for many.

What one might assume was a moment of triumph and glory, the ratification of the Twenty-Sixth Amendment in summer 1971, which was the affirmation of the political power young people had spent a decade trying to achieve, barely received notice in the student newspapers in northern Appalachia. The momentous occasion slipped by with little more notice than a blurb in the national news section of the paper. Perhaps this lackluster response was due to the anticlimactic nature of the ratification in July 1971. For more than a year, the inevitability of the 18-year-old vote had hung over the country, ever since Senator Edward Kennedy offered an amendment to the Voting Rights Act in March 1970. Kennedy's amendment lowered the voting age for federal, state, and municipal elections, arguing, "A society that imposes the extraordinary burden of war and death on its youth should also grant the benefit of full citizenship and representation, especially in sensitive and basic areas like the right to vote."[37]

However, in December 1970, the Supreme Court struck down the requirements for state and municipal elections in the case *Oregon* v. *Mitchell*. The decision of the court reaffirmed the right of 18-year-olds to vote in federal elections, meaning young people could register and local boards of elections would have to maintain separate voter rolls. The bureaucratic nightmare this created compelled many states to seek to lower their voting age requirements to 18. It also sparked a national movement to amend the Constitution, and West Virginia Senator Jennings Randolph introduced a joint resolution in January 1971 to lower the voting age. From Congressional passage to ratification, the Twenty-Sixth Amendment moved more rapidly than any previous amendment; Ohio became the 38th, and deciding, state to ratify the amendment a mere three months after it cleared both houses of Congress. Yet the amendment, like much to do with electoral politics in the early 1970s, seems to have not phased many students at northern Appalachian universities.[38]

Students felt turned off from the 1972 presidential election by the seeming lack of a candidate worth supporting and because of the triumph of the

New Left message of the broken nature of American electoral politics. Assuredly, Senator George McGovern (Democratic candidate from South Dakota) did speak to many students' issues, including, but not exclusively, the war in Vietnam. However, the revelation of VP nominee Thomas Eagleton's medical history—his depression, hospitalization, and electro-shock therapy—and the manner in which McGovern handled the situation caused a debacle for the candidate. McGovern's vacillation and his eventual decision to drop Eagleton in favor of Sargent Shriver led to a sense among some movement activists that McGovern was just another opportunist politician.[39]

McGovern's longshot and blundering candidacy may have kept young voters from the polls, but the New Left had been saying for years that electoral politics in America was broken. According to a survey of Pitt students conducted on the eve of the election, while "they unanimously agree that they are in favor of the legislation which gave them the right to vote, they view the election and their part in it with indifference." Local boards of election had hassled students when they tried to register to vote, now they felt less than enthused at their choices.[40]

Students expressed a sense that it did not really matter anyway because their single vote could not stop the machine arrayed against them. A poll conducted in February 1972 by the Student Government Board at OU showed "a full 69 per cent of the responding students said they felt [that] 'American politics were beyond the influence of the electoral process' . . . . Twenty-six per cent felt it was no longer worthwhile to participate in the electoral process." One Pitt senior gave voice to many in his cohort, "McGovern's programs are groovy and they're what we need. But nine of 10 of his promises he'll never be able to fulfill. He just isn't a dynamic enough politician." In the end, only 48.3 percent of eligible 18-to-20-year-olds voted in the 1972 election, a percentage only slightly below the national trends for over-21-year-olds. By 1972, student newspapers were again decrying student apathy, just as they had in 1964–65, as students became less convinced of their ability to affect change on a national scale.[41]

One can see the return of student disinterest in the way students engaged with the 1972 presidential election. In 1964 and 1968, the campuses of northern Appalachia buzzed with activities surrounding electoral politics. Campuses held mock Republican conventions and mock elections. Students openly, loudly, and regularly debated party platforms and sided with potential presidential candidates. In 1972, little of this happened.

One may argue there was no need for the mock conventions or elections since students were now able to participate in the real thing. However, as the editors of the *Post* pointed out in advocating for a mock political convention, the fact that students had earned the franchise possibly made these mock events more important. The editors contended that "college students are vitally interested in political issues and participation in such an organized activity can only help to channel potential votes into a true political force." A mock convention could have served as a bell-weather or an unofficial primary and would potentially draw major political candidates into a region of the country they may not visit otherwise—just as the 1964 and 1968 events had done.[42] However, these arguments failed to sway students and they held no mock political events. In fact, few official election-related events seemed to happen on these campuses.

While the campus papers offered occasional updates on the campaigns of 1972, electoral politics did not dominate news coverage. For the most part, campus papers retreated to covering campus events, including those things that offered limited controversy or, if controversial, focused on the campus community. The national news returned to the publication of wire stories or syndicated columns, as the newspapers had been doing a decade earlier. In many ways, the campus papers of 1972 shared more in common with those of 1964 than say 1968 or 1969. Syndicated national columnists replaced student opinions on national events. Editorials became shorter and less pointed, less likely to attack administrations (college or presidential). The idea of the mid-1960s of a community of engaged student-citizens fed by a strong voice in the campus media was, for all intents and purposes, dead. At the exact moment students received an official voice in American politics, they seemed no longer to want it.

Despite the seeming lack of interest in the election of 1972, students were not completely inactive. Struggles over ROTC, women's hours, and racial discrimination continued. Students continued to argue the changes so far made, while positive, did not go far enough to integrate the student voice into campus decision-making. However, the war in Vietnam continued to be one of the most important issues that generated student activism.

In May 1972, Athens police arrested over seventy students at OU for an antiwar protest that included a nighttime occupation of Lindley Hall, which housed the campus ROTC, to protest the program's existence on campus. Earlier that same night, May 9, nearly one thousand students had participated in an antiwar rally in Memorial Auditorium. As the students inside the auditorium debated what to do next, about 250 students moved to Lindley Hall, occupying various floors for several hours. On the second floor, a peaceful sit-in became a teach-in as students discussed whether ROTC had a legitimate place on campus. The second-floor students argued that as citizens of the university and the nation they had a right to debate the merits of military training at a public university. Police and campus officials ordered students to evacuate the building; over 170 left while chanting, "All we are saying, is give peace a chance." In the end, police arrested 77 people and charged them with violations under Ohio's anti-riot bill, known as HB 1219.[43]

Passed in the aftermath of the Kent State riots in May 1970, HB 1219 gave wide powers to administrators to arrest students and enforced harsh penalties on students arrested for disturbances. The punishments included suspension of students, prior to a conviction in a court of law, and a potential ban on admission into any state-sponsored college or university based on participation in an ambiguously defined "disruptive" demonstration. The act made little distinction between the riotous actions of May 1970 and the peaceful events of May 1972. After months of wrangling, the local prosecutors resolved the cases of the "Athens 77" without imposing the draconian measures of HB 1219, as students pled guilty to lesser charges not covered by the anti-riot act.[44]

The events of May 1972 suggest that the fires of student passions had not fully burned out, though it does raise interesting questions about student engagement with the presidential election that year. Since it seems that students were passionate enough to face stiff penalties for protesting the war, the question becomes, why were they unwilling to fight as hard for the McGovern campaign? It seems that the low voter participation amongst young people did not emanate from a lack of concern over the issues taken up by the McGovern campaign. Rather, some disconnect existed between the student-citizen impulse to activism and the act of voting. Perhaps this was born from years of lacking the vote, or maybe it came from a sense of pessimism and disillusionment about the ability of electoral politics to fulfill the wishes of the citizenry. Although it appears that many young voters chose not to participate in the 1972 election in the wake of the Eagleton affair, which painted McGovern as just another politician.[45] Regardless, young people had received the franchise and their first act with it was to withhold their vote.

If anything, the McGovern campaign and the weak youth turnout in the 1972 presidential election demonstrated that there would be no revolution.

Young people in northern Appalachia, like their counterparts around the country, supported McGovern, yet their support was not sufficient to overcome the Nixon landslide. The McGovern candidacy had represented the multi-faceted anti-establishment movement in all its disjointed, convolute, and contradictory glory. However, McGovern's nomination victory was also the seal of his general election loss as he represented a minority view that had failed for nearly a decade to gain widespread support within mainstream politics. While some aspects of McGovern's campaign, such as the antiwar message, had increased mainstream support, the domestic and foreign policy changes he called for were largely not appealing to most Americans. Nixon was a relatively, all things considered, popular incumbent who seemed to many to be the best option for ending the war and promoting the domestic well-being.[46] McGovern's failures, however, were not universal. His very nomination demonstrated how far American politics had moved in a dozen years since the Greensboro sit-ins. Although his nomination may have also stemmed from the fact that he had helped to rewrite the rules for nominating a candidate in the Democratic Party in order to allow greater voice for those who would be his supporters, rather than a manifestation of changing ideals among the electorate.[47] Regardless, it is safe to say the political voice of minorities, students, and women had grown exponentially, and northern Appalachian campuses marked these changes.

Conclusion

The Moratorium had been the high-water mark for organized national student protest. However, the Moratorium had not been a call to action, as many had hoped it would be, but a sort of cathartic moment of national expression of frustration. Most participants appeared happy to take a momentary break from their lives to express their concerns and then resume their daily actions the next day as if they had accomplished something. In the end, the Moratorium failed. It failed to end the war, and it failed to generate an impetus for continued mass protest. The peaceful nature of the day made it stand out as a singular moment, a thing accomplished rather than a step in an on-going process. If it succeeded at all, it did so by helping to empower local organizers; however, with the drift away from mass protest, this seems like a minor victory at best.

The immense tragedy of Kent State served as the spark to light the explosive frustrations building on campuses around the nation. The proximity to Kent State and potential for friends and family to be among the victims brought the tragedy home to northern Appalachian campuses in a way it may not have done at other schools. However, the shock and terror of the events gave rise to visceral responses—uncoordinated, local, and, at times, violent. Many campuses saw students target ROTC buildings—burning some or trashing them (as what happened in a limited way at WVU). It seemed the worst fears had come true and the frustrations at the long train of failures and delays turned irrational violence into an acceptable response. If one could simply be killed for peaceful protest, what was the point?

The Student-Citizen Identity, Northern Appalachia, and the Sixties

In May 1971, one year after closing the University down in the wake of the Kent State tragedy, students at Ohio University held a small antiwar demonstration. Promoters were adamant this would be "both a legal and peaceful action." The plan was to picket the local Athens draft board and to have draft-eligible men go in and ask a constant stream of questions to keep the board so busy they could not process any draft notices or engage in any other functions.[1]

At 8:00 a.m. about thirty students began what they hoped would be a daylong peaceful action; however, shortly after 10:00 a.m. the event changed when the police arrested one of the protesters. Kim Levitch was one of the draft-aged men who marched to the Athens draft board and while demonstrating outside he waved a National Liberation Front flag. Athens Police Captain Charles Cochran confiscated the flag, placing it in his squad car. When Levitch attempted to retrieve his flag Cochran arrested him for disorderly conduct. In response to Levitch's arrest, his fellow protesters called for an emergency meeting on the College Green, to which only 150 people came. After some marching around town and back to campus, the protesters dissipated and a rally later that night drew barely 100 people.[2]

The Levitch incident highlights the possibility of student burnout and the waning of protest-based activism. The student-protester model of engagement simply did not excite the level of participation in this case as it had in the previous three or four years. Despite the breathless claims by the May 1971 demonstrators that "constitutional rights . . . are increasingly becoming constitutional luxuries for even the most peaceful of war protesters," there appeared to be few on the Athens campus willing to do much about it. In previous years, by contrast, thousands of students turned out for antiwar protests.[3] A final aftershock of mass student protest at OU would occur the following May when Athens police arrested seventy-seven students during a protest and occupation of Lindley Hall.[4] For years now, students had felt, and in a very real sense were, disenfranchised. The lack of a political voice and the frustration at authority figures' indifference had turned many off from the mass rally politics of the previous few years.

By 1972, the campuses of northern Appalachia had seen a great deal of change yet maintained a significant degree of continuity with their 1964 selves. In loco parentis as a governing philosophy was all but dead, yet schools continued to exert a degree of control over student morality through codes of conduct, often constructed by the students themselves and frequently with administration guidance. Students gained a degree of access to decision-making processes, mostly in judicial processes and as members of committees, but they never attained an equal share of administrative powers. Curricula expanded to include a wider array of possible fields of study, but the notion of the free university—of education untethered to career preparation—largely did not take hold. The war was not yet over, the draft was still present (though phasing out), ROTC remained, and the university as research center for the military and corporate worlds continued: in these ways one may note the failures of student activism. Even with the triumph of the Twenty-Sixth Amendment that lowered the voting age to eighteen, the end result was anticlimactic as large numbers of young people sat out the 1972 presidential election.

Student-Citizen Identity and Northern Appalachia

Contrary to popular images of Appalachia in the Sixties—as a region disconnected from wider national trends—there was a great deal of student political and social activism in the mountains. The students at Ohio University, the University of Pittsburgh, and West Virginia University felt the same impulses and faced the same concerns as young people around the nation during the Vietnam War era; they were full participants in the debates and upheavals of the period. Historians have falsely silenced these students from the historiographies of the Sixties and of the region, believing them sequestered in the bucolic Appalachian countryside. By focusing on northern Appalachia

and exploring how these students debated and constructed concepts such as patriotism and citizenship, gaps in existing scholarship can begin to close.

Memory and myth create false images of Appalachia in the Sixties. For well over a century, Appalachia has existed in the popular and scholarly imagination as a backward region, serving as a foil for arguments of progress and modernity. These images have lampooned the people of Appalachia as hillbillies and rednecks, while derisively calling their culture "quaint" and "folksy." Appalachia exists as a land forgotten by time and out of step with the modern world. Its quasi-Southern image projects virulent racism along-side rural poverty, both born from the twin tragedies of ignorance and want. Furthermore, these constructions strip the citizens of Appalachia of their agency, seeing them as set upon by avaricious outsiders (mostly in the form of mining corporations). These visions of the region perpetuate an assumption that Appalachia could not be a part of the Sixties, because Appalachia had not truly entered the modern world. As such, with Thomas Kiffmeyer's notable exception, scholarship on the Sixties and of the region has overlooked the role of Appalachian student political and social activism.[5]

While issues surrounding poverty, unions, and out-migration from the region were undoubtedly endemic during these years, they do not tell the whole story of the region and its people. By exploring student political and social activism during the Vietnam War era, Appalachia's supposed isolation from the rest of America melts away. Indeed, Appalachia may not have experienced the Sixties the same way as other regions of the country. However, all regions of the country experienced these turbulent years in slightly different ways, as Kenneth Heineman, Marc Gilbert, Robbie Lieberman, and Andrew Grose have demonstrated in their various works on Sixties student activism.[6]

In constructing their own experience of the Sixties, northern Appalachian students found intersections with students around the country. When Dr. King called for people to march in Alabama in 1965, Appalachians answered the call alongside thousands from around the nation. Appalachians joined with hundreds and thousands of other citizens who were angry at the war in Vietnam and U.S. policies at home and marched on the Pentagon in 1967. Just like millions of their fellow Americans, Appalachians recoiled in fear and sorrow at the 1968 assassinations of Martin Luther King and Robert Kennedy, and they, like so many around the nation, lashed out in terror and frustration after the killing of four of their fellow young people at Kent State in 1970. As young people around the nation joined civil rights organizations, demanded greater say in university decision-making processes, refused the draft, and challenged the federal government's foreign and domestic policies, so too did they in Appalachia. While Appalachian emphasis on antipoverty activism may have been greater than in some other regions, especially during the height of the federal War on Poverty, the impulse to generate empowered communities capable of asserting their rights and improving their circumstances was a largely national impulse among American youth of the Sixties.

By-and-large, the period 1964 to 1972 saw a dramatic outburst of student unrest. However, many misinterpret this spike in activity, misreading large demonstrations as indicators of student activism, and wonder why activism faded so rapidly after the events at Kent State University in May 1970. In truth, the marches and rallies were only one part of student expression of discontent. There were two different tracks of student activism, one in which students observed events and discussed issues in the campus newspapers and a second form of active engagement. Student active engagement with social and political issues also expressed itself in two ways: one emphasizing community empowerment and one focused on large displays of frustrations. Historical observers see the differences between the two forms of activism readily when comparing the Freedom Summer in 1964 to the Selma march in 1965. Students from around the nation, including Appalachia, moved to Mississippi in the summer of 1964 to occupy the state and help build empowered black communities, and in the spring of 1965 busloads of students traveled to Alabama for a few days to march and demonstrate. The goals of these two actions differed significantly, from empowerment to voicing discontent. These tensions, easily observed in the civil rights movement, existed in all forms of student political and social activism during the Vietnam War era—from campus issues to antipoverty work, from the war to the draft, student activism oscillated between community building and empowerment to boisterous expressions of frustration and concern.

Within a few years of the Selma march, the pendulum had swung most decidedly toward demonstration and away from community organizing. Mass demonstrations became more frequent and widespread. Initially, activists localized their demonstrations to national centers—Washington, D.C., New York, or San Francisco—drawing tens of thousands of protesters to a single location for the purposes of a rally, march, or demonstration that lasted anywhere from a single day to a long weekend. The protesters would then leave after voicing their frustrations. These events represented massed individual acts of protest, each participant there for their own reasons and to express their own frustrations or concerns, a reality seen in the diversity of signs and placards as well as actions taken during these events.

The importance of individual acts of protest as spectacle also helps explain the rising tide of draft resistance ceremonies and the rallies held in support of resisters as they actively refused induction or stood trial. These acts of resistance were a form of theater and held power only in as much as others observed them, in the same way that mass rallies and demonstrations only had power if they in some way disrupted the daily routines of others and penetrated the public space. Draft resistance ceremonies conducted in or around churches, like in Pittsburgh in December 1967 or Morgantown in April 1968, were meant to convey the solemnity of religious conviction as well as the community of faithful that made up the resistance.[7]

The October 1969 Moratorium shifted the emphasis of massed rallies back to the local communities. One of the arguments for this shift was that, rather than having tens of thousands of people travel to one location for a single event, staging hundreds of events around the nation on a single day would force people throughout the country to confront the realities of the war. However, following the October Moratorium the frequency of large rallies, local or national, faded significantly. There was a large demonstration in November that drew several hundred thousand people to cities on the coasts, but massive, local protests coordinated at a national level did not continue. Thus, it was not the events of Kent State that signaled the end of the student-protester model of engagement, but the Moratorium. The post-Kent State riots and disturbances represented an outburst of pain and frustration, and while activists held a few large demonstrations after these events, it seems that prior to May 1970 many activists had chosen to forego these tactics.

Student activism did not end in 1970, rather one form of student expression of unrest faded. Mass rallies and demonstrations failed to affect meaningful change in the war policies of the administrations in Washington. In part, these failures resulted from the tactical decision to use mass rallies and demonstrations that mobilized individuals for a limited period to voice frustrations. The goal of these actions was to express views and raise awareness, not to resolve the issues that generated the protest. However, one should not dismiss the mass rally form of activism, as it served an important function of expressing deep felt frustrations and demonstrated how widespread such frustrations were within the population.

Successes, like changes to women's hours and adding courses in black studies, limited though they may have been, came from community building and empowerment, which required a deeper, longer, and, at times, harder commitment than simply a few hours on a given day. This form of student activism predated the mass rallies and continued, if subdued, during the rise of the rally years. This locally focused form of activism emphasized affecting positive change through expanding access to the decision-making power within a given community. Activism along these lines required an identity based in the assumption that all citizens have a right to participate in their communities.

In the student case, this was the formation of the student-citizen identity. The process of forming this identity emerged in the early-to-mid 1960s and became the basis for much of the activism of students. Even during the years when mass protests overshadowed community building, the concept of the student-citizen identity was present. Students claimed the right to express their frustrations in massed individual protest because of their status as students and citizens. In a June 1966 opinion editorial, Pitt student Frank Couvares explained the student-citizen position, saying, "The University student is in a unique position. During his college years, he confronts, usually for the first time, the problems of integrity, identity and his obligations as an individual in a social context. His ability to think conceptually is intensely exploited and demanded. His sense of community is stimulated and challenged. As a result he is expected to form opinions, to articulate them, and to defend and advocate them."[8] The following year, in a letter to the editors of the *Post*, John T. Nixon explained the link between student activism and the wider society:

> The university is, to use an overworked but nonetheless apt idea, an assembly-line in which a student (reduced to a number) is processed through a diploma mill, very seldom even meeting their faculty. . . . The protest then is lodged with the university, because that is where the student is. But, unfortunately, the protest is much more deeply lodged than that. The protest is actually against the whole of contemporary society. . . . The university is seen as a microcosm of society, which the student views before he enters it, a culture characterized by impersonality in business, in living arrangements, even in social life—a culture in which nobody dares to be himself, and everybody wears a mask for fear he may be found to be in deviation at some point from conformity.[9]

Couvares and Nixon both recognized the university as a unique space, a place where the student developed a sense of citizenship duty through confrontation with a similar set of stimuli as the wider society. This unique space allowed students to claim simultaneously citizenship in the wider society and that of the university, in both places an active citizen must have been willing to engage with the issues of that community. They noted that the impulses that drove engaged citizenship in one realm carried over into the other.

The many impulses of activism in the Sixties—antiwar and antipoverty, civil and students' rights—provided a cross-causal basis for the student-citizen identity. Perhaps one of the best examples of this cross-causal student-citizen identity comes from WVU student Harry Shaw. Shaw, a West Virginia native, was a vocal critic of the war in Vietnam, a draft resister in contact with the resistance movement in Pittsburgh, a founding member of the WVU campus chapter of Students for a Democratic Society as well as an initial organizer of the Student Action Against Poverty (which later rebranded as Student Action for Appalachian Progress), a local Vietnam Summer coordinator, and he traveled to Alabama in 1965 to march, following the tragedy at the Edmund Pettis Bridge. With Shaw at the helm, the WVU chapter of SDS circulated anti-discrimination petitions to desegregate local barbershops; he also led the organization in their first attention getting protest against the Vietnam War when they picketed a student-organized variety show performance that the University had falsely promoted as a statement of unanimous WVU student support for the war. Shaw argued that his conscience dictated him to act to improve the world around him and not to destroy it, rejecting discrimination, exploitation, and war in equal measure. Simultaneously, Shaw encouraged his fellow students to become active in their campus, local, state, and national communities, to exercise their voices, and to change that which they saw as inappropriate in society. In 1967, Shaw described the society he hoped to help foster, "a society built on responsible freedom where the individual has his right to share in the decisions directly affecting his life; a social organ to encourage independence in man."[10] Shaw embodied the very notion of a student-citizen, the dual identity of a person equally connected to the world of the university and to that of the wider community so that the obligations and duties of one intimately and unavoidably linked to the other.

By exploring the activism of individuals like Harry Shaw and the students of northern Appalachian universities, one gains a deeper insight into student political and social activism during the Vietnam War era. By 1964, students were becoming increasingly aware of larger social and political issues within and beyond their campuses. The primary focus initially was civil rights and anti-poverty activism. Students sought to help build empowered communities capable of exerting their political rights, and in so doing developed techniques and strategies they applied to their own empowerment on campus, as student-citizens. By 1967, activism began to orbit the war in Vietnam as the central focus of attention. Students increasingly used mass mobilizations to demonstrate and express their frustrations at the lack of political power and their desires to end the war and discrimination. Students also linked the events of their campuses with larger national struggles. However, beginning in 1969, the emphasis shifted again from the national to the local with the Moratorium and then the killings at Kent State, which sent a shockwave through the student community. Though activism did not completely end, the era of the large demonstration, brief though it was, had ended by the early 1970s and once students had the political voice that had long been denied them, they found little desire to wield this power in the 1972 presidential election.

From the conflicted campuses of the early-to-mid 1960s as students began to conceptualize themselves as a distinct social group, through the turbulent years at the end of the decade when the world seemed to be falling apart around them, one sees the organization and development of a student-citizen identity. Assuredly, the activist model of student citizenship that dominated throughout the Sixties had begun to fade by 1972, but the idea that students as citizens of the university and citizens of the nation had rights that college and community leaders were obligated to respect did not disappear. The changes that emerged from the Sixties may not have been as radical, revolutionary, or far-reaching as many of the activists pushing for them had hoped, but they did represent a shift in the relationship between students, the university, and the community. In loco parentis was nearly dead, students had some new voice in university and political decision-making, the war and the draft ended, and while civil rights and poverty are still works in progress, undeniable advances occurred because of the activism of students during the Sixties—though they may remind us that progress is not an attainable goal but a continuing process. Furthermore, exploring how students at these northern Appalachian universities engaged with issues that generally reached beyond their region, one helps to challenge notions of Appalachian isolation and victimhood, as well as suggest there is a great deal more to the story of Appalachia in the Sixties than poverty, unions, and out-migration.

Notes

1. David H. Kurtzman, "Commencement Address," (speech, Pittsburgh, PA, May 31, 1967), Chancellor of the University of Pittsburgh, David H. Kurtzman (Acting), Administrative Files, 1966–1967, UA.2.10.1966–1967, Archives Service Center, University of Pittsburgh [hereafter referred to as ASC].

2. Michael Ferber and Staughton Lynd, *The Resistance* (New York: Beacon Press, 1971); Kirkpatrick Sale, *SDS: The Rise and Development of the Students for a Democratic Society* (New York: Random House, 1973); Nancy Zaroulis and Gerald Sullivan, *Who Spoke Up? American Protest Against the War in Vietnam, 1963–1975* (New York: Doubleday, 1984); Todd Gitlin, *The Sixties: Years of Hope, Days of Rage* (New York: Bantam Books, 1987); Tom Hayden, *Reunion: A Memoir* (New York: Random House, 1988); W.J. Rorabaugh, *Berkeley at War: The 1960s* (New York: Oxford University Press, 1989); Melvin Small and William Hoover, eds., *Give Peace a Chance: Exploring the Vietnam Antiwar Movement* (Syracuse, NY: Syracuse University Press, 1992); Terry Anderson, *The Movement and the Sixties: Protest in America from Greensboro to Wounded Knee* (New York: Oxford University Press, 1995).

3. Kenneth J. Heineman, *Campus Wars: The Peace Movement at American State Universities in the Vietnam Era* (New York: New York University Press, 1992).

4. Marc J. Gilbert, ed., *The Vietnam War on Campus: Other Voices, More Distant Drums* (New York: Praeger, 2000); Rusty L. Monhollon, *"This is America?" The Sixties in Lawrence, Kansas* (New York: Palgrave, 2002); Mary Ann Wynkoop, *Dissent in the Heartland: The Sixties at Indiana University* (Bloomington, IN: Indiana University Press, 2002); Robbie Lieberman, *Prairie Power: Voices of 1960s Midwestern Protest* (Columbia, MO: University of Missouri Press, 2004); Andrew Grose, "Voices of Southern Protest during the Vietnam War Era: The University of South Carolina as a Case Study," *Peace & Change*, 32, 2 (April 2007): 153–67; Thomas Weyant, "Pittsburgh in the Time of Protest: Draft Resistance and Contending Definitions of Patriotism during the Vietnam Era," in *Lesser Civil Wars: Civilians Defining War and the Memory of War*, ed. Marsha R. Robinson (Newcastle, UK: Cambridge Scholars Press, 2012), 151–73.

5. President's Appalachian Regional Commission [PARC], *Appalachia: A Report By the President's Appalachian Regional Commission, 1964* (Washington, D.C.: Government Printing Office, 1964), xv.

6. Thomas Kiffmeyer, *Reformers to Radicals: The Appalachian Volunteers and the War on Poverty* (Lexington, KY: University Press of Kentucky, 2008).

7. Paul C. Shaw, "The Urban University Student: A Political Profile," *Research in Higher Education* 2, 1 (March 1974), 65–79; Robert C. Alberts, *Pitt: The Story of the University of Pittsburgh, 1787–1987* (Pittsburgh, PA: University of Pittsburgh Press, 1986); Barbara J. Howe, *Tales from the Tower: If Woodburn Hall Could Speak* (Morgantown, WV: West Virginia University Eberley College of Arts and Sciences, 1997); Betty Hollow, *Ohio University, 1804–2004: The Spirit of a Singular Place* (Athens, OH: Ohio University Press, 2003).

8. For a discussion of current subregions, including a map of designated counties, see

Appalachian Regional Commission [ARC], "Subregions in Appalachia," accessed on February 10, 2013, http://www.arc.gov.

9. Allen Batteau, *The Invention of Appalachia* (Tucson, AZ: University of Arizona Press, 1990), 7.

10. Jack E. Weller, *Yesterday's People: Life in Contemporary Appalachia* (Lexington, KY: University of Kentucky Press, 1965); Henry D. Shapiro, *Appalachia on Our Minds: The Southern Mountains and Mountaineers in American Consciousness, 1870–1920* (Chapel Hill, NC: University of North Carolina Press, 1978); John Gaventa, *Power and Powerlessness: Quiescence and Rebellion in an Appalachian Valley* (Urbana, IL: University of Illinois Press, 1980); Ronald D. Eller, *Miner, Millhands, and Mountaineers: Industrialization of the Appalachian South, 1880–1930* (Knoxville, TN: University of Tennessee Press, 1982); Bruce Ergood and Bruce E. Kuhre, eds., *Appalachia: Social Context Past and Present*, 2nd ed. (Dubque, IA: Kendall/Hunt, 1983); Paul Salstrom, *Appalachia's Path to Dependency: Rethinking a Region's Economic History, 1730–1940* (Lexington, KY: University Press of Kentucky, 1994); Ada F. Haynes, *Poverty in Central Appalachia: Underdevelopment and Exploitation* (New York: Garland Publishing, 1997); Dwight B. Billings and Kathleen M. Blee, *The Road to Poverty: The Making of Wealth and Hardship in Appalachia* (New York: Cambridge University Press, 2000); Robert B. Drake, *A History of Appalachia* (Lexington, KY: University Press of Kentucky, 2001); John Alexander Williams, *Appalachia: A History* (Chapel Hill, NC: University of North Carolina Press, 2002); Richard A Straw and H. Tyler Blethen, eds., *High Mountain Rising: Appalachia in Time and Place* (Urbana, IL: University of Illinois Press, 2004); Ronald D. Eller, *Uneven Ground: Appalachia since 1945* (Lexington, KY: University Press of Kentucky, 2008); Gregory S. Wilson, *Communities Left Behind: The Area Redevelopment Administration, 1945–1965* (Knoxville, TN: University of Tennessee Press, 2009).

11. Roul Tunley, "The Strange Case of West Virginia," *Saturday Evening Post*, February 6, 1960, 19–20, 64–66.

12. Thomas R. Ford, ed., *The Southern Appalachian Region: A Survey* (Lexington, KY: University of Kentucky Press, 1962).

13. Harry M. Caudill, *Night Comes to the Cumberlands: A Biography of a Depressed Area* (Boston, MA: Little, Brown, and Co., 1963).

14. J.D. Vance, *Hillbilly Elegy: A Memoir of a Family and Culture in Crisis* (New York: Harper, 2016); Anthony Harkins and Meredith McCarroll, eds., *Appalachian Reckoning: A Region Responds to* Hillbilly Elegy (Morgantown, WV: West Virginia University Press, 2019).

15. PARC, *Appalachia*, 28; John Friedmann, "Poor Regions and Poor Nations: Perspectives on the Problem of Appalachia," *Southern Economic Journal* 32, 4 (April 1966), 165–75; Michael E. Latham, *Modernization as Ideology: American Social Science and "Nation Building" in the Kennedy Era* (Chapel Hill, NC: University of North Carolina Press, 2000).

16. John Alexander Williams, *West Virginia: A History* (Morgantown, WV: West Virginia University Press, 2001); Jerry Bruce Thomas, *An Appalachian Reawakening: West Virginia and the Perils of the New Machine Age, 1945–1972* (Morgantown, WV: West Virginia University Press, 2010).

17. *U.S. Census of Population, 1960: Vol. I, Characteristics of the Population, Number of Inhabitants, General Population Characteristics, General Social and Economic Characteristics, and Detailed Characteristics: Part I, United States Summary* (Washington, D.C.: Government

Printing Office, 1962); *U.S. Census of Population, 1970: Vol. I, Characteristics of the Population: Part 1, United States Summary: Section 1* (Washington, D.C.: Government Printing Office, 1973); "The New Appalachian Subregions and Their Development Strategies," in *Appalachia: Social Context Past and Present*, 2nd ed., ed. Bruce Ergood and Bruce E. Kuhre (Dubuque, IA: Kendall/Hunt, 1983), 22–30; Williams, *Appalachia*, 334–35.

18. David E. Whisnant, *Modernizing the Mountaineer: People, Power, and Planning in Appalachia*, rev. ed. (Knoxville, TN: University of Tennessee Press, 1994), 3–39; Thomas J. Kiffmeyer, "From Self-Help to Sedition: The Appalachian Volunteers in Eastern Kentucky, 1964–1970," *Journal of Southern History* 64, 1 (February 1998), 68.

19. Suzanne Mettler, *Soldiers to Citizens: The G.I. Bill and the Making of the Greatest Generation* (New York: Oxford University Press, 2005); Glenn C. Altschuler and Stuart M. Blumin, *The GI Bill: A New Deal for Veterans* (New York: Oxford University Press, 2009).

20. Kenneth T. Jackson, *Crabgrass Frontiers: The Suburbanization of the United States* (New York: Oxford University Press, 1985); Elaine Tyler May, *Homeward Bound: American Families in the Cold War Era* (New York: Basic Books, 1999); Stephanie Coontz, *The Way We Never Were: American Families and the Nostalgia Trap* (New York: Basic Books, 2000); Lizabeth Cohen, *A Consumer's Republic: The Politics of Mass Consumption in Postwar America* (New York: Alfred A. Knopf, 2003); Centers for Disease Control and Prevention, "Vital Statistics of the United States, 2003, Volume I, Natality," Table I-I "Live Births, Birth Rates, and Fertility Rates, by Race: United States, 1909–2003" (Washington, D.C.: Government Printing Office, 2003); Victor B. Brooks, *Boomers: The Cold War Generation Grows Up* (Chicago: Ivan R. Dee, 2009); Sandra L. Colby and Jennifer M. Ortman, *The Baby Boom Cohort in the United States: 2012 to 2060*, Current Population Reports P25-1411 (Washington, D.C.: U.S. Census Bureau, 2014), 2–5.

21. Victoria M. Grieve, *Little Cold Warriors: American Childhood in the 1950s* (New York: Oxford University Press, 2018).

22. "A Young $10 Billion Power: The US Teen-age Consumer Has Become a Major Factor in the Nation's Economy," *Life*, August 31, 1959, 78–84; James U. McNeal, *Children as Consumers* (Austin, TX: Bureau of Business Research University of Texas, 1964); Cohen, *A Consumer's Republic*, 298–309.

23. Tommy Boyce and Bobby Hart, "(Theme from) The Monkees," *The Monkees*, Colgems, 1967.

24. Nicholas von Hoffman, *The Multiversity: A Personal Report on What Happens to Today's Students at American Universities* (New York: Holt, Rinehart, and Winston, 1966); S.E. and Zella Luria, "The Role of the University: Ivory Tower, Service Station, or Frontier Post?" in *The Embattled University*, ed. Stephen R. Graubard and Gino A. Ballotti (New York: George Braziller, 1970); Helen Lefkowtiz Horowitz, *Campus Life: Undergraduate Cultures from the End of the Eighteenth Century to the Present* (New York: Alfred A. Knopf, 1987); John R. Thelin, *A History of American Higher Education* (Baltimore, MD: Johns Hopkins University Press, 2004); John C. Scott, "The Mission of the University: Medieval to Postmodern Transformation," *Journal of Higher Education* 77, 1 (Jan–Feb 2006): 1–39.

25. von Hoffman, *The Multiversity*, 60–73, 122–30; Horowitz, *Campus Life*, 11–14, 26, 39; Daniel A. Clark, "'The Two Joes Meet—Joe College, Joe Veteran': The G.I. Bill, College Education, and Postwar American Culture," *History of Education Quarterly* 38, 2 (Summer

1998), 175–78; Thelin, *A History of American Higher Education*, 20–28, 65–69, 158–69, 191–94, 254; Mettler, *Soldiers to Citizens*, 52–59, 67–68, 71–76; Altschuler and Blumin, *The GI Bill*, 86–96, 108–16.

26. Hugh Davis Graham and Nancy Diamond, *The Rise of American Research Universities: Elites and Challengers in the Postwar Era* (Baltimore, MD: Johns Hopkins University Press, 1997), 11, 26–50; Clark Kerr, *The Uses of the University*, 5th ed. (Cambridge, MA: Harvard University Press, 2001), 93; Henry A. Giroux, *The University in Chains: Confronting the Military–Industrial–Academic Complex* (Boulder, CO: Paradigm Publishers, 2007), 13–17; James Ledbetter, *Unwarranted Influence: Dwight D. Eisenhower and the Military–Industrial Complex* (New Haven, CT: Yale University Press, 2011), 154–59.

27. J. William Fulbright, *The Arrogance of Power* (New York: Vintage Books, 1966), 40–42; Ellen W. Schrecker, *No Ivory Tower: McCarthyism and the Universities* (New York: Oxford University Press, 1986); Lionel S. Lewis, *Cold War on Campus: A Study of the Politics of Organizational Control* (New Brunswick, NJ: Transaction Books, 1988); Sigmund Diamond, *Compromised Campus: The Collaboration of Universities with the Intelligence Community, 1945–1955* (New York: Oxford University Press, 1992).

28. Kerr, *The Uses of the University*, 15–22.

29. Jane Sanders, *Cold War on Campus: Academic Freedom at the University of Washington, 1946–1964* (Seattle, WA: University of Washington Press, 1979); Schrecker, *No Ivory Tower*; Charles H. McCormick, *This Nest of Vipers: McCarthyism and Higher Education in the Mundel Affair, 1951–52* (Champaign, IL: University of Illinois Press, 1989); Noam Chomsky, Laura Nader, Immanuel Wallerstein, R.C. Lewontin, Richard Ohmann, Ira Katznelson, David Montgomery, Ray Siver, and Howard Zinn, eds., *The Cold War & the University: Toward an Intellectual History of the Postwar Years* (New York: New Press, 1997); William J. Billingsley, *Communists on Campus: Race, Politics, and the Public University in Sixties North Carolina* (Athens, GA: University of Georgia Press, 1999).

30. Kenneth Keniston speaks of varying impulses that gave rise to competing definitions of student and youth identity. See Keniston, "Youth Culture as Enforced Alienation," in *The Cult of Youth in Middle-Class America*, Richard L. Rapson, ed. (Lexington, MA: D.C. Heath and Company, 1971), 85–87.

31. Benedict Anderson identified similar components as necessary for the creation of nationalism within imagined communities, see Benedict Anderson, *Imagined Communities: Reflections on the Origins and Spread of Nationalism* (New York: Verso, 1983).

32. Horowitz, *Campus Life*.

33. Several studies of New Left and New Right origins, development, and goals exist; for a non-exhaustive list, see Charles DeBenedetti, *An American Ordeal: The Antiwar Movement of the Vietnam Era* (Syracuse, NY: Syracuse University Press, 1990); Gitlin, *The Sixties*; Anderson, *The Movement and the Sixties*; John A. Andrew, III, *The Other Side of the Sixties: Young Americans for Freedom and the Rise of Conservative Politics* (New Brunswick, NJ: Rutgers University Press, 1997); Rebecca E. Klatch, *A Generation Divided: The New Left, the New Right, and the 1960s* (Berkeley, CA: University of California Press, 1999); Maurice Isserman and Michael Kazin, *America Divided: The Civil War of the 1960s*, 3rd ed. (New York: Oxford University Press, 2008).

34. Derek Heater, *What is Citizenship?* (Malden, MA: Polity Press, 1999); Catriona McKinnon and Iain Hampsher-Monk, "Introduction," in *The Demands of Citizenship*, eds. Catriona McKinnon and Iana Hampsher-Monk (New York: Continuum, 2000), 1–9.

Chapter 1

1. "16 'U' Coeds Will Vie for Homecoming Queen," *Daily Athenaeum*, October 2, 1964; Nancy Fuchs, "Sour Sixties Theme, Fighting Irish, Set for Homecoming," *Pitt News*, October 2, 1964; Editorial, "More Spirit(s)?" *Daily Athenaeum*, October 7, 1964; "IFC Votes to Have Homecoming Floats If Frats Say Yes," *Pitt News*, October 9, 1964; "Two Seniors, One Junior Vie for Homecoming Queen," *Daily Athenaeum*, October 13, 1964; "Week's Results Given for Spirit Competition," *Pitt News*, October 16, 1964; "Queen Candidates Announced," *Pitt News*, October 19, 1964; "Campus Groups Aid In Shaping Weekend," *Daily Athenaeum*, October 20, 1964; "Wanted– a Crown for Homecoming," *Daily Athenaeum*, October 22, 1964; Bob Graham, "Parade to Initiate Homecoming Events," *Daily Athenaeum*, October 23, 1964; "New Theme Set for Homecoming Is 'Famous Firsts'," *Pitt News*, October 23, 1964; Jacki Katz, "Banners Approved," *Pitt News*, October 23, 1964; Editorial, "No Queen Announcement," *Post*, October 23, 1964; Julie Stickel, "Weekend Activities to Include Traditional Parade, Game, Dance," *Post*, October 23, 1964; Bob Welling, "Phi Sigs, DG's Take First In Parade Competition," *Daily Athenaeum*, October 24, 1964; Scott Bosley, "Chilly, But Lively Parade Kicks Off WVU Celebration," *Daily Athenaeum*, October 24, 1964; Editorial, "New System, Better Weekend," *Daily Athenaeum*, October 24, 1964; "Campus Greeks, Dorms Plan Receptions, Parties Today," *Daily Athenaeum*, October 24, 1964; "Homecoming Candidates," *Pitt News*, October 26, 1964; "Homecoming Queen Voting to Take Place Today, Must Pick 5," *Pitt News*, October 30, 1964; "Spirit Award Results Announced; Tri-Delt, Sigma Chi Rated Tops," *Pitt News*, October 30, 1964; "Here They Are: Homecoming Queen Finalists," *Pitt News*, November 2, 1964; 'Pep Rally Kicks Off Events for Homecoming Weekend," *Pitt News*, November 2, 1964; "Homecoming Queen Voting Procedure Discussed by CAC," *Post*, November 3, 1964.

2. Nicholas von Hoffman, *The Multiversity: A Personal Report of What Happens to Today's Students at American Universities* (New York: Holt, Rinehart, and Winston, 1966), 69–73, 122–30; Helen Lefkowitz Horowitz, *Campus Life: Undergraduate Cultures from the End of the Eighteenth Century to the Present* (New York: Alfred A. Knopf, 1987), 11–14, 26, 39; John R. Thelin, *A History of American Higher Education* (Baltimore, MD: Johns Hopkins University, 2004), 20–28, 65–69, 158–69, 191–97, 254.

3. Horowitz, *Campus Life*, 15–19.

4. Daniel A. Clark, "'The Two Joes Meet—Joe College, Joe Veteran': The G.I. Bill, College Education, and Postwar American Culture," *History of Education Quarterly* 38, no. 2 (Summer 1998), 175–78; Suzanne Mettler, *Soldiers to Citizens: The G.I. Bill and the Making of the Greatest Generation* (New York: Oxford University Press, 2005), 52–59, 67–68, 71–76; Glenn C. Altschuler and Stuart M. Blumin, *The GI Bill: A New Deal for Veterans* (New York: Oxford University Press, 2009), 86–96, 108–16.

5. Hugh Davis Graham and Nancy Diamond, *The Rise of American Research Universities: Elites and Challengers in the Postwar Era* (Baltimore, MD: Johns Hopkins University Press,

1997), 11, 26–50; Clark Kerr, *The Uses of the University*, 5th ed. (Cambridge, MA: Harvard University Press, 2001), 93; Henry A. Giroux, *The University in Chains: Confronting the Military–Industrial–Academic Complex* (Boulder, CO: Paradigm Publishers, 2007), 13–17; James Ledbetter, *Unwarranted Influence: Dwight D. Eisenhower and the Military–Industrial Complex* (New Haven, CT: Yale University Press, 2011), 154–59.

6. J. William Fulbright, *The Arrogance of Power* (New York: Vintage Books, 1966), 40–42; Ellen W. Schrecker, *No Ivory Tower: McCarthyism and the Universities* (New York: Oxford University Press, 1986); Lionel S. Lewis, *Cold War on Campus: A Study of the Politics of Organizational Control* (New Brunswick, NJ: Transaction Books, 1988); Charles H. McCormick, *This Nest of Vipers: McCarthyism and Higher Education in the Mundel Affair, 1951–52* (Champaign, IL: University of Illinois Press, 1989); Sigmund Diamond, *Compromised Campus: The Collaboration of Universities with the Intelligence Community, 1945–1955* (New York: Oxford University Press, 1992); William J. Billingsley, *Communists on Campus: Race, Politics, and the Public University in Sixties North Carolina* (Athens, GA: University of Georgia Press, 1999).

7. Kerr, *The Uses of the University*, 15–22.

8. Jane Sanders, *Cold War on Campus: Academic Freedom at the University of Washington, 1946–1964* (Seattle, WA: University of Washington Press, 1979); Ellen Schrecker, *No Ivory Tower: McCarthyism and the Universities* (New York: Oxford University Press, 1986); Noam Chomsky, Laura Nader, Immanuel Wallerstein, R.C. Lewontin, Richard Ohmann, Ira Katznelson, David Montgomery, Ray Siver, and Howard Zinn, eds., *The Cold War & the University: Toward an Intellectual History of the Postwar Years* (New York: New Press, 1997).

9. Thomas N. Hoover, *The History of Ohio University* (Athens, OH: Ohio University Press, 1954), 16–25; Betty Hollow, *Ohio University, 1804–2004: The Spirit of a Singular Place* (Athens, OH: Ohio University Press, 2003), 13–14, 183.

10. Hoover, *The History of Ohio University*, 85–98, 121–25; Hollow, *Ohio University, 1804–2004*, 31–33, 42–56.

11. Hoover, *The History of Ohio University*, 126, 196–97, 225–37; Hollow, *Ohio University, 1804–2004*, 45, 55–76, 91–93, 111–14, 132–46, 149.

12. Hoover, *The History of Ohio University*, 250–51.

13. Ohio University, *Ohio University Bulletin: For the Biennium, 1958–1960* (Athens, OH: Ohio University, 1958), iv, http://www.archive.org.

14. "LBJ Selects Dr. Alden to Command Poverty War," *Post*, March 26, 1964; Hollow, *Ohio University, 1804–2004*, 180–85; Ohio University, *Ohio University Bulletin: For the Biennium, 1964–1966* (Athens, OH: Ohio University, 1964), 13, http://www.archive.org.

15. Robert C. Alberts, *Pitt: The Story of the University of Pittsburgh, 1787–1987* (Pittsburgh, PA: University of Pittsburgh Press, 1986), 8–12, 18–23, 33–34, 49, 56.

16. Alberts, *Pitt*, 41–42, 64–72, 115–17, 124, 160, 181.

17. Alberts, *Pitt*, 185–88, 194–95, 211–19; Graham and Diamond, *The Rise of American Research Universities*, 38.

18. Paul C. Shaw, "The Urban University Student: A Political Profile," *Research in Higher Education* 2, 1 (March 1974), 65–79; Alberts, *Pitt*, 255–58, 266–69, 272–87, 300–07, 317–23.

19. Alberts, *Pitt*, 144–56, 292–69.

20. There appears to be no singular institutional history of West Virginia University, though several authors have pieced together some aspects; for example, see James Dawson,

WVU: An Early Portrait (Morgantown, WV: 1971), 2–3, 12; Barbara J. Howe, *Tales from the Tower: If Woodburn Hall Could Speak* (Morgantown, WV: West Virginia University Eberley College of Arts and Sciences, 1997), 2–7; J. William Douglas, *The School of Physical Education at West Virginia University: An Historical Perspective, 1891–1999* (Morgantown, WV: West Virginia University School of Physical Education, 2000), 13, 21.

The Dawson source provides no information on a publisher. It is a series of images with interspersed, unsourced text. It appears that someone or some group associated with the University published the short pamphlet; it may have been part of a class project as the pamphlet describes Dawson as a WVU graduate.

21. Dawson, *WVU*, 10; Howe, *Tales from the Tower*, 27–28; Douglas, *The School of Physical Education at West Virginia University*, 5, 21, 37; Susan Buehler, "Frosh Week 'Successful'; Beanie-Wearing Ends Tomorrow," *Daily Athenaeum*, September 8, 1967.

A memoir written in 1975 by Berlin Basil Chapman recounts his experiences at WVU during the 1920s. In the very short pamphlet, Chapman discusses his participating in ROTC and the excitement of football games, especially against rival Pittsburgh. Chapman also describes courses and some of the administrative issues students encountered providing a window into the college experience at WVU in the years immediately following the First World War; see Berlin Basil Chapman, *West Virginia University: A Memoir* (Parsons, WV: McClain Publishing Co, 1975).

22. Dawson, *WVU*, 16; Howe, *Tales from the Tower*, 26–31; Douglas, *The School of Physical Education at West Virginia University*, 38–39, 55–57; "Enrollment tally Hits Another Record High: President 'Gratified' At Enrollment Gains," *Daily Athenaeum*, September 14, 1967; Memo, "Student Social Regulations," [unknown author, presumably Office of Student Life], January 11, 1971, A&M 2833, WVU Office of Student Life Collection, West Virginia and Regional History Collection, West Virginia University, Morgantown, West Virginia [hereafter referred to as: WVRHC].

23. Ronald L. Lewis, *Aspiring to Greatness: West Virginia University since World War II* (Morgantown, WV: West Virginia University Press, 2013), 1–8, 29–36, 45–49, 63–68, 104–22, 180–82.

Part 1

1. "Freshmen Hear Miller," *Daily Athenaeum*, September 15, 1964.

2. "Freshmen Hear Miller," *Daily Athenaeum*, September 15, 1964.

3. Robert F. Kennedy, "Day of Affirmation—South Africa" (speech, University of Capetown, South Africa, June 6, 1966), http://rfkcenter.org.

4. Students for a Democratic Society, "The Port Huron Statement," in *"Takin' It To The Streets": A Sixties Reader*, 2nd ed., ed. Alexander Bloom and Wini Breines (New York: Oxford University Press, 2003), 50–61.

5. Many sources on students and the university in the 1960s reference the ideas of isolation and estrangements as well as concepts of empowerment and independence, especially of the individual. See Nicholas von Hoffman, *The Multiversity: A Personal Report on What Happens to Today's Students at American Universities* (New York: Holt, Rinehart, and Winston, 1966), xv–xx, 122–23, 136, 151–52; Jerry Farber, *The Student as Nigger: Essays and Stories*

(New York: Pocket Books, 1970); Clark Kerr, *The Uses of the University*, 5th ed. (Cambridge, MA: Harvard University Press, 2001), 14–15, 31–34; SDS, "The Port Huron Statement," in *"Takin' It To the Streets,"* 50–61; Doug Rossinow, *The Politics of Authenticity: Liberalism, Christianity, and the New Left in America* (New York: Columbia University Press, 1998), 18.

6. Victoria Grieve provides an instructive discussion on youth political participation in the early Cold War. Her work highlights youth participation in prescribed and adult directed activities, demonstrating that Cold War youth were political participants despite claims of their apolitical existence. See Grieve, *Little Cold Warriors: American Childhood in the 1950s* (New York: Oxford University Press, 2018).

Chapter 2

1. Beth Bailey, *Sex in the Heartland* (Cambridge, MA: Harvard University Press, 1999), 82–102.

2. Nicholas von Hoffman, *The Multiversity: A Personal Report of What Happens to Today's Students at American Universities* (New York: Holt, Rinehart, and Winston, 1966), xi–xiii, 10–11, 122–23, 128–30; Jerry Farber, "The Student and Society: An Annotated Manifesto," in *The Student as Nigger: Essays and Stories*, ed. Jerry Farber (New York: Pocket Books, 1970), 17–23, 27–28, 32–33; Bailey, *Sex in the Heartland*, 79–96.

3. Richard Pesin, "When the Real is Fantasy," *Post*, April 19, 1967.

4. Baily, *Sex in the Heartland*; Elaine Tyler May, *Homeward Bound: American Families in the Cold War Era* (New York: Basic Books, 1999); Stephanie Coontz, *The Way We Never Were: American Families and the Nostalgia Trap* (New York: Basic Books, 2000); Stephanie Coontz, *A Strange Stirring: The* Feminine Mystique *and American Women at the Dawn of the 1960s* (New York: Basic Books, 2012).

5. Bailey, *Sex in the Heartland*, 82.

6. "Betty Friedan to Speak on Feminine Illusions at Midday Wednesday," *Pitt News*, January 13, 1964; Bill Niederberg, "Author Demands Female Equality," *Pitt News*, January 17, 1964; "Noted Author to Speak on Feminine Identity," *Daily Athenaeum*, October 13, 1964; Joyce Breach, "Author States Women Should Face Challenge," *Daily Athenaeum*, October 15, 1964.

7. "Noted Author to Speak on Feminine Identity," *Daily Athenaeum*, October 13, 1964.

8. Nancy Fuchs, "A Forced Equality," *Pitt News*, March 11, 1964.

9. Stu Sharpe, Letter to the Editor, *Post*, February 20, 1964.

10. Bailey, *Sex in the Heartland*, 82–102.

11. Ned Whelan, Letter to the Editor, *Post*, February 24, 1964.

12. Sandi Wolff, Sandy Kovanes, Sandy Given, and Jan Linnert, Letter to the Editor, *Post*, February 25, 1964.

13. Contemporary authors and later historians have tangentially addressed the connections students made between their roles in society as students and as citizens. See Jerry Farber, "The Student as Nigger," in *The Student as Nigger: Essays and Stories*, ed. Jerry Farber (New York: Pocket Books, 1970), 90–100; Irving Louis Horowitz and William H. Friedland, *The Knowledge Factory: Student Power and Academic Politics in America* (Chicago, IL: Aldine Publishing, 1970), 12–15, 19–26; Helen Lefkowitz Horowitz, *Campus Life: Undergraduate*

Cultures from the End of the Eighteenth Century to the Present (New York: Alfred A. Knopf, 1987), 222–25, 229–33, 236; Terry H. Anderson, *The Movement and the Sixties: Protest in America from Greensboro to Wounded Knee* (New York: Oxford University Press, 1995), 48–50, 57–60; Bailey, *Sex in the Heartland*, 82–86.

14. Barbara Olivitto, "AWS Institutes New Policy," *Daily Athenaeum*, October 19, 1966; Merideth Robb, "Unenforced Outdated Law Needs New Modification," *Daily Athenaeum*, October 19, 1966; Editorial, "Leave 'em Alone," *Daily Athenaeum*, October 25, 1966; Editorial, "Abolish those Childish Rules," *Daily Athenaeum*, October 27, 1966.

15. Judy Weimer, "RA's Submit Proposal for Elimination of Hours," *Post*, September 30, 1966; Editorial, "Hours Unlimited," *Post*, October 11, 1966; Deena Mirrow, "Education Expert Calls Women's Hours 'Trivia,'" *Post*, October 18, 1966; RAs Revise No-Hours Plan," *Post*, October 28, 1966; Editorial, "'Fairly Well Satisfied,'" *Post*, November 11, 1966; Judith Brown, Letter to the Editor, *Post*, November 14, 1966.

16. Editorial, "Talk," *Post*, March 2, 1964.

17. "Mock Convention Positions Open for Delegation Heads," *Post*, January 13, 1964; Dick Kamradt, "Mock Political Staff Prepare for April Event," *Post*, February 11, 1964; "Big Screening for Convention Starts Sunday," *Post*, February 20, 1964; "Wanted: 2600 Delegates, Applications Open Now," *Post*, February 28, 1964; Raymond H. Gusteson, Letter to the Editor, *Post*, March 19, 1964; "Mock Convention Planned April 10," *Daily Athenaeum*, March 25, 1964; Editorial, "Students to Voice Decision," *Daily Athenaeum*, April 3, 1964; "Laurence Rockefeller Will Nominate Uncle," *Daily Athenaeum*, April 8, 1964; Delia Devine, "400 Students Will Attend Mock Convention," *Daily Athenaeum*, April 10, 1964; Warren S. Napier, Letter to the Editor, *Daily Athenaeum*, April 10, 1964; "MPC Rally Draws Reps of Aspirants," *Post*, April 14, 1964; Dave Cummings, "Over 500 Attend Mock Convention," *Daily Athenaeum*, April 14, 1964; Editorial, "Mock Convention Successful," *Daily Athenaeum*, April 14, 1964; Rhona Saunders, "Chanting Delegates Rally as 'Fever' Sweeps Ohio," *Post*, April 17, 1964; Joe Eszterhas, "College MPCs Support Lodge, but Kent State Adopts Platform with Strong Conservative Vein," *Post*, April 17, 1964; "Poor Communication Hurt Barry," *Post*, April 21, 1964.

Pitt did not hold a mock Republican convention, though during the summer and fall they took several polls of student opinion and held a mock election. See "Poll Shows Johnson Favored 4–1," *Pitt News*, June 22, 1964; Marvin Zelkowitz, "Second 'News' Poll Indicates Students Still Favor Johnson," *Pitt News*, July 27, 1964; "Students Do Mock Voting Wednesday," *Pitt News*, October 23, 1964; "Johnson, Scott Both Victors in University Mock Election as Students Split Ballots," *Pitt News*, October 30, 1964.

18. For an in-depth look at the political participation of American youth in the early Cold War, see Victoria M. Grieve, *Little Cold Warriors: American Childhood in the 1950s* (New York: Oxford University Press, 2018).

19. "Police Plan Protection for Johnson," *Daily Athenaeum*, September 18, 1964; Bob Welling, "Tall Texan Brings Thrill, Worry Too," *Daily Athenaeum*, September 22, 1964; Ron McMillen, "Young Attacks Taft Jr., Sen. Goldwater in Speech," *Post*, September 25, 1964; Penny Lowe, "Early Dismissal Allows Student Turn-Out at Rally for Senator Goldwater," *Post*, September 28, 1964; Dick Belsky, "Democrat Cause War—Goldwater," *Post*, October 1, 1964; Morris Baines, "Barry's Defensive Stand Forgets Traditional Rules," *Post*, October 2,

1964; Cecilie Smith, "Moore Sums Up GOP's Platform," *Daily Athenaeum*, October 8, 1964; Larry Bernfeld, "Humphrey on Campus Thursday: Only Local Speech Set for CL Lawn," *Pitt News*, October 12, 1964; Nancy Copeland, "Republicans, Democrats Clash Over Political Issues at Forum," *Post*, October 15, 1964; Jackie Katz and Chris Martin, "Humphrey Thrills Crowded Rally," *Pitt News*, October 19, 1964; Al Janezic, "100-Man Guard Protects Senator; 2 Dozen Spectators Rumble Over GOP Placards," *Pitt News*, October 19, 1964; "Candidates Join Humphrey for Rally on Cathedral Lawn; 6000 Hear Election Appeals," *Pitt News*, October 19, 1964; "Johnson, Goldwater Appear at Two Civic Arena Rallies," *Pitt News*, October 26, 1964; "Goldwater Calls National Control Unconstitutional," *Pitt News*, October 28, 1964; Jackie Katz, "14,000 Greet Pres. Johnson," *Pitt News*, October 30, 1964; Alex D'Ippolito, "Barry Bowls 'em Over Thursday," *Pitt News*, November 2, 1964.

20. Challenges to ROTC and its place in the university can be found during the 1930s as part of both pacifist and isolationist traditions of the period. See Thomas N. Hoover, *The History of Ohio University* (Athens, OH: Ohio University Press, 1954), 225–26; George W. Knepper, *New Lamps for Old: One Hundred Years of Urban Higher Education at The University of Akron* (Akron, OH: University of Akron Press, 1970), 229–32; Eileen Eagan, *Class, Culture, and the Classroom: The Student Peace Movement of the 1930s* (Philadelphia, PA: Temple University Press, 1981), 33, 57–61; Robert C. Alberts, *Pitt: The Story of the University of Pittsburgh, 1787–1987* (Pittsburgh, PA: University of Pittsburgh Press, 1986), 147–48; Robert Cohen, *When the Old Left was Young: Student Radicals and America's First Mass Student Movement, 1929–1941* (New York: Oxford University Press, 1993), 79–84.

21. Ruth Levikoff, "Students for Peace, PLUS Formed on Univ. Campus," *Pitt News*, April 5, 1965; Alan Disler, "Students for Peace Violate Pitt Preview Solicitation Regulations," *Pitt News*, March 23, 1966; Editorial, "Jurisprudence in Recognition," *Pitt News*, March 23, 1966; Vicki Epstein, "Students for Peace Group Retain Campus Recognition," *Pitt News*, March 25, 1965; Bill Weber and Paul LeBlanc, Letter to the Editor, *Pitt News*, March 30, 1966.

In September 1965, a group of students initiated the New Student Left (NSL) organization at Pitt to serve as a coordinating body for various student organizations with similar goals. The group brought together representatives from the Hill Education Project and civil rights groups, as well as antiwar groups and members of a Pittsburgh city chapter of the W.E.B. DuBois Club. While the NSL never sought, nor received, official sanction by the University, it did represent the existence of a growing liberal-to-radical core of students at Pitt and in the Pittsburgh area. And while neither SFP nor SDS were mentioned in the article describing the formation of NSL, it seems that both of these organizations would have had some connection to or have been born from the NSL. See Alex D'Ippolito, "Liberals Form New Organization," *Pitt News*, September 20, 1965. Student groups like NSL left virtually no archival trace and become visible to historians only through the historical record of the student newspapers.

Both OU and WVU had chapters of SDS (official or not) or other New Left-leaning organization form between 1965 and 1967. See Stu Berger, "Radical Groups Help Establish Democracy," *Daily Athenaeum*, November 2, 1965; "Students Begin Chapter of 'Democratic Society,'" *Post*, March 3, 1966; Tom Price, "SDS May Not Be Formed Here," *Post*, March 7, 1966; "Local S.D.S. Chapter to Join National Society," *Post*, September 26, 1966; Joel Forrester, Letter to the Editor, *Post*, September 27, 1966; Robert L. Newton, "The New Left," *Post*, October 19, 1966; Ohio Chapter of Students for a Democratic Society, Letter to the Editor, *Post*, November 16, 1966; Julian Martin, Rich Anderson, Harry Shaw, Linda Helmstetter, Jane Sullivan, Letter to the Editor, *Daily Athenaeum*, February 16, 1967.

22. Frank Couvares, "Obligation to Dissent," *Pitt News*, June 13, 1966; "Peace Group Questions ROTC," *Pitt News*, June 16, 1966; Frank Couvares, "ROTC in Perspective," *Pitt News*, June 16, 1966; "Students for Peace Attack Rushes Decision on ROTC," *Pitt News*, June 20, 1966; Robert Zavos, "SFP Cite Literature Censorship," *Pitt News*, June 27, 1966; Dan Booker, "ROTC in Orientation," *Pitt News*, June 29, 1966.

23. Couvares, "Obligation to Dissent," *Pitt News*, June 13, 1966.

24. Tom Price, "Students Sought to Staff Cafeterias," *Post*, March 6, 1967; June Kronholz, "Students Condone Walkout," *Post*, March 6, 1967; Rick Rozenman, "Congress' Three Bills Back Strike," *Post*, March 6, 1967; Editorial, "Backing the Strike," *Post*, March 6, 1967; Deena Mirrow, "Sunday Was Rough, But Tomorrow . . .," *Post*, March 6, 1967; Susan Leibensperger, Letter to the Editor, *Post*, March 6, 1967; Rick Rozenman, "Student Supporters Hear Workers' Side," *Post*, March 7, 1967; Tom Price, "University Sees No Discussions," *Post*, March 7, 1967; Editorial, "Don't Sub," *Post*, March 7, 1967; Tom Price, "Strikers Talk With Alden But Reach No Settlement," *Post*, March 8, 1967; Rick Rozenman, "Students Urged to Resist," *Post*, March 8, 1967; Deena Mirrow, "Employees Prepared To Stick It Out," *Post*, March 8, 1967; Editorial, "9.41 v. Hagerman," *Post*, March 8, 1967; Bob Holmes, Bob Tomcho, Ronald G. Schlayer, Richard T. Rehn, Gary N. Schatmeyer, Richard Moysey, George H. Luckey, Bill Keller, Pat Hoban, Tom Burns, Dean Duffey, and Craig Duffey, Letter to the Editor, *Post*, March 8, 1967; Rick Rozenman, "Congress Reaffirms Full Support," *Post*, March 9, 1967; June Kronholz, "Board Job Boycott is Saturday Threat," *Post*, March 9, 1967.

25. "DeNicola Wins Student Presidency," *Post*, May 3, 1966; Bill Sievert, "Rethinking Time," *Post*, December 5, 1966; Rick Rozenman, "Congress' Three Bills Back Strike," *Post*, March 8, 1967; Bill Sievert, "Alden Faces Cheering, Booing Crowd," *Post*, March 9, 1967; Daniel DeNicola, email message to author, June 1, 2015.

26. Bill Sievert, "Alden Faces Cheering, Booing Crowd," *Post*, March 9, 1967; Editorial, "Editorial," *Post*, March 9, 1967; Tom Price, "Alden Will Meet Saxbe in Columbus Today," *Post*, March 10, 1967; "Alden Says Strike Won't Close O.U.," *Chillicothe Gazette* [Chillicothe, OH], March 10, 1967; Tom Price, "University Returns to 'Normal' After Workers' Demands Met," *Post*, March 20, 1967; "Academic Calendar for 1966–1967," in *Ohio University Bulletin: General Catalog Issue 1966–1967* (Athens, OH: Ohio University Printing Office, 1966), 5; Daniel DeNicola, email message to author, June 1, 2015.

27. Clarence Page, "Reactions Mixed on End of Strike," *Post*, March 20, 1967; Rick Rozenman, "Recent Acts of Congress Defended," *Post*, March 23, 1967.

28. John T. Nixon, Letter to the Editor, *Post*, April 6, 1967.

29. Nixon, Letter to the Editor, *Post*, April 6, 1967.

Even fifty years later, Nixon believed that his action was motivated from "an obligation as a citizen." John T. Nixon, email messages to author, February 8 & 9, 2018.

30. Joe Eszterhas, "We are Kooks, Because We Dissent," *Post*, November 8, 1965.

1. Doug McAdam, *Freedom Summer* (New York: Oxford University Press, 1988), 4–7, 12–13, 127, 161–67, 173; Doug Rossinow, *The Politics of Authenticity: Liberalism, Christianity, and the New Left in America* (New York: Columbia University Press, 1998), 4–12, 15–20.

2. John F. Kennedy, "Acceptance Address, 1960," in *The Great Society: A Sourcebook of Speeches*, ed. Glenn R. Capp (Belmont, CA: Dickenson Publishing, 1967), 14; Lyndon B. Johnson, "Remarks in Athens at Ohio University. May 7, 1964" (speech, Athens, OH, May 7, 1964), http://www.presidency.ucsb.edu; John A. Andrew, III, *Lyndon Johnson and the Great Society* (Chicago, IL: Ivan R. Dee, 1998), 56–94; Robert Dallek, *Flawed Giant: Lyndon Johnson and His Times, 1961–1973* (New York: Oxford University Press, 1998), 108–10; Thomas Kiffmeyer, *Reformers to Radicals: The Appalachian Volunteers and the War on Poverty* (Lexington, KY: University Press of Kentucky, 2008), 11, 49–50; Gregory S. Wilson, *Communities Left Behind: The Area Redevelopment Administration, 1945–1965* (Knoxville, TN: University of Tennessee Press, 2009), xiv–xxii, 1–5, 9–11, 15–17, 83–104.

3. John Dittmer, *Local People: The Struggle for Civil Rights in Mississippi* (Urbana, IL: University of Illinois Press, 1994); Mary L. Dudziak, *Cold War Civil Rights: Race and the Image of American Democracy* (Princeton, NJ: Princeton University Press, 2000); Nancy MacLean, *Freedom Is Not Enough: The Opening of the American Workplace* (Cambridge University Press, 2006).

4. Martha Biondi, *To Stand and Fight: The Struggle for Civil rights in Postwar New York City* (Cambridge, MA: Harvard University Press, 2003); Matthew J. Countryman, *Up South: Civil Rights and Black Power in Philadelphia* (Philadelphia, PA: University of Pennsylvania Press, 2007).

5. Michael B. Friedland, *Lift Up Your Voice Like a Trumpet: White Clergy and the Civil Rights and Antiwar Movements, 1954–1973* (Chapel Hill, NC: University of North Carolina Press, 1998); Simon Hall, *Peace and Freedom: The Civil Rights and Antiwar Movements of the 1960s* (Philadelphia, PA: University of Pennsylvania Press, 2006);

6. "Lewis Reviews Civil Rights," *Tartan* [Carnegie Institute of Technology], March 4, 1964; "Non-Violence Leader to Talk Here Friday," *Pitt News*, March 4, 1964; "SNCC Chairman Lewis Lectures This Afternoon," *Duke* [Duquesne University], March 6, 1964; Margie Donaldson, "Slavery in White South," *Pitt News*, March 11, 1964; "SNCC Freedom Singers Entertain for Carnegie Tech Liberal Club," *Tartan*, March 11, 1964; "Civil Rights to Return in Discussion Groups," *Post*, March 17, 1964; Tom Johnson, "Two Ohio Civil rights' Drivers Risk Arrest to Deliver Athens' Aid to Southern Negroes," *Post*, March 20, 1964; Benjamin F. McKeever, "Rights Leader Briggs Finds Education as Key to Segregation Problem," *Post*, March 20, 1964; "Appearance by Gregory Aids 'Rights,'" *Post*, April 13, 1964; Joe Eszterhas, "Gregory Looks to Ohio for Prejudice Examples," *Post*, May 1, 1964.

7. "SNCC Freedom Singers Entertain For Carnegie Tech Liberal Club," *Tartan*, March 11, 1964.

8. Editorial, "'Y' to Aid Negro Voters," *Daily Athenaeum*, March 3, 1964; "Venture in South Told by 'Y' Panel," *Daily Athenaeum*, April 9, 1964; Joseph L. Kuykendall, Letter to the Editor, *Daily Athenaeum*, April 17, 1964; Susan Hofstetter, Letter to the Editor, *Daily Athenaeum*, April 22, 1964.

9. "'Y' To Hold Voter Drive," *Tartan*, May 13, 1964; Richard Fernandez, Untitled Flyer, undated [presumably prior to May 16, 1964], Civil Rights Folder, Collection on Student Activism, UA00046, [hereafter referred to as: CSA] Ohio University, Athens, Ohio [hereafter referred to as: OU]; Untitled Flyer, undated [presumably on or about May 17, 1964], Civil Rights Folder, CSA, OU; Editorial, "Go South!" *Pitt News*, May 20, 1964; Roger Zepernick, "ACRAC Sends Money, Clothes to Help Civil Rights Fight," *Post*, June 23, 1964; "Can Rights Law Be Enforced?" *Daily Athenaeum*, July 9, 1964.

10. Joe William Trotter Jr. and Eric Ledell Smith, *African Americans in Pennsylvania: Shifting Historical Perspectives* (University Park, PA: Pennsylvania State University Press, 1997); Joe W. Trotter and Jared N. Day, *Race and Renaissance: African Americans in Pittsburgh Since World War II* (Pittsburgh, PA: University of Pittsburgh Press, 2010); Ralph Proctor, *Voices from the Firing Line: A Personal Account of the Pittsburgh Civil Rights Movement* (Pittsburgh, PA: Introspec Press, 2013).

11. "Local Citizen Group Organizes to Protest Oakland Renewal," *Pitt News*, October 7, 1963; Nancy Fuchs, "Oaklanders Against Oak-Corp Planners," *Pitt News*, October 9, 1963; "HEP Aims to Lower School Drop-Out Rate," *Pitt News*, January 22, 1964; Editorial, "Go South!" May 20, 1964; Jacki Katz and Marsha Rehns, "Area Students Bus South," *Pitt News*, March 17, 1965.

12. The OU chapter of Student Peace Union (SPU) was part of a larger national organization created in 1959 by Ken Calkins and held a broader anti-militarism focus than later Vietnam-centered antiwar organizations. The chapter at OU had been in existence for at least one year by the time members engaged in a limited discussion of militarism in American society, especially in higher education, via the editorial page of the *Post* in January 1964. However, SPU at OU was not limited to issues of militarism, it (and its members) also engaged in civil rights activism. See SPU, Untitled Flyer, undated [presumably on or prior to November 4, 1963], Civil Rights Folder, CSA, OU; Student Peace Union, Letter to the Editor, *Post*, January 15, 1964; George Clark, Letter to the Editor, *Post*, January 17, 1964; Bonnie Guy, Letter to the Editor, *Post*, January 21, 1964; Maurice Isserman, *If I Had a Hammer . . . : The Death of the Old Left and the Birth of the New Left* (New York: Basic Books, 1987), 194–203.

13. See "Ohio Students in Civil Rights Drive," *Post*, June 30, 1964; "Ohio Student Attacked," *Post*, July 14, 1964; Bonnie Guy, "Students Accept Bitter Life in Mississippi Summer Project," *Post*, July 14, 1964; Bonnie Guy, "Ohio Student Writes on 'Freedom' as Practiced in Rural Mississippi," *Post*, July 28, 1964; Bonnie Guy, "Negro Homes in South Depict Extreme Poverty," *Post*, August 4, 1964; "Ohio Graduate to Work with SNCC Freedom School Project," *Post*, August 4, 1964; "ACRAC Gives," *Post*, August 4, 1964; Bonnie Guy, "Mississippi Negro Youths Challenge Nonviolent Means," *Post*, August 11, 1964.

In September, Vicki Epstein filed a report with the *Pitt News* about four Pitt students' participation in Freedom Summer. However, no additional references or connections to Freedom Summer could be found. See Vicki Epstein, "Local Civil Rights Volunteers Give 'Report on Mississippi,'" *Pitt News*, September 16, 1964.

14. "Civil Rights Act Suffers Setback," *Daily Athenaeum*, September 18, 1964; "CORE Director Talks Wednesday," *Pitt News*, September 21, 1964; Fred Frank, "Farmer Calls All to Rights Fight," *Pitt News*, September 25, 1964; Morris Baines, "The Civil Rights Choice: Constitution or Equality," *Post*, October 9, 1964.

15. Ruth Levikoff, "Reverend Joins in March; NAACP to Sponsor Drive," *Pitt News*, March 12, 1965; Dick Belsky, "Leaders Seek Funds, Marchers to Selma," *Post*, March 15, 1965; "Rights March," *Post*, March 15, 1965; "Federal Officials May Register Voters," *Post*, March 15, 1965; "CAC Approves Project to Solicit NAACP Funds," *Post*, March 16, 1965; Editorial, "Solution—In the Heart," *Daily Athenaeum*, March 17, 1965; L.O. Bloom, Letter to the Editor, *Daily Athenaeum*, March 17, 1965; Jacki Katz and Marsha Rehns, "Area Students Bus South," *Pitt News*, March 17, 1965; Marsha Rehns and Jacki Katz, "800 Gather in Oakland March to Honor Memory of Rev. Reeb," *Pitt News*, March 17, 1965; Allan Schlosser, "Protests in Alabama," *Pitt News*, March 17, 1965; Arch Woodruff, III, Letter to the Editor, *Pitt News*, March 17, 1965; Dick Belsky, "Two Coeds to Join Protest in Alabama," *Post*, March 18, 1965; Bill Cabin, "Students Were Non–Violent; Stern Claims Police Inhuman," *Pitt News*, March 19, 1965; "Demonstrations Proves Terrifying Experience; Citizens Wanted Blood," *Pitt News*, March 19, 1965; Marsha Rehns, "Rankin Calls Trip Good Experience," *Pitt News*, March 19, 1965; Marcia Bernstein, "Horror Seems Unbelievable as Students Recount Events," *Pitt News*, March 19, 1965; "Rabbi Rubenstein Praises Action of Students While in Alabama," *Pitt News*, March 19, 1965; Nancy Delaney, "Montgomery Briefing Awakens Marchers," *Pitt News*, March 19, 1965; Dick Belsky, "More Students Will March from Selma to Montgomery," *Post*, March 19, 1965; Jacki Katz, "Tech Student Recounts Trouble for First Bus Starting in Birmingham," *Pitt News*, March 22, 1965; "University Marchers Arrested," *Pitt News*, March 22, 1965; Dick Belsky, "Seven Leave Campus for Alabama March," *Post*, March 22, 1965; Jill Foreman, "Tension, Hostility Prevail," *Post*, March 22, 1965; Dick Belsky, "Bystanders Jeer 'March of Love,'" *Post*, March 23, 1965; Mary Twohig, Letter to the Editor, *Post*, March 23, 1965; Philip Walsh, "Chaplains Praise Demonstrators," *Pitt News*, March 24, 1965; Mary Forester, "130 Students March in Alabama Protest," *Tartan*, March 24, 1965; "Other Campuses," *Daily Athenaeum*, April 1, 1965.

16. Patti Silverman, "Students Voice 'Bama Views," *Pitt News*, March 19, 1965; "Student Body Alters Sentiments About Trip," *Pitt News*, March 19, 1965; "What They Did in Montgomery, Alabama," *Pitt News*, March 22, 1965; Vicki Epstein, "Apathetic Student Disappears As Civil Rights Movement Grows," *Pitt News*, March 24, 1965.

In early April, Dr. Richard Rubenstein from Pitt spoke to the Monongalia County chapter of the NAACP and WVU students about the experience he and approximately 135 Pittsburgh area students had during their Alabama adventures. He described the violence they faced connecting their experiences with those of WVU students who participated but had not confronted police violence. See "Local NAACP Hears Rights March Story," *Daily Athenaeum*, April 7, 1965.

17. Susan Eisenfelder, Letter to the Editor, *Pitt News*, April 5, 1965; "Appalachia Will Get Summer Student Aid," *Daily Athenaeum*, April 23, 1965; "Student Group Plans Region Poverty War," *Post*, April 27, 1965; John Seidman, Letter to the Editor, *Pitt News*, May 5, 1965; Warren Brennan, "More Than Protest," *Pitt News*, May 12, 1965; "Cooperative Action Now Group Promises to Remain on Campus," *Post*, May 21, 1965; Peter Kemeny, "Project Studies March," *Pitt News*, June 21, 1965; "Ohio University Grads Will Participate in New Jersey Civil Rights Project," *Post*, June 24, 1965; Peter Kemeny, "Marchers Continue Rights Work," *Pitt News*, June 28, 1965; Melanie Smith, "Grad Says 'Rights' Work Gives Hope," *Post*, August 12, 1965.

18. "Christmas Vacation Set for Civil Rights Project," *Post*, November 17, 1965; Editorial, "Time to Act," *Post*, November 18, 1965; "Cabinet Endorses Civil Rights Project," *Post*, November 19, 1965; ACRAC, *Help Mississippi Now*, undated [presumably mid–to–late November to mid–December 1965], Civil Rights Folder, CSA, OU; John Bates, "Ohio Students Help in South," *Post*, March 2, 1966; Robert Schulman, "It's Hard to Call Winstonville a 'Town,'" *Post*, March 2, 1966; David Steeds, "Will the Races Learn to Trust?" *Post*, March 2, 1966.

19. "KA's Forbidden To Fly Confederate Flag; 'U' Invokes Ultimatum, Breaks Tradition," *Daily Athenaeum*, November 23, 1965; "Dean Judges KA Issue," *Daily Athenaeum*, December 2, 1965; Brent Diefenbach, Letter to the Editor, *Daily Athenaeum*, December 2, 1965; Editorial, "Setting Dangerous Precedent?" *Daily Athenaeum*, December 3, 1965; Linda Leckie, "100–Year History of KA's Reviewed," *Daily Athenaeum*, December 3, 1965; Charles M. Robb, Letter to the Editor, *Daily Athenaeum*, December 7, 1965; Charles D. Trembly, Letter to the Editor, *Daily Athenaeum*, December 7, 1965; Danny G. Tilson, Letter to the Editor, *Daily Athenaeum*, December 10, 1965; Edward Balog, Letter to the Editor, *Daily Athenaeum*, December 10, 1965; Editorial, "Banning Flag Termed 'Silly,'" *Daily Athenaeum*, December 16, 1965; Ira Beth Rogers, Letter to the Editor, *Daily Athenaeum*, December 17, 1965.

20. David W. Blight, *Race and Reunion: The Civil War in American Memory* (Cambridge, MA: Harvard University Press, 2001); Anne E. Marshall, *Creating a Confederate Kentucky: The Lost Cause and Civil War Memory in a Border State* (Chapel Hill, NC: University of North Carolina Press, 2013).

21. Edward Balog, Letter to the Editor, *Daily Athenaeum*, December 10, 1965.

22. Julian Martin, Rick Anderson, Harry Shaw, Linda Helmstetter, and Jane Sullivan, Letter to the Editor, *Daily Athenaeum*, February 16, 1967; Martin Coy, "SDS Pursues 'Individual Decisions,'" *Daily Athenaeum*, February 21, 1967; Sue Serenella, "SDS Denounced Vietnam Conflict," *Daily Athenaeum*, February 28, 1967; Biographical Sketch, undated, Harry F. Shaw Jr. Papers (AIS.1974.03) Harry F. Shaw Jr. Personal Files series [hereafter referred to as: Shaw Papers], Box 1, Folder 1, ASC.

23. "Program May Cause SDS Demonstration," *Daily Athenaeum*, March 10, 1967; Martin Coy, "SDS Pickets Show for the 'Other Side,'" *Daily Athenaeum*, March 14, 1967; "SDS Petition to Place Barbers 'Under Fire,'" *Daily Athenaeum*, March 15, 1967; "SDS Petitions Local Barbers," *Daily Athenaeum*, March 21, 1967; Editorial, "Segregation Petitioned," *Daily Athenaeum*, March 21, 1967.

A plethora of letters to the editor appeared in *Daily Athenaeum* between March 15 and April 19 discussing various aspects of SDS, many critical and almost as many defending the actions of the group.

24. Editorial, "Segregation Petitioned," *Daily Athenaeum*, March 21, 1967; Glen Cain and Ron Chisler, Letter to the Editor, *Daily Athenaeum*, April 4, 1967; Scott King, Letter to the Editor, *Daily Athenaeum*, April 7, 1967; Teresa Rash, "Cabinet Solicits to Petition Integration," *Daily Athenaeum*, April 13, 1967.

25. Thomas Kiffmeyer, *Reformers to Radicals: The Appalachian Volunteers and the War on Poverty* (Lexington, KY: University Press of Kentucky, 2008).

26. "Federal Program Will Aid Poverty–Stricken Children," *Daily Athenaeum*, February 5, 1964; Susie Thurmond, "'U' May Aid Kanawha County Youth, Poverty Program," *Daily Athenaeum*, February 20, 1964; Robert F. Kennedy, "Address by Attorney General Robert F.

Kennedy to a Joint Meeting of the Kanawha County Parent–Teachers Council and Members of Action for Appalachian Youth, Inc.," (speech, Charleston, West Virginia, April 29, 1965), https://www.justice.gov.

27. Bob Graham, "Problems of Appalachia Studied by 'U' Students," *Daily Athenaeum*, October 16, 1964.

28. "HEP Aims To Lower School Drop-Out Rate," *Pitt News*, January 22, 1964; "HEP Recruiting For Projects," *Pitt News*, April 27, 1964; "HEP To Recruit Volunteer Tutors Starting Monday," *Pitt News*, September 18, 1964; "Tuesday Meeting Begins Season for HEP Tutors," *Pitt News*, September 25, 1964; "Home Duty Aim of New Peace Corps," *Daily Athenaeum*, November 12, 1964; "Ohio Meeting to give Briefing on Economic Opportunity Act," *Post*, November 13, 1964; Tom Price, "President Alden Commends Work on Poverty 'War,'" *Post*, November 19, 1964; Editorial, "VISTA: Domestic Peace Corps," *Daily Athenaeum*, November 20, 1964.

29. "VISTA Hosts Two University Students," *Pitt News*, March 31, 1965; Michael Marcuse, "The Face of Poverty," *Pitt News*, March 31, 1965.

30. Marsha Rehns, "VISTA Aids U.S. Poor," *Pitt News*, April 2, 1965.

31. "PiKA's Aid VISTA In Serving Pittsburgh Area," *Pitt News*, April 15, 1965.

32. "PiKA's Aid VISTA In Serving Pittsburgh Area," *Pitt News*, April 5, 1965; "Betty Furness Speaks for VISTA," *Pitt News*, April 28, 1965; Marsha Rehns, "VISTA Needs Much Ingenuity Betty Furness Tells Audience," *Pitt News*, May 3, 1965; "University Students Aid in Renewal," *Pitt News*, May 12, 1965; Warren Brennan, "More than Protest," *Pitt News*, May 12, 1965; Thomas Kiffmeyer, "Looking Back to the City in the Hills: The Council of the Southern Mountains and a Longer View of the War on Poverty in the Appalachian South, 1913–1970," in *The War on Poverty: A New Grassroots History, 1964–1980*, ed. Annelise Orleck and Lisa Gayle Hazirjian (Athens, GA: University of Georgia Press, 2011), 359–86.

33. Judith Weimer, "'Poverty is Loneliness' Caudill Tells Audience," *Post*, April 8, 1966; Dennis Hefferman, "Spirit Paves Way to Future," *Post*, April 13, 1966; Lucy Puccio, "Students Aid Youngtown Action Effort," *Post*, April 13, 1966; Tom Price, "People of All Kinds Seen at Meeting," *Post*, April 13, 1966; Tome Shipka, "Ohio Students Aid Dropouts," *Post*, April 13, 1966; Joe Eszterhas, "Winning THE War," *Post*, April 13, 1966.

34. Deena Mirrow, "Portsmouth: A Lesson in Caring," *Post*, November 7, 1966; Ron Clement, Sharon Siegel, Bob Vanderwyst, David Brightbill, Tom Knight, John Porter, Judi Hudspeth, and Susan Leibensperger, Letter to the Editor, *Post*, November 10, 1966; Bob Vanderwyst, "Portsmouth Revisited by Students," *Post*, December 2, 1966.

35. "HEP Aims To Lower Drop-Out Rate," *Pitt News*, January 22 ,1964; Joni Hartman, "University Student Volunteers Tutor Underprivileged Children," *Post*, October 25, 1965; Editorial, "The Meaning of SOOP," *Post*, December 8, 1965; Clarence Page, "Tutoring Program Aids Area Youths," *Post*, September 26, 1966; Suzanne Jett, "Students Experience Life in Poverty-Stricken Areas," *Daily Athenaeum*, January 17, 1967; Martin Coy, "Osage Homes Pilot Project," *Daily Athenaeum*, January 17, 1967; "Three Organizations Join in Recruit Drive," *Daily Athenaeum*, January 24, 1967; "Volunteers Needed for SOOP," *Post*, February 8, 1967; "'U' Students Discuss Youngstown Poverty," *Daily Athenaeum*, February 21, 1967; Martin Coy, "SAAP Recruitment Termed Successful," *Daily Athenaeum*, March 7, 1967; "SAAP Ends 1967 Activities with Free Sunday Supper," *Daily Athenaeum*, April 7, 1967; "SAAP May In-

crease Area Tutoring Work," *Daily Athenaeum*, April 11, 1967; Mary J. Kirklan to Harry Shaw, April 25, 1967, Shaw Papers, Harry F. Shaw Jr. Personal Files series, Box 1, Folder 2, ASC.

Chapter 4

1. Kirkpatrick Sale, *SDS: The Rise and Development of the Students for a Democratic Society* (New York: Random House, 1973), 93, 97–103; Fred Halstead, *Out Now! A Participant's Account of the American Movement Against the Vietnam War* (New York: Monad Press, 1978), 24–44; Stewart Burns, *Social Movements of the 1960s: Searching for Democracy* (Boston, MA: Twayne Publishers, 1990), 67–69; Kenneth J. Heineman, "'Look Out Kid, You're Gonna Get Hit!': Kent State and the Vietnam Antiwar Movement," in *Give Peace Chance: Exploring the Vietnam Antiwar Movement*, ed. Melvin Small and William D. Hoover (Syracuse, NY: Syracuse University Press, 1992), 201–222; Todd Gitlin, *The Sixties: Years of Hope, Days of Rage*, rev. ed. (New York: Bantam Books, 1993), 177–85; Rhodri Jeffreys–Jones, *Peace Now! American Society and the Ending of the Vietnam War* (New Haven, CT: Yale University Press, 1999), 61–92; Mary Ann Wynkoop, *Dissent in the Heartland: The Sixties at Indiana University* (Bloomington, IN: Indiana University Press, 2002), 22–48.

2. Marilyn B. Young, *The Vietnam Wars, 1945–1990* (New York: HarperCollins, 1991), 117–20; Edwin E. Moise, *Tonkin Gulf and the Escalation of the Vietnam War* (Chapel Hill, NC: University of North Carolina Press, 1996); George C. Herring, *America's Longest War: The United States and Vietnam, 1950–1975*, 4th ed. (Boston: McGraw Hill, 2002), 142–48.

3. The near complete silence on the Gulf of Tonkin Incident and Resolution seems odd, especially given the depth of scholarly focus on the incident and resolution. However, it seems, due to the lack of coverage in the campus newspapers, students did not see these as issues of great concern.

4. Ruth Woodside, "Marchers Protest U.S. in Viet Nam," *Post*, February 15, 1965; James Lynch, Letter to the Editor, *Post*, February 16, 1965; J.E. Harrison, Letter to the Editor, *Post*, February 16, 1965.

5. Irv Garfinkle, "Vietnam 'Democracy,'" *Pitt News*, March 1, 1965; Irv Garfinkle, "Why We Are Fighting," *Pitt News*, March 3, 1965; Irv Garfinkle, "Withdrawal From Vietnamese War Advocated," *Pitt News*, March 5, 1965.

6. Alex D'Ippolito, "The Real Issue," *Pitt News*, March 19, 1965.

7. Tim Bigelow, "Viet Nam: What Will Come Next?" *Daily Athenaeum*, February 12, 1965; Harry Baisden, "Biggest Problem of All: Defining Viet Nam Problem," *Daily Athenaeum*, February 26, 1965.

8. Richard Pesin, "Viet Nam War Not to be Won," *Post*, March 16, 1965; Joe McKeefer, Letter to the Editor, *Post*, March 23, 1965.

9. Halstead, *Out Now!*, 24–44; Nancy Zaroulis and Gerald Sullivan, *Who Spoke Up? American Protest Against the War in Vietnam, 1963–1975* (New York: Holt, Rinehart and Winston, 1984), 38–42; Mark Hamilton Lytle, *America's Uncivil Wars: The Sixties Era from Elvis to the Fall of Richard Nixon* (New York: Oxford University Press, 2006), 180–82; Carl Oglesby, *Ravens in the Storm: A Personal History of the 1960s Antiwar Movement* (New York: Scribner, 2008), 44–45.

10. "Student War March Protests Viet Nam," *Post*, April 22, 1965. Neither the archival

records, nor the student newspapers from Pitt or WVU provided any indication of student participation in the Washington protest in April 1965.

11. Devra Lee Davis, "Teachers and Students to Attend Nat'l. Viet Protest Discussion," *Pitt News*, May 5, 1965; Devra Lee Davis, "Faculty Set Teach-In for Saturday," *Pitt News*, May 10, 1965; Editorial, "The Teach-In—A Trap for the University," *Pitt News*, May 10, 1965; Devra Lee Davis, "Teach-In Plan Changes Announced," *Pitt News*, May 12, 1965; Irv Garfinkle, "A Boon for Democracy," *Pitt News*, May 12, 1965; "Vietnam 'Teach In' Slated, Broadcast to University," *Tartan*, May 12, 1965; Merrily Kodis, "Non-Surprise," *Pitt News*, May 17, 1965; Fred Frank, "Teach-In Debates Crisis," *Pitt News*, May 19, 1965; Marsha Rehns, "University Debate Seen 'Scholarly'," *Pitt News*, May 19, 1965; Karen Tokar, "Profs Pleased at Teach-In," *Pitt News*, May 19, 1965; Editorial, "Vive la Difference," *Pitt News*, May 19, 1965; Halstead, *Out Now!*, 50–54; Gitlin, *The Sixties*, 187–88.

12. "Vietnam Teach-In Finds No Solution," *Pitt News*, October 15, 1965; "Peace Marchers to Protest U.S. Military Intervention In Vietnam," *Pitt News*, October 15, 1965. Despite apparently being a fairly well organized student group, Students for Peace left no archival trace. Constructing their actions thus relies heavily on the only available textual source for their thoughts and motivations, the campus newspapers.

13. David Mitchell, Letter to the Editor, *Pitt News*, October 18, 1965. David Mitchell refused induction in May 1964; however, his trial did not occur until the fall of 1965. At roughly the same time, a man with a very similar name, David J. Miller, burned his draft card as part of a rally in New York City on October 15, 1965, in conjunction with the First International Days of Protest. His action has often been cited as the trigger for other draft card burnings and as the starting point for growing resistance to the draft. However, draft resistance, especially in the form of draft card burning, had existed before Miller's brazen act. The first publicized case of draft card burning came in May 1964 when 12 men in New York City destroyed their draft cards as part of a counterdemonstration to on-going Armed Forces Day festivities. This action came on the heels of "We Won't Go" pledges beginning to circulate college campuses and printed in local newspapers. See Zaroulis and Sullivan, *Who Spoke Up?*, 51–58, 225; Stephen M. Kohn, *Jailed for Peace: The History of American Draft Law Violators, 1658–1985* (Westport, CT: Greenwood Press, 1986), 76–79; George Q. Flynn, *The Draft, 1940–1973* (Lawrence, KS: University Press of Kansas, 1993), 74–81; Melvin Small, *Antiwarriors: The Vietnam War and the Battle for America's Hearts and Minds* (New York: SR Books, 2002), 13, 32–33; Michael S. Foley, *Confronting the War Machine: Draft Resistance During the Vietnam War* (Chapel Hill, NC: University of North Carolina Press, 2003), 29.

One of the first instances of draft resistance in the city of Pittsburgh came when local youth, Thomas Rodd, announced his intentions to refuse to register for the Selective Service and staged a one-man sit-in at the federal building downtown hoping to be arrested so he could bring a legal case against conscription in late March 1964. See "Rodd Moves Peace Sit-In," *Pittsburgh Post-Gazette*, March 27, 1964. Rodd's actions will be explored in greater detail in Chapter Six.

14. Harvey F. Dahut and William G. McGeorge, Letter to the Editor, *Pitt News*, October 22, 1965.

15. Richard D. Peters, Letter to the Editor, *Pitt News*, October 22, 1965; Stuart A. Arn-

heim, Letter to the Editor, *Pitt News*, October 25, 1965; Cris Hogg, Carl Garofalo, and Richard Milo, Letter to the Editor, *Pitt News*, October 25, 1965.

16. Alex Frank, Letter to the Editor, *Pitt News*, November 8, 1965.

17. "50 YAF Counter Pickets; Support Pres. Johnson," *Duquesne Duke*, October 27, 1965; "Pro-Vietnam Policy Group Gains Petition Support For Mass Rally," *Pitt News*, October 27, 1965; "YAF Petition Backs LBJ on Viet-Nam," *Duquesne Duke*, November 10, 1965; Linda Goldstein, "Students Write Letter to President To Show Support for American Servicemen In Vietnam," *Pitt News*, November 12, 1965.

Duquesne University had a recognized YAF chapter by the fall of 1965, which formed sometime in academic year 1964-1965; an exact date could not be found in records of the *Duquesne Duke*, nor other sources. However, a Conservative Society did exist prior to the formation of YAF, suggesting an existing conservative base on the campus. No official chapters of YAF appear to have existed at either Pitt or Carnegie Tech at this time, though both had active Young Republicans and other conservative-leaning student groups. Similarly, OU and WVU lacked official YAF chapters, but ad hoc, unofficial conservative student groups popped up around the 1964 presidential election on various northern Appalachian campuses. Jim Cross, OU Young Republican president, became the state chairman for YAF in 1965 despite the lack of a YAF chapter at OU. Further, it appears that as liberal-to-New Left activism grew locally and nationally between 1965 and 1967, conservative student organizations began to develop. Pitt, OU, and WVU all had functioning YAF chapters (or other officially recognized conservative groups) by 1968. See Pat Phillips and Larry Bloom, "Conservative Shoots for GOP," *Post*, March 12, 1965; Mike Shane, "Radical Right Now Respectable," *Daily Athenaeum*, January 12, 1966; John Avant, "Political Group Counteracts 'Berkeley Image'," *Post*, March 23, 1966; Lou Gillick, "Publication Due Soon From OUSI," *Post*, December 2, 1966; Sherri O'Dell, "YAF's Beliefs Include Victory Over Coexistence," *Daily Athenaeum*, April 26, 1967; Ned Crews, "Stump-Speaker Stresses Need for Conservatives," *Daily Athenaeum*, April 27, 1967.

18. Editorial, "Viet Rally—A Hope?" *Pitt News*, October 29, 1965; Alan Disler, "Rally Supporting GI's in Vietnam Draws Peaceful Crowd of 1500," *Pitt News*, October 29, 1965; Alex D'Ippolito, "The Right Method," *Pitt News*, November 1, 1965; Berni McLeod, "Polls Show Pitt Students Favor Rally," *Pitt News*, November 1, 1965; E.C. Baird, Letter to the Editor, *Pitt News*, November 5, 1965.

19. Randi Dokken, Judy Glotzer, and Beth Anne Waithe, Letter to the Editor, *Pitt News*, November 5, 1965.

20. Diane Ruppen, ed., *The Owl [1966]/The Annual of the University of Pittsburgh* (Pittsburgh, PA: University of Pittsburgh Press, 1966), 30 [online], http://digital.library.pitt.edu.

21. Dick Belsky, "Blood and Vietnam," *Post*, October 28, 1965; Dick Belsky, "Whalen Calls meeting to Plan 'Bleed-In' Here," *Post*, November 2, 1965; "Student Cabinet Plans to Lead Campus 'Bleed-In' for Vietnam," *Post*, November 4, 1965; Richard Pesin, "Cabinet Backs Blood Drive for GIs Fighting in Vietnam," *Post*, November 5, 1965.

22. Dick Putney, Letter to the Editor, *Post*, November 1, 1965; Joe Eszterhas, "Cabinet—Dissent," *Post*, November 5, 1965; Jerry Paschke, Letter to the Editor, *Post*, November 8, 1965; Janet E. Harrison, Letter to the Editor, *Post*, November 8, 1965; Richard Pesin, "Dabbling

in Politics," *Post*, November 9, 1965; Edward Hecht, Letter to the Editor, *Post*, November 12, 1965; Clarence Page, "230 Students Give Blood for Viet GIs," *Post*, December 1, 1965.

This unnamed group demonstrates the ephemeral nature of student activism, popping up here to organize around a specific event and then disappearing. This group left no archival sources for future historians, who are left with only passing references to the group in campus papers.

23. Linda Ball, "Ballot to Give Students Chance to Express Views on Vietnam," *Post*, December 9, 1965; "Vietnam Poll Results Favor U.S. Policies," *Post*, February 8, 1966.

24. Editorial, "One–Sided Compassion & Vietnam," *Post*, November 2, 1965.

25. Daniel Giovannitti, "Gen. Lewis Hershey Challenges Demonstrators and Drop Outs," *Duquesne Duke*, December 9, 1965; "Deferments May Hinge on Grades," *Post*, January 12, 1966.

26. "Draft to Change," *Pitt News*, February 4, 1966; "Tests, Standings, Criteria Listed," *Daily Athenaeum*, February 8, 1966; Editorial, "Protest: Be Drafted," *Post*, February 8, 1966; Lt. Col. John B. Hetzel, "Students and Draft," *Pitt News*, February 9, 1966; Tom Price, "Questions About Deferments Face College Men," *Post*, February 16, 1966; "Draft Sanctuary May No Longer Harbor Student," *Duquesne Duke*, February 16, 1966; Tom Price, "The Draft Helps 'Maintain Effective National Economy'," *Post*, February 17, 1966; Anonymous, Letter to the Editor, *Daily Athenaeum*, February 25, 1966; "First 'Deferment' Test to be Given May 14," *Post*, February 28, 1966.

27. "Draft Card Fireproofing Conducted," *Pitt News*, May 4, 1966.

28. Hobart Harris, "Professors Debate Importance and Goals of Dissent; Views Differ Concerning the Vietnamese Conflict," *Pitt News*, February 7, 1966; "POST to Sponsor Vietnam Forum," *Post*, February 21, 1966; Editorial, "Perspective," *Post*, February 21, 1966; Tom Price, "War Attacked at 'Perspective;' Cady, Whealey Lead Discussions," *Post*, March 1, 1966; "Debate Discusses Vietnam Issues," *Pitt News*, March 7, 1966.

29. "Gen. Taylor Will Talk on Crisis in Vietnam," *Post*, February 21, 1966; Joe Eszterhas, "Tailoring Taylor," *Post*, February 21, 1966; "Student Groups to Protest While Taylor Talks," *Post*, February 23, 1966; Joe Eszterhas, "Thursday Committee: The Challenge," *Post*, February 23, 1966; Joseph Grant Ledgerwood, Letter to the Editor, *Post*, February 24, 1966; Richard Pesin, "Taylor Wants Action Not Words," *Post*, February 25, 1966; Editorial, "Closed Debate, Says Who?" *Post*, February 25, 1966.

30. "Students Begin Chapter of 'Democratic Society'," *Post*, March 3, 1966; Tom Price, "SDS May Not be Formed Here," *Post*, March 7, 1966.

31. Bob Verbasky, "Humphrey Main Speaker During 'Festival of Ideas'," *Daily Athenaeum*, September 14, 1966; Ken Baker, "Signature, Donations Called for in Protest," *Daily Athenaeum*, September 27, 1966; Charles Gardner, "Campus Protest Face Opposition," *Daily Athenaeum*, September 29, 1966; Merideth Robb, "HHH Discusses Viet Nam, Challenges of Changing Age," *Daily Athenaeum*, October 11, 1966; Editorial, "Humphrey Reiterated Our Goals," *Daily Athenaeum*, October 11, 1966; "HHH's Visit Provokes Advertisement," *Daily Athenaeum*, October 13, 1966.

32. Robert E. Rankin, Letter to the Editor, *Daily Athenaeum*, September 30, 1966; Buzz Wagner, Letter to the Editor, *Daily Athenaeum*, October 4, 1966; Craig T. Rainey, Letter to the Editor, *Daily Athenaeum*, October 4, 1966.

33. Baker, "Signature, Donations Called for in Protest," *Daily Athenaeum*, September 27, 1966; "HHH's Visit Provokes Advertisement," *Daily Athenaeum*, October 13, 1966.

34. Jim Gilkerson, "Freedom of Speech Must Be Exercised," *Daily Athenaeum*, November 15, 1966.

35. "SFP Sponsors [*sic*] Rally, Distribute Literature In National Program," *Pitt News*, November 2, 1966; "Politicians, Profs Compare Ideas At Viet Meeting," *Tartan*, November 2, 1966; "Thornburgh, Moorhead In Pitt Debate," *Pittsburgh Post-Gazette*, November 2, 1966; Paul Stoller, "Thornburgh and Moorhead Discuss Campaign Issues," *Pitt News*, November 4, 1966; Hobart Harris, "US Vietnam Policies Questioned," *Pitt News*, November 7, 1966; "Local Speak-Out Protests Aspects of Vietnam War," *Tartan*, November 9, 1966; Richard A. Rieker, "'War Nobody Wants' Prompts 'Speak Out'," *Pittsburgh Point*, November 10, 1966.

36. "Students Plan Two-Day Vietnam Vigil," *Post*, November 30, 1966; Editorial, "Answers, Please," *Post*, December 1, 1966; Editorial, "Responsible Protest," *Post*, December 1, 1966; Editorial, "Let's Withdraw," *Post*, December 5, 1966.

37. "Coed Proposes Noon Peace Demonstration," *Post*, January 11, 1967; "Quaker Group Begins Vigil; Hopes for Peace in Vietnam," *Pitt News*, January 27, 1967; Elaine Anne Herald, Letter to the Editor, *Post*, February 7, 1967; Ivan Abrams, "Pittsburgh Collegians Peacefully Protest US Policy in Vietnam with Silent Peace Vigils Here," *Pitt News*, March 10, 1967.

38. Editorial, "The Other Dissenters," *Post*, January 6, 1967.

39. Ronald Meltzer, Letter to the Editor, *Post*, January 10, 1967.

40. The importance of the individual, especially in the political process can be seen in both New Left and New Right rhetoric. For examples of scholarship on the similarities and differences on New Left and New Right visions of individuality in terms of freedom, liberty, and equality, see Paul Lyons, *New Left, New Right, and the Legacy of the Sixties* (Philadelphia, PA: Temple University Press, 1996), 53–72; John A. Andrew III, *The Other Side of the Sixties: Young Americans for Freedom and the Rise of Conservative Politics* (New Brunswick, NJ: Rutgers University Press, 1997), 22–24, 56–60; Rebecca K. Klatch, *A Generation Divided: The New Left, the New Right, and the 1960s* (Berkeley, CA: University of California Press, 1999), 30–36; Lytle, *America's Uncivil Wars*, 80–95; Gerard J. DeGroot, *The Sixties Unplugged: A Kaleidoscopic History of a Disorderly Decade* (Cambridge, MA: Harvard University Press, 2008), 243–47; Maurice Isserman and Michael Kazin, *America Divided: The Civil War of the 1960s*, 3rd ed. (New York: Oxford University Press, 2008), 174–78, 223–24.

41. Joel Forrester, "Napalm and the Man from Dow," *Post*, February 10, 1967; Tom Price, "Napalm Producers Draw Protests," *Post*, February 14, 1967; Editorial, "Vital Role?" *Post*, February 14, 1967.

42. Garry Walsh, Letter to the Editor, *Post*, February 20, 1967; John Wood, Letter to the Editor, *Post*, February 20, 1967; Ellen Jones, Letter to the Editor, *Post*, February 28, 1967.

43. "Towers Variety Show to Benefit Servicemen," *Daily Athenaeum*, March 9, 1967; "Program May Cause SDS Demonstration," *Daily Athenaeum*, March 10, 1967; Pat Gilbert, "Variety Show Gets Praised," *Daily Athenaeum*, March 10, 1967.

44. "Program May Cause SDS Demonstration," *Daily Athenaeum*, March 10, 1967; "Benefit Program Nets Over $400," *Daily Athenaeum*, March 14, 1967; Martin Coy, "SDS Pickets Show for the 'Other Side'," *Daily Athenaeum*, March 14, 1967.

45. Editorial, "Getting Pushy," *Daily Athenaeum*, March 14, 1967; Rev. Joe Rainey, Rev.

Richard Margold, and Rev. Edward Hofler, Letter to the Editor, *Daily Athenaeum*, March 16, 1967; David Harter, Letter to the Editor, *Daily Athenaeum*, March 16, 1967; James S. Rick, Letter to the Editor, *Daily Athenaeum*, March 16, 1967; Editorial, "An American Right," *Daily Athenaeum*, March 17, 1967; Fred Nillinger, Letter to the Editor, *Daily Athenaeum*, March 17, 1967.

46. W. L. Abraham, Letter to the Editor, *Daily Athenaeum*, March 17, 1967; "Student Cabinet Offers SDS Representative," *Daily Athenaeum*, March 21, 1967; Editorial, "Autonomy or Aggression," *Daily Athenaeum*, March 22, 1967; Thomas M. McIntire, Letter to the Editor, *Daily Athenaeum*, March 22, 1967; James A.L. Rice, Letter to the Editor, *Daily Athenaeum*, March 22, 1967; Editorial, "'Representation' Misunderstood," *Daily Athenaeum*, March 31, 1967; R. B. Benefield, Letter to the Editor, *Daily Athenaeum*, March 31, 1967; Richard Eckerhd, Letter to the Editor, *Daily Athenaeum*, April 4, 1967; Cathy Howard, Letter to the Editor, *Daily Athenaeum*, April 4, 1967; Marsha A. Montgomery, Letter to the Editor, *Daily Athenaeum*, April 5, 1967; Thomas L. Hopkins, Letter to the Editor, *Daily Athenaeum*, April 5, 1967; "SDS to Clarify Stand Concerning Viet War," *Daily Athenaeum*, April 7, 1967; Scott King, Letter to the Editor, *Daily Athenaeum*, April 7, 1967.

47. "YAF Forms Against SDS," *Daily Athenaeum*, March 22, 1967; Glen Cain and Ron Chrisler, Letter to the Editor, *Daily Athenaeum*, April 4, 1967.

48. Harry Shaw Jr., Letter to the Editor, *Daily Athenaeum*, March 22, 1967; Joan O'Connor, "Stump Speaker States SDS Stand on War," *Daily Athenaeum*, April 13, 1967; Sutton Breiding, Letter to the Editor, *Daily Athenaeum*, April 13, 1967; Courtyard Talks End in Anger," *Daily Athenaeum*, April 18, 1967; T. W. Cavanaugh, III, Letter to the Editor, *Daily Athenaeum*, April 18, 1967; Jerald Cox, Letter to the Editor, *Daily Athenaeum*, April 18, 1967; William Branham, Letter to the Editor, *Daily Athenaeum*, April 19, 1967.

49. Committee on Un-American Activities, U.S. House of Representatives, *Communist Origin and Manipulation of Vietnam Week (April 8–15, 1967)*, 90th Cong., 1st sess., March 31, 1967.

50. Ohio Valley Region Peace Conference, *Campus Handbook for Vietnam Week* (Cleveland, OH: Regional Coordinating Committee for the Spring Mobilization, 1967), 2–7; Bob Vanderwyst, "Ohio Students to Attend Massive War Protest," *Post*, April 10, 1967; Joel Forrester, "Mobilizing Against the Vietnam War," *Post*, April 12, 1967; Walt Borton and Bob Vanderwyst, "70 From Here in Peace March," *Post*, April 17, 1967; "SDS Marches in New York," *Daily Athenaeum*, April 18, 1967.

There is no specific mention of Pitt students traveling to New York City to participate in the rally; however, it does not seem outside the realm of possibility that some may have made the journey.

51. "Local Students Coordinate For National Viet Protest," *Tartan*, February 22, 1967; "'Angry Arts' Protest War; Features Dr. Montgomery," *Pitt News*, April 5, 1967; "Students for Peace Show 'Angry Arts'," *Tartan*, April 5, 1967; Advertisement, *Pittsburgh Press*, April 6, 1967; Poster, "Stop the Bombing," April 6, 1967, Shaw Papers, Organizations series, Box 2, Folder 81, ASC; "Crowd Jams Field House For 'Angry Arts', March," *Tartan*, April 12, 1967; "Tech Profs. Examine War's Many Effects," *Tartan*, April 12, 1967; Mike Martin, "Rally Held for Peace In Viet Nam," *Duquesne Duke*, April 14, 1967.

The number of those participating in the candlelit march was alternately reported as 400 and 800.

Part 2

1. David Caute, *The Year of the Barricades: A Journey through 1968* (New York: Harper & Row, 1988); Irwin Unger and Debi Unger, *Turning Point, 1968* (New York: Scribner, 1988); Todd Gitlin, *The Sixties: Years of Hope Days of Rage*, rev. ed. (New York: Bantam Books, 1993); Terry H. Anderson, *The Movement and the Sixties: Protest in America from Greensboro to Wounded Knee* (New York: Oxford University Press, 1995); Mark Kurlansky, *1968: The Year That Rocked the World* (New York: Random House, 2005); Maurice Isserman and Michael Kazin, *America Divided: The Civil War of the 1960s*, 3rd ed. (New York: Oxford University Press, 2008).

Chapter 5

1. Patricia Wagner, ed., *The Owl [1968]/The Annual of the University of Pittsburgh* (Pittsburgh, Pa: University of Pittsburgh Press, 1968), 8–9 [online], http://digital.library.pitt .edu. The state legislature reinforced Posvar's point when they moved to have participants in obstructionist actions denied state loans and/or scholarships. "Bill Halts Loans to Protestors," *Pitt News*, May 10, 1968.

2. Editorial, "Do Parents Care About Hours," *Post*, April 29, 1968; Melinda Swezey and Barb Lucey, Letter to the Editor, *Post*, May 3, 1968; Virginia Joyce, "Women Want Social, Sexual Freedom," *Pitt News*, July 30, 1968; John Felton, "Trustees Revamp Beer Policy, Women's Hours," *Post*, September 25, 1968; Editorial, "Two Classes to Go," *Post*, September 26, 1968; Editorial, "Coed Hours Seen as Necessary Evil," *Daily Athenaeum*, October 11, 1968; Peggy Allen, "Curfews: 'Who's Going to Take Care of Me When I Graduate'," *Pitt News*, October 14, 1968; "AWS Will Present Findings to Harlow," *Daily Athenaeum*, November 22, 1968; Editorial, "Do 2 a.m. Permissions Mean More Problems?" *Daily Athenaeum*, November 22, 1968; John Felton, "No Official Action Planned to End Sophomore Hours," *Post*, December 4, 1968.

3. Carol Towarnicky, "Students, Faculty Reveal Racial Discrimination in Housing," *Post*, November 2, 1967; Carol Towarnicky, "Officials 'Will Use Power' if Bias Practice is Clear," *Post*, November 15, 1967; Tom Hodson, "Congress Passes Fair Housing Bill, Adopts Files Plan," *Post*, April 22, 1968; Tom Hodson, "SC Passes Open Housing Bill, Condemns Vietnam Effort," *Post*, April 29, 1968; "White Group to Work for Open Housing," *Post*, April 30, 1968; Editorial, "Action Tonight," *Post*, May 1, 1968; Cathy Martindale, "Housing Chairmen Explain Referendum," *Post*, May 7, 1968; Editorial, "Vote Yes Mon." *Post*, May 10, 1968; Editorial, "Vote Yes," *Post*, May 13, 1968; William J. Day, Letter to the Editor, *Post*, May 13, 1968; Paul O. Gillette, Letter to the Editor, *Post*, May 13, 1968; "Open Housing Referendum Defeated, 2–1," *Post*, May 14, 1968; Cathy Martindale, "Open-housing Bill 'Wasn't Understood'," *Post*, May 15, 1968; Rick Rozenmann, Letter to the Editor, *Post*, May 16, 1968; Robert Jemess, Letter to the Editor, *Post*, May 16, 1968; Teresa Rash, "Citys Open Housing Law Could Be Better Written," *Daily Athenaeum*, July 3, 1968; Andrew Alexander, "SC Considers Bill on Outside-Housing," *Post*, November 11, 1968.

4. June Kronholz, "SC Presents Ultimatum to Alden," *Post*, April 1, 1968.

5. Mark Roth, "Local 1699 Threatens Strike If 'Inequalities' Not Corrected," *Post*, May 8, 1968; Mark Roth, "Union's Ultimatum Called 'Unrealistic'," *Post*, May 10, 1968; Mark Roth, "Union Strike Still Possible If Top Jobs Not Filled Soon," *Post*, May 13, 1968; Mark Roth,

"Union Strike Looms Closer as Separate Positions Held," *Post*, May 15, 1968; Mark Roth, "No Union–University Talks Set Before Monday Strike Deadline," *Post*, May 16, 1968; Mark Roth, "Opposing Sides Fail to Meet on Issues," *Post*, May 17, 1968; Mark Roth and Andrew Alexander, "Union Strike Averted," *Post*, May 19, 1968; Carol Towarnicky, "Decision Pleases Administrators," *Post*, May 19, 1968; Andrew J. Chonko, Maj Arty, Ohio ARNG, Asst. Adj., "After Action Report on Ohio University Student Disturbance," May 23, 1968, CSA, Ohio National Guard—Athens Riot 1968 Folder [hereafter referred to as: Athens Riot 1968], OU.

6. Bruce Jorgenson, "'We Want Out' Begins March," *Post*, May 20, 1968; Carol Towarnicky, "Building Damage, Injuries Result from Disturbances," *Post*, May 20, 1968; Margaret Kantz, Letter to the Editor, *Post*, May 20, 1968; Andrew Alexander and John Felton, "Students Riots Cool as Troops Stand By," *Post*, May 21, 1968; "Disturbances Incites Campus Comment," *Post*, May 21, 1968; Bruce Jorgenson, "Second Night Difference," *Post*, May 21, 1968; Janet A. Smith, Letter to the Editor, *Post*, May 21, 1968; Chonko, "After Action Report," May 23, 1968, CSA, Athens Riot 1968, OU.

7. "Demands," May 21, 1968, CSA, OU; Andrew Alexander, "3000 Students List Grievances; Non-violence Urged; Meeting is Planned," *Post*, May 22, 1968; Editorial, "Again and Again," *Post*, May 22, 1968; Andrew Alexander and John Felton, "Congress Supports Student Grievances," *Post*, May 23, 1968; Robert Vogel, Letter to the Editor, *Post*, May 23, 1968.

8. Vernon R. Alden, "Official Statement issued by Ohio University President Vernon R. Alden, May 22, 1968," CSA, Public Statements Folder, OU.

9. "Disturbance Incites Campus Comment," *Post*, May 21, 1968.

10. "Leaders Outline Policies at Weekend Conference," *Daily Athenaeum*, September 10, 1968.

11. Clark Kerr, *The Uses of the University*, 5th ed. (Cambridge, MA: Harvard University Press, 2001), 21–29.

12. Like the OU student group that opposed the bleed-in in December 1965, the Committee for Student Rights represented a transitory organization that may have been quite active for a short time and perhaps exerted influence over student actions; however, it left no archival sources, making newspaper coverage the only textual source available to observe their actions.

Committee for Student Rights, *Protect Your Rights! Vote 'No' on Student Code*, August 28, 1968, A&M 2833, W.V.U. Office of Student Life Collection [hereafter referred to as: Student Life], WVRHC; Committee for Student Rights, *Concerned About Signing for the Regent's Code of Conduct*, August 1968 [presumably on or after August 28], A&M 2833, Student Life, WVRHC.

13. J. Timothy Philipps, Letter to the Editor, *Daily Athenaeum*, September 11, 1968; R. B. Walker Jr., Letter to the Editor, *Daily Athenaeum*, September 11, 1968; "Legislature Meet to Discuss Code," *Daily Athenaeum*, September 19, 1968; "Faculty Consensus Says Code 'Student Matter'," *Daily Athenaeum*, September 19, 1968; David Zinn, Rick Becker, and John F. Nutter, Letter to the Editor, *Daily Athenaeum*, September 19, 1968; Jackie Hallinan, Letter to the Editor, *Daily Athenaeum*, September 19, 1968; Editorial, "Code Referendum Should be Moved," *Daily Athenaeum*, September 19, 1968; "Vote Yes Today for Student Progress," *University Bulletin*, September 25, 1968; "Student Power—Responsible Student Involvement," *University Bulletin*, September 25, 1968; Bob Arnold, "Students Reject Conduct Code in Close Vote," *Daily Athenaeum*, September 26, 1968.

14. Bob Berlan, "Students Attack Code," *Daily Athenaeum*, September 19, 1968.

15. Committee for Student Rights, *Protect Your Rights! Vote 'No' on Student Code*, August 28, 1968, A&M 2833, W.V.U. Office of Student Life Collection [hereafter referred to as: Student Life], WVRHC; J. Timothy Philipps, Letter to the Editor, *Daily Athenaeum*, September 11, 1968; R. B. Walker Jr., Letter to the Editor, *Daily Athenaeum*, September 11, 1968; Bob Berlan, "Students Attack Code," *Daily Athenaeum*, September 19, 1968; "Legislature Meet to Discuss Code," *Daily Athenaeum*, September 19, 1968; "Faculty Consensus Says Code 'Student Matter'," *Daily Athenaeum*, September 19, 1968; David Zinn, Rick Becker, and John F. Nutter, Letter to the Editor, *Daily Athenaeum*, September 19, 1968; Jackie Hallinan, Letter to the Editor, *Daily Athenaeum*, September 19, 1968; Editorial, "Code Referendum Should be Moved," *Daily Athenaeum*, September 19, 1968; "Vote Yes Today for Student Progress," *University Bulletin* [WVU], September 25, 1968; "Student Power—Responsible Student Involvement," *University Bulletin*, September 25, 1968; Bob Arnold, "Students Reject Conduct Code in Close Vote," *Daily Athenaeum*, September 26, 1968.

16. Editorial, "Alden's Last Year," *Post*, September 25, 1968; Editorial, "Choosing a President," *Post*, September 30, 1968; Andrew Alexander, "Student Voice Omitted in Alden Replacement," *Post*, October 1, 1968; Andrew Alexander, "Dispute on Student Voice Continues," *Post*, October 4, 1968; Editorial, "A Student View," *Post*, October 7, 1968; Andrew Alexander, "Veto 'Final' on Student Choice; Stivison's Message Due Tonight," *Post*, October 8, 1968.

17. Andrew Alexander, "Stivison Calls for 'Disruption'; Result of Student Voice Omission," *Post*, October 9, 1968; Andrew Alexander, "Stivison—'Disruption is Not Destruction'," *Post*, October 10, 1968; Andre Alexander, "HC Ballot May Contain Referendum," *Post*, October 21, 1968; Andrew Alexander, "Balloting Today on Referendum for Selection of Next President," *Post*, October 24, 1968; Andrew Alexander, "Referendum Passes 2–1; Record Turnout Credited," *Post*, October 29, 1968; Andrew Alexander, "Students Awarded Power in Selection of President," *Post*, November 7, 1968; Andrew Alexander, "Presidential Selectors Begin Screenings Soon," *Post*, November 13, 1968.

18. Clarence Page, "Campus Force Must Disarm," *Post*, November 20, 1968; Untitled Flyer, [re: Campus Police Disarmament], November 1968 [presumably on or about November 19, 1968], James J. Whalen, Executive Vice-President Records [hereafter: Whalen Records], Box 8, SDS Folder, OU. The OU chapter of SDS left no archival collection, rather historians see them only through the files of University administrators. At Pitt, SDS is virtually nonexistent in the archival collection. Of the three, WVU's chapter of SDS had the greatest archival sources, the result of the Papers of Harry F. Shaw Jr. and Scott Bills; however, the organization itself left no independent records.

19. Memo, Mike Long to James Whalen, November 20, 1968, Whalen Records, Box 8, SDS Folder, OU; Charles F. Myers, Letter to the Editor, *Post*, November 21, 1968; Rick Irvine, "SDS Statement," *Post*, November 21, 1968; Steven G. Garniss, Letter to the Editor, *Post*, November 22, 1968; James Whalen to SDS, November 22, 1968, Whalen Records, Box 8, SDS Folder, OU; "SDS's Gun Demand Denied," *Post*, November 25, 1968; Andrew Alexander, "Twenty SDS Members Arrested Following Sit–In," *Post*, November 26, 1968; Bruce Jorgensen, "Police Close In on Sit–In," *Post*, November 26, 1968.

20. O. E. Frank, Letter to the Editor, *Post*, November 26, 1968; John Felton, "Choosing Issues," *Post*, November 26, 1968; Clarence Page, "SDS Members Face Trial for Security Office

Sit-In," *Post*, December 3, 1968; Clarence Page, "17 SDS Members Found Guilty, of Trespassing, Fined $50 Apiece," *Post*, December 5, 1968.

21. Clarence Page, "Negro Unit Protests Athens Gun Classes," *Post*, April 11, 1968; L. R. Ray, Letter to the Editor, *Daily Athenaeum*, April 16, 1968; D. Michael Worley, Letter to the Editor, *Post*, April 18, 1968; Darl L. Stephenson, Letter to the Editor, *Post*, April 18, 1968; Editorial, "Gun Control," *Pitt News*, June 14, 1968; "University Students Head Committee for Gun Control," *Pitt News*, June 18, 1968; Peggy Allen, "NRA Cites Fear of Future United States Dictatorship," *Pitt News*, June 21, 1968; "Local Rifle Clubs Oppose Gun Laws," *Daily Athenaeum*, July 3, 1968; Editorial, "Gun Control Now," *Post*, October 3, 1968; "B.A.S. 'News' Asks—'Why Arm Campus Police?'" *Pitt News*, October 4, 1968; Eugene Moore, Nelson Linnabary, Thomas Becker, Steve Sandrock, David Wallace, Letter to the Editor, *Post*, October 11, 1968; Steven Raush, Letter to the Editor, *Post*, October 11, 1968; Frank W. Tipton, Letter to the Editor, *Post*, October 14, 1968; Rob Roberts, Gib Guthrie, Dave Smith, Bill Wright, Jon Cornell, Letter to the Editor, *Post*, October 14, 1968; Editorial, "More On Guns," *Post*, October 17, 1968; Michael B. Jackson, Letter to the Editor, *Post*, October 23, 1968.

22. Pat Dorner, Marty Denlinger, Erick Fralick, Letter to the Editor, *Post*, December 5, 1968.

23. Examples of this trend include Timothy B. Tyson, *Radio Free Dixie: Robert F. Williams and the Roots of Black Power* (Chapel Hill, NC: University of North Carolina Press, 1999); Adam Fairclough, *Better Day Coming: Black and Equality, 1890–2000* (New York: Penguin Books, 2001); Lance Hill, *The Deacons for Defense: Armed Resistance and the Civil Rights Movement* (Chapel Hill, NC: University of North Carolina Press, 2004); Nihkil Pal Singh, *Black is a Country: Race and the Unfinished Struggle for Democracy* (Cambridge, MA: Harvard University Press, 2004).

24. Carol Towarnicky, "Black 'Greeks' Combine Common Goals to Form SACC," *Post*, February 12, 1968; Peggy Allen, "Racism Hit By Faculty Committee," *Pitt News*, June 25, 1968; Editorial, "The B.A.S." *Pitt News*, June 28, 1968; Sheila Travis, "Black Unity; Campus Group Serves Dual Purpose: Functions Socially, Fights Discrimination," *Daily Athenaeum*, July 18, 1968; Virginia Joyce, "UCR Continues Probe Into Racial Problems," *Pitt News*, July 23, 1968.

25. "King Assassinated; Riots Spread," *Post*, April 5, 1968; "Unrest, Violence Erupt, Johnson Postpones Tour," *Daily Athenaeum*, April 5, 1968; Don Marbury, "'I Have a Dream,' Said God's Minister," *Pitt News*, April 6, 1968; George Lies, "His Death Caused Fearful Wet Eyes," *Pitt News*, April 6, 1968; "Memorium: A Prayer Racial Unity," *Pitt News*, April 6, 1968; Untitled Handbill [MLK Memorial Service], April 1968 [on or about April 7, 1968], A&M 2506, W.V.U. Student Anti-War Movement, WVRHC; Cathy Martindale, "Steele Speaks at Sitdown Staged After 'Dedication'," *Post*, April 8, 1968; "Racial Unrest Hits at Least 62 Cities," *Post*, April 8, 1968; "Blacks Plan Boycott Day," *Post*, April 9, 1968; Robert I. Vexler, ed., *Pittsburgh: A Chronological & Documentary History, 1682–1976* (New York: Oceana Publications, 1977), 63, 138–39; Patrick J. McGeever, *Rev. Charles Owen Rice: Apostle of Contradiction* (Pittsburgh, PA: Duquesne University Press, 1989), 185–86.

26. Petition, "WVU Discrimination Petition," April 18, 1968, A&M 2043, WVU Discrimination Petition, WVHRC.

27. "Black Action Society Lists Demands to Administration," *Pitt News*, June 25, 1968; Bruce Levenson, "Demands Must Be Met," *Pitt News*, June 25, 1968; Editorial, "The B.A.S.," *Pitt News*, June 28, 1968.

28. "Needs and Demands," undated [presumably, December 2, 1968], Executive Vice President James J Whalen Office Files, 1968–69, Box 2, Black Students Folder, Mahn Archives; Andrew Alexander, "Black Demand List Handed to Alden," *Post*, December 3, 1968; Carol Towarnicky, "'Racism' Charge Directed at University Community," *Post*, December 4, 1968.

29. Ken Schueler, "Militancy and Responsibility," *Pitt News*, June 28, 1968.

30. Towarnicky, "'Racism' Charge Directed at University Community," *Post*, December 4, 1968.

31. Schueler, "Militancy and Responsibility," *Pitt News*, June 28, 1968; William R. Ott, Letter to the Editor, *Pitt News*, June 28, 1968; Barbara Sargent, Letter to the Editor, *Pitt News*, July 12, 1968; Zuberi Mwamba, Letter to the Editor, *Pitt News*, July 30, 1968; Wesley W. Posvar, "Chancellor Probes Role of Black Man," *Pitt News*, September 16, 1968; Barbara Sargent, Letter to the Editor, *Pitt News*, September 18, 1968; Carol Towarnicky, "Alden Hopes for Meeting Soon with Black Leaders," *Post*, December 5, 1968; Memo, untitled [RE: black demands], December 6, 1968, James J. Whalen, Executive Vice-President Records, OUN0943, [hereafter referred to as: Whalen Records], Box 2, Black Student Development Center Folder, OU ; Minutes, "Meeting of Deans with Provost Smith," December 1968 [between December 5 and December 9], Whalen Records, OU.

32. "The B.A.S.," *Pitt News*, June 28, 1968; Editorial, "Discussion is Needed," *Post*, December 4, 1968; Towarnicky, "Alden Hopes for Meeting Soon with Black Leaders," *Post*, December 5, 1968.

33. Memo, "Possible Responses to Black Demands," December 3, 1968, Whalen Records, OU; Memo, Long to Whalen, December 5, 1968, Whalen Records, OU.

34. Beverly Loy Taylor, "HEP Holds Orientation," *Pitt News*, October 2, 1967; Tom Hodson, "ASV Discusses Plans for Projects," *Post*, October 4, 1967; "Tutoring Service Provided for Athens County Children," *Post*, October 6, 1967; John Felton, "ASV Work May Halt for Lack of Funds," *Post*, October 12, 1967; June Kronholz, "To Be Or Not to Be—Apathetic, That Is," *Post*, October 13, 1967; "ASV's Plan Novel 'Live-In'," *Post*, November 29, 1967; Jim Axelrod, "SOOP: To Give and Gain," *Post*, January 10, 1968; "HEP Needs Pitt Students to Tutor Underprivileged," *Pitt News*, January 12, 1968; Carol Towarnicky, "SOOP Tutor Program Aids Youth; Volunteers, Students Show Results," *Post*, April 16, 1968; "SAAP Fights Poverty With Student Help," *Daily Athenaeum*, September 20, 1968; George Spicer, "SAAP Volunteers Help Disadvantaged," *Daily Athenaeum*, October 15, 1968; Nancy Nickell, "Poor and Students Linked by Program," *Post*, October 23, 1968.

At some point WVU's Student Action Against Poverty changed its name to Student Action for Appalachian Progress. There was not discussion of this name change in the *Daily Athenaeum* and appears to have happened during the summer of 1967; however, exact dates and reasons why are not readily available.

35. Thomas Kiffmeyer has explored the radicalization of the Appalachian Volunteers and has shown that by the mid-1960s cooperation with local officials, tutoring programs, and renovation efforts became less desirable as students embraced radical calls for social justice. See Thomas Kiffmeyer, *Reformers to Radicals: The Appalachian Volunteers and the War on Poverty* (Lexington, KY: University Press of Kentucky, 2008).

36. Vincent P. Knipfing, "Attitudes of Seniors Toward the ROTC Program at a State University," (master's thesis, Ohio University, 1966), 23, 30–34, 41–42; Special Committee on

ROTC and George C. S. Benson, *Report of the Special Committee on ROTC to the Secretary of Defense* (Washington, D.C.: U.S. Department of Defense, 1969), 8–11; Robert L. Holmes, "University Neutrality and ROTC," *Ethics* 83, no. 3 (April 1973), 188–89; Michael S. Neiberg, *Making Citizen Soldiers: ROTC and the Ideology of American Military Service* (Cambridge, MA: Harvard University Press, 2000).

37. On February 9, 1933, the Oxford Union debating society of Oxford University in England voted 275 to 173 to adopt a pledge to never again support "King and Country" in war. When the pledge came to the United States the references to the monarchy were, obviously, dropped but the sentiment remained the same. Students at Brown University constructed a widely circulated version with six central tenets, including the futility of war as a means of international peace and the refusal to train or serve in the military unless invasion directly threatened America or its interests. See Mulford Q. Sibley and Philip E. Jacob, *Conscription of Conscience: The American State and the Conscientious Objector, 1940–1947* (Ithaca, NY: Cornell University Press, 1952), 28; Eileen Eagan, *Class, Culture, and the Classroom: The Student Peace Movement of the 1930s* (Philadelphia, PA: Temple University Press, 1981), 57–71; Charles DeBenedetti, "Peace History, in the American Manner," *The History Teacher* 18, 1 (November 1984), 91–92; Lawrence S. Wittner, *Rebels Against War: The American Peace Movement, 1933–1983* (Philadelphia, PA: Temple University Press, 1984), 4–7; Robert Cohen, *When the Old Left Was Young: Student Radicals and America's First Mass Student Movement, 1929–1941* (New York: Oxford University Press, 1993), 79–83.

38. Thomas N. Hoover, *The History of Ohio University* (Athens, OH: Ohio University Press, 1954), 225–26; Knipfing, "Attitudes of Seniors Toward the ROTC Program at a State University," 37, 45–46; Special Committee on ROTC and George C. S. Benson, *Report of the Special Committee on ROTC to the Secretary of Defense*, 5–6; Norman P. Auburn, *The First Hundred Years Are the Hardest: The Story of The University of Akron* (New: Newcomen Society in North America, 1970), 16–17; George W. Knepper, *New Lamps from Old: One Hundred Years of Urban Education at The University of Akron* (Akron, OH: University of Akron Press, 1970), 229–32; Eagan, *Class, Culture, and the Classroom*, 33, 57–61; Robert C. Alberts, *Pitt: The Story of the University of Pittsburgh, 1787–1987* (Pittsburgh, PA: University of Pittsburgh Press, 1986), 147–48; Cohen, *When the Old Left was Young*, 79–84.

39. Ron Wilson, "Optional ROTC? Officials Present View," *Daily Athenaeum*, March 4, 1965; Bob Verbosky, "Changes Considered in ROTC Program," *Daily Athenaeum*, December 7, 1966; "Optional ROTC Bill Not to Hurt Program," *Daily Athenaeum*, February 14, 1967; "Board Makes ROTC Optional," *Daily Athenaeum*, June 22, 1967.

40. Ken Baker, "Vital Student Choice: Await Draft or Enlist," *Daily Athenaeum*, April 5, 1966; Dan Booker, "ROTC Enrollment Up 70 Percent," *Pitt News*, September 16, 1966; Paul Yeager, "Men May Lose Deferments," *Pitt News*, April 3, 1967.

41. Knipfing, "Attitudes of Seniors Toward the ROTC Programs at a State University," 42, 50; Dan Booker, "ROTC Enrollment Up 70 Percent," *Pitt News*, September 16, 1966; "Optional ROTC Bill Not to Hurt Program," *Daily Athenaeum*, February 14, 1967; Paul Yeager, "Men May Lose Deferments," *Pitt News*, April 3, 1967; "Students for Peace Continue Protest Against ROTC Academic Standing," *Pitt News*, November 3, 1967; Linda Founds, "Military, Anti-Ball to Coexist," *Post*, March 1, 1968; Jim Jordan, "Jordan's Jargon," *Daily Athenaeum*,

September 20, 1968; Bob Berlan, "Riffs," *Daily Athenaeum*, October 1, 1968; Ted Goertzel and Acco Hengst, "The Military Socialization of University Students," *Social Problems*, 19, no. 2 (Autumn 1971), 262.

42. Jim Jordan, "Jordan's Jargon," *Daily Athenaeum*, September 20, 1968; Bob Berlan, "Riffs," *Daily Athenaeum*, October 1, 1968; Lewis Barker, Letter to the Editor, *Post*, October 11, 1968; George Delaney, Letter to the Editor, *Pitt News*, November 1, 1968; "MDC Supports ROTC," *Pitt News*, November 4, 1968; David Ehrenwerth, "ROTC and the Facts," *Pitt News*, November 20, 1968.

43. Dan Booker, "Military in Society," *Pitt News*, November 8, 1967.

44. Ed Berger, Larry Flatley, John Frisch, Mayda Gottlieb, Judy Haisley, Peter Karsten, Larry Pexton, and William Worrest, "ROTC, Mylai and the Volunteer Army," *Foreign Policy* (Spring 1971), 135–60.

45. Berger, *et al.*, "ROTC, Mylai and the Volunteer Army," 157–58.

46. Rise Weinberg, "Academic Cabinet States Recommendations on ROTC," *Pitt News*, July 12, 1968; Editorial, "R.O.T.C.," *Pitt News*, July 12, 1968; S. M. Davis, Letter to the Editor, *Pitt News*, July 19, 1968; Jim Jordan, "Jordan's Jargon," *Daily Athenaeum*, September 20, 1968; David Rosenblum, "ROTC Issues, Where Are You? The Facts Seem to be Missing," *Pitt News*, November 6, 1968.

47. Editorial, "Same Old Thing," *Pitt News*, November 13, 1968; Peggy Allen, "SG Bill Says, 'End ROTC Credit'," *Pitt News*, November 22, 1968.

48. Editorial, "A Lesson," *Pitt News*, December 4, 1968.

49. Holmes, "University Neutrality and ROTC," 177–95.

50. "Students for Peace Continue Protest Against ROTC Academic Standing," *Pitt News*, November 3, 1967; "Students Protest Against ROTC," *Pitt News*, November 3, 1967.

51. S. M. Davis, Letter to the Editor, *Pitt News*, July 19, 1968.

52. Greg Lichko, Letter to the Editor, *Post*, October 11, 1968.

53. Editorial, "ROTC Opponents Hurt Freedoms," *Daily Athenaeum*, October 22, 1968; Bill Yetto, "Alienation, Conscience, Freedom—Issues Relevant to ROTC Attack," *Pitt News*, October 25, 1968; Don Marbury, "ROTC Students Confront Dr. Rose," *Pitt News*, October 28, 1968; George Delaney, Letter to the Editor, *Pitt News*, November 1, 1968; "MDC Supports ROTC," *Pitt News*, November 4, 1968; David Ehrenwerth, "ROTC and the Facts," *Pitt News*, November 20, 1968.

54. "ROTC Bulletin," *Pitt News*, October 28, 1968; Editorial, "Cleanse and Purify," *Pitt News*, October 28, 1968; Don Marbury, "ROTC Credit: A Controversy Near Crisis?" *Pitt News*, November 4, 1968; David Rosenblum, "ROTC Conference Turns Into 'Debate'," *Pitt News*, November 13, 1968; Damaine Martin, "The Good Guys vs. the Bad Guys," *Pitt News*, November 25, 1968; Dave Kuhns, "ROTC 'Dis-credited'," *Pitt News*, December 4, 1968.

Chapter 6

1. Fred Halstead, *Out Now! A Participant's Account of the American Movement Against the Vietnam War* (New York: Monad Press, 1978), 311–16, 334–40; Terry H. Anderson, *The Movement and the Sixties: Protest in America from Greensboro to Wounded Knee* (New York: Oxford

University Press, 1995), 177–80; George C. Herring, *America's Longest War: The United States and Vietnam, 1950–1975*, 4th ed. (Boston: McGraw Hill, 2002), 209; Gerard J. DeGroot, *The Sixties Unplugged: A Kaleidoscopic History of a Disorderly Decade* (Cambridge, MA: Harvard University Press, 2008), 380–81.

2. "SDS Attend Washington Rally," *Daily Athenaeum*, October 20, 1967; Tom Price, "War Protesters Persist; 150 March for Ohio," *Post*, October 23, 1967; Hobart Harris, "March on Washington Draws Big Crowd," *Pitt News*, October 23, 1967.

3. "Peace Torch Arriving in Pittsburgh Oct. 15," *Pittsburgh Peace and Freedom News*, September–October 1967; "City Marchers Join National War Protest," *Pittsburgh Post-Gazette*, October 17, 1967; Myles Saunders, "Peace Torch Stops Here; Stays Briefly," *Pitt News*, October 18, 1967; Amy Peal, "Peace Runners Bring Torch Through City," *Duquesne Duke*, October 27, 1967.

4. E. W. Seeley, "Peace Demonstration Held on Campus," *Tartan*, October 18, 1967; Editorial, "How Not to Protest," *Tartan*, October 25, 1967; Andrew Schwartz, Stephen Walfish, George Kavanagh, and Lynn Sterman, Letter to the Editor, *Tartan*, October 25, 1967.

In 1967, Carnegie Institute of Technology and the Mellon Institute joined to form Carnegie-Mellon University. Another major transition occurred in 1969 when the university decided to phase out the associate women's college, Margaret Morrison Carnegie College, to form a College of Humanities and Social Science, and make CMU a coeducational institution. See Edwin Fenton, *Carnegie Mellon, 1900–2000: A Centennial History* (Pittsburgh, Pa: Carnegie Mellon University Press, 2000), 162–63.

5. Harry Shaw to National Mobilization Committee, September 25, 1967, Shaw Papers, Series III: Organizations, Box 1 Folder 29, AFSC—Peace Education Committee, 1967–1968, ASC; Harry Shaw to Ronnie Sue, September 27, 1967, Shaw Papers, Series I, Box 1 Folder 2, ASC; Harry Shaw to Young Peoples Draft/War Survey, October 10, 1967, Shaw Papers, Series III, Box 2 Folder 53, ASC; Patty Preston, "SDS Antidraft, Antiwar Drive Small Part of National Protest," *Daily Athenaeum*, October 18, 1967; Fellowship of Reconciliation to Harry Shaw, October 18, 1967, Shaw Papers, Series III, Box 2 Folder 53, ASC; Young Peoples Draft/War Survey, undated, Shaw Papers, Series III, Box 2 Folder 53, ASC; "SDS to Attend Washington Rally," *Daily Athenaeum*, October 20, 1967; Kitty Melville, "Three 'U' Students Arrested," *Daily Athenaeum*, October 24, 1967.

6. Phil Semas, "Anti-War Rally Expected to Draw Thousands Oct. 21," *Post*, October 6, 1967; Editorial, "Speak Out," *Post*, October 11, 1967; "Peace March," *Post*, October 12, 1967; "200 to Go to March," *Post*, October 17, 1967; "Viet Protest Assemblage Scheduled for Saturday," *Post*, October 19, 1967; Tom Price, "War Protesters Persist; 150 March for Ohio," *Post*, October 23, 1967; Editorial, "Washington," *Post*, October 23, 1967; Bob Vanderwyst, "Pentagon Confrontation—A Learning Situation," *Post*, October 24, 1967; Editorial, "Action, Again," *Post*, October 25, 1967.

7. Editorial, "The Growing Dissent," *Pitt News*, October 23, 1967.

8. "Vietnam Group Seeks Approval," *Post*, January 31, 1968; *Feb 20th Tuesday*, February 1968, CSA, Student Commentary Folder, OU; Untitled Handbill, [undated], re: Vietnam Dialogue Week, CSA, Student Demonstrations—Student Flyers, 1966–1971 Folder, OU; "Viet Topic of Week-Long Campus Talks," *Post*, February 20, 1968; Untitled Flyer, February 1968,

CSA, Student Commentary Folder, OU; Tom Hodson, "Speeches at Gam Open Viet Dialogue," *Post*, February 21, 1968; Athens Committee to End the War in Vietnam, Untitled Flyer, February 22, 1968, CSA, Student Demonstrations—Student Flyers, 1966–1971 Folder, OU; Julie Snider, "Issue Is Not Vietnam But All of Asia—McGee," *Post*, February 23, 1968; June Kronholz, "Marching for a Reason," *Post*, February 23, 1968; Judy Siehl and Carrie Ator, Letter to the Editor, *Post*, February 27, 1968.

9. Pamphlet, "International Student–Faculty Strike, April 26th," Student Mobilization Committee to End the War in Vietnam, undated [presumably between January 29 and April 26, 1968], CSA, Box 1, Vietnam War Folder, OU; Carol Towarnicky, "Students Organize War, Racial Boycott," *Post*, April 16, 1968; Victor Zinn, Letter to the Editor, *Post*, April 19, 1968; Student Mobilization Committee to End the War in Vietnam, *Bring Our Men Home From Vietnam NOW!*, April 1968 [sometime on or about April 20], CSA, Box 1, Vietnam War Folder, OU; Athens Committee to End the War in Vietnam, *Schedule of Activities*, April 1968 [sometime on or before April 20], CSA, Box 1, Vietnam War Folder, OU; "Class Boycott Protests Prejudice, War, Draft," *Post*, April 26, 1968; Editorial, "Support the Boycott," *Post*, April 26, 1968; Bob Rogers, photos and caption, *Athens Messenger*, April 28, 1968.

While Pitt did not participate in the International Student Strike and Boycott, students at Duquesne University did. It is not possible to know with certainty, but given previous interactions between Pitt and Duquesne students, some Pitt students may have attended the films, discussions, speeches, or the "Is the War Over?" dance. See "Duquesne University—Vietnam Day April 26th," *Pittsburgh Peace and Freedom News*, April 1968; "Strike for Peace," *Duquesne Duke*, April 26, 1968.

10. *Demonstration*, November 1967 [on or about November 14], CSA, Student Demonstrations—Student Flyers, 1966–1971 Folder, OU; Bob Vanderwyst, "Response 'Peaceful' to Dow Recruiting Here," *Post*, November 14, 1967; Athens Committee to End the War in Vietnam, Untitled Handbill, November 1967 [on or about November 14], CSA, Student Demonstrations—Student Flyers, 1966–1971 Folder, OU; Bob Vanderwyst, "70 March in Vietnam Protest; Dow Rep Meets Demonstrators," *Post*, November 15, 1967; Editorial, "The Dow Thing," *Post*, November 15, 1967; Editorial, "A Matter of Principle," *Pitt News*, November 15, 1967; Alice Goldsmith, "The Right to Recruit," *Pitt News*, November 15, 1967; J. Matthew Simon, David R. Morrison, Charles Springer, Martin A. Volker, Letter to the Editor, *Pitt News*, November 15, 1967; Daniel E. Cogan, Letter to the Editor, *Pitt News*, November 15, 1967; Paul Stoller, "Marchers Stage Peaceful Protest Against Dow Chemicle [*sic*]," *Pitt News*, November 15, 1967; Direct Action Committee to Harry Shaw, November 16, 1967, Shaw Papers, Series III, Box 1 Folder 40, ASC; Alan Meyer and John Silisky, "Pickets March Two Days to Protest Dow Recruiting," *Pitt News*, November 17, 1967; Bill Sheridan, Letter to the Editor, *Post*, November 20, 1967; Lewis Mollica, Letter to the Editor, *Post*, November 20, 1967.

11. Ivan Abrams and Joshua Chasan, Letter to the Editor, *Pitt News*, November 20, 1967.

12. Bob Berlan, "SDS-Marine Recruiters Confrontation Planned, *Daily Athenaeum*, October 1, 1968; Peggy Workman, "SDS Clash Avoided, Recruiters Moved," *Daily Athenaeum*, October 2, 1968.

13. Michael S. Foley, *Confronting the War Machine: Draft Resistance During the Vietnam War* (Chapel Hill, NC: University of North Carolina Press, 2003), 113–30.

14. Mulford Q. Sibley and Philip R. Jacob, *Conscription of Conscience: The American State and the Conscientious Objector, 1940–1947* (Ithaca, NY: Cornell University Press, 1952), 28; Eileen Eagan, *Class, Culture, and the Classroom: The Student Peace Movement of the 1930s* (Philadelphia, PA: Temple University Press, 1981), 57–71; Charles DeBenedetti, "Peace History, in the American Manner," *The History Teacher* 18, 1 (November 1984), 91–92; Lawrence S. Wittner, *Rebels Against War: The American Peace Movement, 1933–1983* (Philadelphia, PA: Temple University Press, 1984), 4–7; Robert Cohen, *When the Old Left was Young: Student Radicals and America's First Mass Student Movement, 1929–1941* (New York: Oxford University Press, 1993), 79–83.

15. Sibley and Jacob, *Conscription of Conscience*, 17–47, 332–50; U.S. President's Commission on Campus Unrest, *The Report of the President's Commission on Campus Unrest* (Washington, D.C.: Government Printing Office, 1971), 20–21; Eagan, *Class, Culture, and the Classroom*, 221–25; Stephen M. Kohn, *Jailed for Peace: The History of American Draft Law Violators, 1658–1985* (Westport, CT: Greenwood Press, 1986), 45–48, 59–60; Lee Kennett, *G.I.: The American Soldier in World War II* (New York: Charles Scribners' Sons, 1987), 8, 12–13; Cohen, *When the Old Left was Young*, 311–12; David M. Kennedy, *Freedom from Fear: The American People in Depression and War, 1929–1945* (New York: Oxford University Press, 1999), 632–33; Justus Doenecke, *Storm on the Horizon: The Challenge to American Intervention, 1939–1941* (Lanham, MD: Rowman & Littlefield, 2000), 115–16; Kenneth D. Rose, *Myth and the Greatest Generation: A Social History of Americans in World War II* (New York: Routledge, 2008), 61, 110.

The creation of the "World War II as good war" myth traces largely to the mid-1980s and the Pulitzer Prize winning work of writer and historian Studs Terkel. See Terkel, *"The Good War": An Oral History of World War II* (New York: Pantheon Books, 1984). Terkel explained that the title was ironic and a construction of Cold War memory. See "Studs Terkel on 'The Good War'," *NBC Today Show*, New York: NBC Universal, October 22, 1984, https://archives .nbclearn.com. Some efforts at cracking the popular memory of World War II have also begun to appear in the American press over the past decade. See Geoffrey Wheatcraft, "How Good was the Good War," *Boston Globe*, May 8, 2005, http://www.boston.com; Adam Kirsch, "Is World War II Still 'the Good War'," *New York Times*, May 27, 2011, http://www.nytimes.com.

16. "Rodd Moves Peace Sit-In," *Pittsburgh Post–Gazette*, March 27, 1964; Thomas Rodd, untitled statement, *Tartan*, April 29, 1964; "Jail or Peace Corps, Judge Tells Pacifist, 18," *Pittsburgh Press*, August 18, 1964; "Draft Protester Must Go to Jail Or Service Group," *Pittsburgh Post–Gazette*, August 19, 1964; Statement, Thomas Rodd, November 1965, Draft and War Resistance Movement Records, Pittsburgh, Pa., 1966–1972 Collection, AIS.1968.18 [hereafter referred to as: DWRM], Series I: Correspondence, Box 2 Folder 1, ASC; "Statement Prepared by Thomas Rodd to be Delivered at a Hearing in Pittsburgh, Pennsylvania Before Judge Louis Rosenberg on January 7, 1966," Thomas Rodd, January 7, 1966, DWRM, Series I, Box 2 Folder 1, ASC; Jack Ryan, "Pacifist Rodd Prepared for Jail, Judge Gives Him 4-Year Term," *Pittsburgh Post–Gazette*, January 8, 1966; "Prison Term Meted Out to Pacifist," *The Spokane–Review* [Spokane, WA], January 8, 1966; Harvey Cohen, Letter to the Editor, *Duquesne Duke*, January 19, 1966; "Draft Protester Leaves Prison," *Star–News* [Wilmington, NC], June 27, 1967.

Rodd's announcement in April 1964 coincided with over 200 other such statements made in national newspapers in April and May 1964. See Melvin Small, *Antiwarriors: The Vietnam War and the Battle for America's Hearts and Minds* (New York: SR Books, 2002), 13.

17. Hobart Harris, "General Lewis Hershey Discusses Philosophy of Selective Service," *Pitt News*, September 18, 1967; Ivan Abrams, "Student Organize 'Greeting' for General Lewis Hershey," *Pitt News*, September 18, 1967.

18. Some reports suggest up to a dozen Vexlermen returned draft cards, see Jack Garner, "Protest Disrupted by Fire in Church," *Pittsburgh Post–Gazette*, December 5, 1967; "National Day of Draft Resistance," *Tartan*, December 6, 1967; John Caywood, "Ministry Peace Service Finds Probable Arson Amidst 'Friendliness'," *Pitt News*, December 6, 1967; Joshua Chasan (speech, December 4, 1967), DWRM, Series I, Box 2, Folder 1, ASC; Patrick J. McGeever, *Rev. Charles Owen Rice: Apostle of Contradiction* (Pittsburgh, PA: Duquesne University Press, 1989), 208–9.

19. Caywood, "Ministry Peace Service Finds Probably Arson Amidst 'Friendliness'," *Pitt News*, December 6, 1967.

20. *No Longer a Card Carrying Member of the Draft*, DWRM, Series I, Box 1, Folder 1, ASC; Statement by David Rittenhouse Morrison, December 4, 1967, DWRM, Series I, Box 2, Folder 1, ASC; "Personal Appearance Before Local Board #58, Lansdowne, Pa.," December 5, 1967, in the David R. Morrison Papers, Swarthmore College Peace Collection.

21. Judith Galardi, "'We Don't Believe in Dodging the Draft, But in Resisting It' – Dave Morrison," *Pitt News*, July 9, 1968.

22. Young Friends of North America, "Draft Non-Cooperators" [list of draft resisters], Committee on Conscription Records, AIS.1969.17, Box1, Folder 6, ASC; Jim Gray, "Possibility of Jail Sentence Faces Pacifist-School Teacher," *Duquesne Duke*, February 16, 1968; *Peacemaker*, March 1968, DWRM, Series I, Box 1, Folder 12, ASC; "200 Support Marsh's Refusal," *Pittsburgh Peace and Freedom News*, January 1968.

23. "Francis Shor of Mt. Lebanon Refuses Induction," *Pittsburgh Peace and Freedom News*, January 1968; Francis Shor, email and written correspondence to author, June 2014.

24. Untitled Advertisement, *Pitt News*, April 3, 1968; "April 3, 1968; Resistance Service at UOM," DWRM, Series I, Box 2, Folder 1, ASC; Sharon Peruzzi, "Draft Resistance by North Hills Man," *Tartan*, May 15, 1968; David L. Worstell, "Statement of Noncompliance," DWRM, Series I, Box 2, Folder 1, ASC; "Pittsburgher to Refuse Induction Monday, Support Demonstration Planned," *Pittsburgh Peace and Freedom News*, April 1968; David R. Morrison, "New Deferment Laws Should be Studied," *Tartan*, May 15, 1968.

25. Pope and Stoner, "Draft Counseling Available," *Daily Athenaeum*, April 3, 1968; "Two Youths Turn in Draft Cards," *Morgantown Post*, April 3, 1968; Evelyn Ryan, "Draft Cards Sent Back to Hershey in Protest," *Daily Athenaeum*, April 4, 1968; Harry F. Shaw, *Letter of Resistance to the Selective Service*, April 3, 1968, A&M 2828, Scott Bills Papers, WVRHC.

26. Joe Hinson, Letter to the Editor, *Daily Athenaeum*, April 10, 1968.

27. Sam Hoye, Letter to the Editor, *Daily Athenaeum*, April 12, 1968.

28. Henry David Thoreau, "Civil Disobedience," in *Walden and Civil Disobedience* (New York: Barnes & Noble Classics, 2003), 286.

29. "Fromm Refuses Draft, May Face Felony Charge," *Post*, May 6, 1968; "Fromm May Have Draft Notice Cancelled by Status Verification," *Post*, May 23, 1968.

30. "Celebration of Freedom Asks Student Support," *Pitt News*, October 2, 1968; Judi

Galardi, "Teaching Assistant Refuses Induction, Defends Constitution," *Pitt News*, October 2, 1968; "Chasen [*sic*] Resists Induction," *Pitt News*, October 4, 1968; Untitled Flyer, DWRM, Series I, Box 2, Folder 1, ASC.

31. *Is the Draft Bugging You?*, DWRM, Series I, Box 1, Folder 12, ASC; Memo, "Letter to C.O. Counselors," DWRM, Series I, Box 1, Folder 1, ASC; *No Longer a Card Carrying Member of the Draft*, DWRM, Series I, Box 1, Folder 12, ASC.

32. The campus newspapers carried stories beginning in February and running through November 1968 about various candidates and the implications of the election. Unfortunately, the papers were largely silent on student activities related to the campaigns aside from a random blurb about upcoming canvassing activities or calls for volunteers. There appear to have been no rallies, demonstrations, or other events organized by students that directly linked to the presidential election. Scholars of the 1968 election have rightly focused a great deal of attention on the Democratic National Convention in Chicago in August, and undoubtedly personal memories of the election campaign have generated impressions about the levels of student involvement. This is not to say that these are in any way false remembrances, rather to say that the lack of archival sources at either of the three universities and limited reporting in the student newspapers makes it difficult to gauge to what extent these students participated.

For recent, in-depth narrative explorations of the 1968 election, see Michael A. Cohen, *American Maelstrom: The 1968 Election and the Politics of Division* (New York: Oxford University Press, 2016); Michael Schumacher, *The Contest: The 1968 Election and the War for America's Soul* (Minneapolis, MN: University of Minnesota Press, 2018).

33. David Baer, "Students To Vote in Choice '68," *Pitt News*, March 27, 1968; "Students to Cast Mock Vote April 24," *Daily Athenaeum*, April 17, 1968; John Felton, "NBC Newsmen Here Today to Film Pre–MPC Activities," *Post*, April 17, 1968; Mark Roth, "Rockefeller Seen as 'Nixon Alternative,' Needs Strong Cross-Over Vote to Win," *Post*, April 17, 1968; Bill Sievert, "Speculation on the Backroom Strategy," *Post*, April 18, 1968; "McCarthy, Kennedy Meet in Choice 68," *Daily Athenaeum*, April 19, 1968; Tom Hauck, "DU Students to Vote in Choice '68 Election," *Duquesne Duke*, April 19, 1968; Ron Guziak, "Students Across Country Will Vote in Mock Election," *Daily Athenaeum*, April 23, 1968; "Nixon Viewed as GOP Unifier," *Post*, April 23, 1968; Wendell R. Cochran, "Choice 68: Mock Election Today Gives Students a Voice," *Daily Athenaeum*, April 24, 1968; "Choice Offers Voice on President, Vietnam," *Post*, April 24, 1968; Editorial, "Choose McCarthy," *Post*, April 24, 1968; "Choice 68: McCarthy Winner In Mock Election," *Daily Athenaeum*, April 25, 1968; Bill Sievert, "The Mock Political Convention," *Post*, April 25, 1968; Brue Jorgensen, "US Policy Revised in MPC Platform," *Post*, April 26, 1968; June Kronholz, "Rockefeller Nominated President," *Post*, April 29, 1968; "Choice '68 Picks McCarthy, RFK," *Post*, May 9, 1968; Earl Jacobs, "'Pitt News' Student Survey Indicates McCarthy Leads," *Pitt News*, May 10, 1968; "McCarthy Takes Choice '68 at DU," *Duquesne Duke*, May 24, 1968; "Choice '68 Statistics," *Duquesne Duke*, May 24, 1968.

Part 3

1. Selective Service System, "Induction Statistics," https://www.sss.gov.

2. "Selective Service Classifications," in Central Committee for Conscience Objection, *CCCO Draft Counselor's Manual* (1972), 1–8; "Student Deferment," in Central Committee for Conscience Objection, *CCCO Draft Counselor's Manual* (1972), 1–2; Richard Nixon, "Executive Order 11497 – Amending the Selective Service Regulation to Prescribe Random Selection," November 26, 1969, http://www.presidency.ucsb.edu; Selective Service System, "Induction Statistics," https://www.sss.gov; Selective Service System, "The Vietnam Lotteries," https://www.sss.gov; Mark Hamilton Lytle, *America's Uncivil Wars: The Sixties Era from Elvis to the Fall of Richard Nixon* (New York: Oxford University Press, 2006), 352.

3. Paul Hoffman, *Moratorium: An American Protest* (New York: Tower Public Affairs, 1970), 200–5; Simon Hall, *Rethinking the American Anti–War Movement* (New York: Routledge, 2012), 137–50.

4. Todd Gitlin, *The Sixties: Years of Hope, Days of Rage*, rev. ed. (New York: Bantam Books, 1993), 411.

5. Hoffman, *Moratorium*, 204.

Chapter 7

1. Maurice Isserman and Michael Kazin, *America Divided: The Civil War of the 1960s* (New York: Oxford University Press, 2008), 197–98, 290–91.

2. George Lies, "'Pressured' Chancellor Complies 'Positively' with Black Demands," *Pitt News*, January 16, 1969; Bruce Levenson, "Blacks Cool It At Office 'Barge-In'," *Pitt News*, January 16, 1969; Don Marbury, "Campus Wakes Up; Understanding Needed," *Pitt News*, January 16, 1969; "Posvar Pledges Action," *Pitt News*, January 20, 1969; Joe W. Trotter and Jared N. Day, *Race and Renaissance: African Americans in Pittsburgh since World War II* (Pittsburgh, PA: University of Pittsburgh Press, 2010), 120.

3. Carol Towarnicky, "University–Black Talks Viewed as 'Profitable'," *Post*, January 9, 1969; Carol Towarnicky, "Black Planning Begins, New Official Sought," *Post*, January 14, 1969; Carol Towarnicky, "'Signs of Progress' Seen on Black Students' Demands," *Post*, March 6, 1969; Robert E. Mahn, *Meeting of Deans with Provost Smith*, April 10, 1969, Whalen Records, Box 3, Deans Meeting Folder, OU; Carol Towarnicky and Rudy Maxa, "Blacks Issue Statement on 'Incidents'," *Post*, May 2, 1969; Carol Towarnicky, "Black Community Achieves Notable Gains in Demands Presented to Administration," *Post*, May 28, 1969.

4. "Blacks Meet with Harlow," *Daily Athenaeum*, April 30, 1969; "Black Students Present Demands to University," *Daily Athenaeum*, August 7, 1969.

5. Sam Liscook and Ken Huber, Letter to the Editor, *Pitt News*, January 20, 1969; Daniel McNary, Letter to the Editor, *Pitt News*, January 23, 1969; University Committee on the Racial Crisis (UCRC), "Confrontation to Continue," *Pitt News*, January 27, 1969; Editorial, "Precarious Position," *Pitt News*, January 27, 1969; David Rosenblum, "White B(l)acklash," *Pitt News*, January 27, 1969.

6. Wesley W. Posvar, "BAS 'Demands' Analyzed," *Pitt News*, January 29, 1969; Jane E.

Griffey, Letter to the Editor, *Pitt News*, January 31, 1969; UCRC, Advertisement, *Pitt News*, January 31, 1969.

7. "No Hours for Jrs. If Parents Sign," *Post*, January 10, 1969; Editorial, "Ending Hours," *Post*, March 6, 1969; Editorial, "To End All Hours," *Post*, March 27, 1969; Rudy Maxa, "Women's Interest Key to Hours Walk-Out Success, *Post*, April 16, 1969; Rudy Maxa, "Walkout Planned to Deny Women's Hours Existence," *Post*, April 17, 1969; Thomas O'Keefe, "Hours Policy in State Institutions," April 19, 1969, Whalen Records, Box 8, Student Activities, O'Keefe, Thomas—Dean of Folder, OU; Andrew Alexander, "Coeds Continue Defying Hours Policy," *Post*, April 21, 1969; Editorial, "Sock It to 'Em, Ladies," *Post*, April 21, 1969; Andrew Alexander, "Normal Action Pledged for Hours Violators," *Post*, April 22, 1969; *Policy Statement*, May 23, 1969, CSA, Student Demonstrations—Student Flyers, 1966–1971 Folder, OU; Dan Hime, "Student Protests Center on Johnson," *Post*, May 26, 1969.

8. Martha Hartle, "'No Curfew' System Won for Women," *Pitt News*, January 10, 1969; "Board of Governors Indecisive on Hours," *Daily Athenaeum*, April 22, 1969; Tom Shumate, "Women Liberated from Dorm Hours," *Daily Athenaeum*, April 23, 1969; Mountaineer Freedom Party of WVU, *Women's Rights*, Fall 1969, A&M 2833, W.V.U. Student Anti-War Movement Collection, WVRHC; "Mountaineer Freedom Party Platform," *Montani Semper Liberi*, Fall 1969, A&M 161, Miscellaneous Controversial Literature—Mountaineer Freedom Party Folder, WVRHC.

9. "American Legion Resolves to Influence Legislature," *Pitt News*, January 31, 1969; Editorial, "Mickey Mouse U?" *Pitt News*, January 31, 1969; Editorial, "Halliday Decision," *Pitt News*, February 3, 1969; James Holland, "Faculty Power Usurped," *Pitt News*, February 3, 1969; Claudia Bernard, "War on the Campus—Athens Style," *Post*, February 7, 1969; Paul Stoller, "ROTC Credit Still 'Hanging'," *Pitt News*, February 7, 1969; Editorial, "Throat Stuffing," *Pitt News*, February 7, 1969; Charles H. Peake, "Provost's Letter Text to Members of FAS," *Pitt News*, February 7, 1969; Bill Rosen, "Demands Presented to Chancellor Posvar," *Pitt News*, February 10, 1969; "American Legion Still Fighting University," *Pitt News*, February 21, 1969; George Lies, "Posvar Attempts to Clarify Issues," *Pitt News*, February 24, 1969; Eric Fralick, "Is a Campus a Place for ROTC?" *Post*, February 28, 1969; Ken Brill, Letter to the Editor, *Post*, March 6, 1969; Fred Bryant, Letter to the Editor, *Post*, March 6, 1969; Bob Berlan, "'U' Students Voice Opinions on ROTC Academic Credit," *Daily Athenaeum*, March 27, 1969; Bob Arnold, "Definition of Academic Credit Root of ROTC College Hassle," *Daily Athenaeum*, March 27, 1969; Bob Arnold, "Military Has Role in Academic Community," *Daily Athenaeum*, March 27, 1969; Scott Bills and Brad Pyles, "ROTC Has No Place in University; Military Should Train Its Leaders," *Daily Athenaeum*, March 27, 1969; Carol Divens, "Fate of ROTC Program Investigated by Committee," *Post*, May 6, 1969; Geoffrey Bauman, "Posvar Reply NG—SDS," *Pitt News*, June 17, 1969; David R. Morrison to Wesley W. Posvar, July 10, 1969, DWRM, Series I, Box 1, Folder 5, ASC.

10. Robert L. Savage, Provost, to Members of the University Community, April 22, 1970, CSA, Selections from Papers of Claude R. Sowle Folder [hereafter referred to as: Sowle Papers], OU; Stanley White, Untitled Memorandum, April 22, 1970, CSA, Sowle Papers, OU; Bill Choyke, "Nine Arrested After Protest," *Post*, April 23, 1970; Ohio University Student Union, Untitled Statement/Flyer, undated [presumably on or after April 23, 1970], CSA, Sowle Papers, OU; W. C. Culp, *Record of Events; April 24, 1970*, CSA, Campus Security Reports, 4/22/70 to 5/15/70

Folder, OU; Andrew Alexander, "ROTC Issue Creating Tension," *Post*, April 27, 1970; Editorial, "ROTC Can Exist—Off Campus," *Post*, April 28, 1970; "Eight of 'Athens 9' Students Plead Not Guilty to Charges," *Post*, April 30, 1970; Thomas Jackson, *Go Back, You Didn't Say "May I"*: *The Diary of a Young Priest* (New York: Seabury Press, 1974), 52–58, 76–68.

11. George V. Voinovich to James J. Whalen, January 8, 1969, Whalen Records, Box 8, SDS (Students for a Democratic Society) Folder [hereafter referred to as: SDS], OU; Editorial, "Fleming Proposal," *Pitt News*, January 20, 1969; James J. Whalen to George V. Voinovich, January 30, 1969, Whalen Records, SDS, OU; Mark Roth, "Bill Would Evict Students Involved in Disruptions," *Post*, January 31, 1969; Editorial, "George Voinovich," *Post*, February 12, 1969.

12. "Zord Seeks Stick to Stymie Student Stir," *Pitt News*, February 10, 1969; Editorial, "Carry a Big Stick," *Pitt News*, February 10, 1969; "Kaufman Raps Fleming," *Pitt News*, February 14, 1969; "Fleming Bill Strikes at Demonstrators Again," *Pitt News*, February 14, 1969; Editorial, "Alas Babylon," *Pitt News*, February 14, 1969; David Rosenblum, "Foot In the Mouth Trick," *Pitt News*, February 14, 1969; Paul Stoller, "Fleming Bill Called 'Unnecessary'," *Pitt News*, February 25, 1969; Peggy Snyder, "Riot Act Aimed at Colleges Passes Legislature," *Daily Athenaeum*, March 20, 1969.

13. Editorial, "Alas Babylon," *Pitt News*, February 14, 1969.

14. Ellipses in original text. Dave Kuhns, "Dear Legislators: We're Only Human Beings," *Pitt News*, February 25, 1969.

15. Editorial, "George Voinovich," *Post*, February 12, 1969; Editorial, "Alas Babylon," *Pitt News*, February 14, 1969; David Rosenblum, "'Foot' in the Mouth Trick," *Pitt News*, February 14, 1969; Dave Kuhns, "SG to Pass Fleming Opposition," *Pitt News*, February 24, 1969; "SG Confirms Resolution Against Fleming 'Riot Act'," *Pitt News*, February 26, 1969; Allan Senio, "Discipline of What Kind?" *Pitt News*, March 3, 1969; Virginia Joyce, "Teach-In Draws 800," *Pitt News*, March 3, 1969; Snyder, "Riot Act Aimed at Colleges Passes Legislature," *Daily Athenaeum*, March 20, 1969; Wesley Posvar, "Statement," *Pitt News*, March 24, 1969; Roy Costa, "West Virginia's Anti-Riot Law Encourages 'Deadly Violence'," *Daily Athenaeum*, July 10, 1969; Paul M. Scott, "House Bill 1219: A Study," *Akron Law Review* 5, no. 1 (Winter 1972), 93–116.

16. For discussion of the implosion of the national organization of SDS, see Kirkpatrick Sale, *SDS: The Rise and Development of the Students for a Democratic Society* (New York: Vintage Books, 1973), 297–320; Fred Halstead, *Out Now! A Participant's Account of the American Movement Against the Vietnam War* (New York: Monad Press, 1978), 463–67; Nancy Zaroulis and Gerald Sullivan, *Who Spoke Up? American Protest Against the War in Vietnam, 1963–1975* (New York: Holt, Rinehart and Winston, 1984), 206–07, 251–55; Todd Gitlin, *The Sixties: Years of Hope, Days of Rage*, Revised Edition (New York: Bantam Books, 1993), 377–408; Isserman and Kazin, *America Divided*, 276–78.

17. Rudy Maxa, "Anti-Inaugural Planned," *Post*, January 13, 1969; "Ohio SDS Will Join 'Inauguration' Events," *Post*, January 13, 1969; Rudy Maxa, "Washington Fears 'Another Chicago' for Inauguration," *Post*, January 14, 1969; "SDS Info," *Post*, January 15, 1969; Rudy Maxa, "Counter-Inaugural Parade Calm, Until . . ." *Post*, January 20, 1969; Steve Shanesy, "D.C. Carnival Atmosphere Becomes Dismal Overnight," *Post*, January 21, 1969; Rudy Maxa, "After the Inaugural, Mobe Still Lives," *Post*, January 22, 1969; Eric Fralick, "Marching Shifts Mood," *Post*, January 27, 1969.

18. Rudy Maxa, "SDS Chapter Molds Future with Self-Education Move," *Post*, January 29, 1969; Rudy Maxa, "Late—New Left By-Word," *Post*, February 11, 1969; Rudy Maxa, "SDS Seeks New Focus," *Post*, February 12, 1969; "SDS Sponsors 'Opposition' Ball," *Post*, February 24, 1969; S. Wayne Helton, "Anti-Mil Ball Promises Fun, Free Freak-Out," *Post*, February 25, 1969; Clarence Page, "Military, Anti-Military Happenings Provide Something for Everybody," *Post*, February 28, 1969.

19. After February 1969, there is no further mention of SDS at OU in the *Post* or archival sources consulted.

20. Concerned Students and Faculty was representative of the ephemeral, transitory student groups of the period that popped up, was quite active for a short period, and disappeared leaving virtually no trace aside from references in the student newspapers. Bruce Levenson, "Demands Aired in Demonstration," *Pitt News*, February 12, 1969.

21. Levenson, "Demands Aired in Demonstration," *Pitt News*, February 12, 1969; "Students, Faculty Demand Innovation," *Pitt News*, February 14, 1969.

22. Virginia Joyce, "A Free University—But Under Which Roof," *Pitt News*, March 12, 1969; Editorial, "A Wise Decision," *Pitt News*, March 12, 1969; Don Marbury, "That 'Free University'—It's There . . . If You Want It . . ." *Pitt News*, March 13, 1969; Concerned Students and Faculty, "Statement—'Concerned' List Proposals in Statement," *Pitt News*, March 14, 1969; Anne Dorn, "Free University Holds Press Conference," *Pitt News*, March 17, 1969; Editorial, "Free Thinking," *Pitt News*, March 17, 1969.

23. Anne Dorn, "Free University Holds Press Conference," *Pitt News*, March 17, 1969.

24. Carla Sydney Stone, "SDS Members Debate Status, Go Independent," *Pitt News*, July 11, 1969; Carla Sydney Stone, "University SDS Disassociates from National," *Pitt News*, July 11, 1969; Pitt SDS, "SDS Recommends 'Social Justice'," *Pitt News*, July 18, 1969.

25. *Why MFP?*, A&M 2828, Scott Bills Papers, WVRHC; Bob Berlan, "Third Campus Party to Begin Operations," *Daily Athenaeum*, January 22, 1969.

26. Editorial, "ACP, MFP, SP Platforms Evaluated," *Daily Athenaeum*, February 27, 1969; "Bills Advocates Changes Now," *Daily Athenaeum*, March 4, 1969.

27. Mountaineer Freedom Party of WVU, Untitled Handbill, A&M 2506, W.V.U. Student Anti-War Movement Collection, WVRHC; Bob Berlan, "Third Campus Party to Begin Operations," *Daily Athenaeum*, January 22, 1969; Editorial, "New Third Party May Overthrow Apathy," *Daily Athenaeum*, January 24, 1969; Steve Poe, "Bills, Comuntzis, Richmond Reveal Platforms," *Daily Athenaeum*, February 14, 1969; Editorial, "ACP, MFP, SP Platforms Evaluated," *Daily Athenaeum*, February 27, 1969; "Bills Advocates Changes Now," *Daily Athenaeum*, March 4, 1969; MFP Campaign Committee, "Mountaineer Freedom Party," *Daily Athenaeum*, March 5, 1969; Steve Poe, "'Doc' Richmond Wins," *Daily Athenaeum*, March 6, 1969; Mountaineer Freedom Party of WVU, *An Introduction to the Mountaineer Freedom Party*, July 1969, A&M 2506, W.V.U. Student Anti-War Movement Collection, WVRHC.

28. *Student Activist League Thirteen Demands*, A&M 2828, Scott Bills Papers, WVRHC.

29. Roy Costa, "Administrators See Demands as Solvable 'Problems Areas'," *Daily Athenaeum*, August 7, 1969; "Harlow Receives 13 SAL Demands," *Dominion News* [Morgantown, WV], January 14, 1970; "Impossible Demands," *Morgantown Post*, January 16, 1970; "Controversy Boils," *Morgantown Post*, January 16, 1970; "SAL Vows Full Airing of Demands," *Domin-*

ion News, January 18, 1970; David A. Milne, "Richmond Tells Press—'Demands Strengthen SG'," *Daily Athenaeum*, January 20, 1970; "Harlow to Keep Meeting," *Morgantown Post*, January 27, 1970; Joseph C. Gluck to Scott Bills, January 27, 1970, A&M 2828, Scott Bills Papers, WVRHC; Paul Burkey and David Poling, "Bills to Visit Harlow Today to Discuss Thirteen Demands," *Daily Athenaeum*, January 28, 1970; David A. Milne, "Harlow, Bills Meet; U Policies Reaffirmed," *Daily Athenaeum*, January 29, 1970; Joseph C. Gluck to Scott Bills, February 9, 1970, A&M 2828, Scott Bills Papers, WVRHC.

30. Milne, "Harlow, Bills Meet," *Daily Athenaeum*, January 29, 1970.

31. Milne, "Harlow, Bills Meet," *Daily Athenaeum*, January 29, 1970.

32. David Blumberg, "Cutler Besieged by 150; Meeting Set with Sowle," *Post*, January 30, 1970; Editorial, "Misdirection," *Post*, January 30, 1970; Gail S. Schnitzer, "Campus Quiet After Protest," *Athens Messenger*, February 1, 1970; "Sowle Wins Praise, Criticism for His Action," *Athens Messenger*, February 1, 1970; Andrew Alexander, "Fires, Teargas Bombing Follow Friday's Riot," *Post*, February 2, 1970; Mi Herzog, "Action by Students on Tuition Increase Urged by Assembly," *Post*, February 2, 1970; Charles R. Sowle to Roger Fay, February 13, 1970, CSA, Sowle Papers, OU.

33. Schnitzer, "Campus Quiet After Protest," *Athens Messenger*, February 1, 1970; Alexander, "Fires, Teargas Bombing Follow Friday's Riot," *Post*, February 2, 1970; Robert E. Mahn, *The Presidency of Claude R. Sowle: August 1, 1969 to September 1, 1974*, Volume II (Athens, OH: Ohio University Libraries, 2007), 1360–70.

34. West Virginia Union of Students (WVUS), *Draft Program of the West Virginia Union of Students* [undated, presumably after May 1970], A&M 2506, W.V.U. Student Anti–War Movement Collection, WVRHC; WVUS, *The North Bend Statement*, August 9, 1970, A&M 2506, W.V.U. Student Anti–War Movement Collection, WVRHC; WVUS, *Draft Constitution of the West Virginia Union of Students*, October 1970, A&M 2506, W.V.U. Student Anti–War Movement Collection, WVRHC.

Chapter 8

1. Vietnam Moratorium Committee, *They Can't Jail a Generation*, October 1969, Shaw Papers, Series III, Box 3, Folder 119, ASC; Paul Hoffman, *Moratorium: An American Protest* (New York: Tower Public Affairs, 1970); Zaroulis and Sullivan, *Who Spoke Up?*, 266–70; Gitlin, *The Sixties*, 379–80; Charles DeBenedetti, *An American Ordeal: The Antiwar Movement of the Vietnam Era* (Syracuse, NY: Syracuse University Press, 1990), 254–57.

2. West Virginia University Moratorium Committee, *An Open Letter to the Office of the President of WVU*, September 22, 1968, A&M 2828, Scott Bills Papers, WVRHC; Student Activist League, *Position Paper on the Moratorium*, October 1969, A&M 2828, Scott Bills Papers, WVRHC; David Thompson, "Student Vietnam Moratorium Committee Seeks Administration Support in Protest," *Daily Athenaeum*, September 23, 1969; David A. Milne, "Harlow Meets Moratorium Group Today," *Daily Athenaeum*, September 25, 1969; Morgantown Vietnam Moratorium Committee (MVMC), *Work for Peace*, October 1969, A&M 2828, Scott Bills Papers, WVRHC; MVMC, *Work for Peace, Moratorium Schedule*, October 1969, A&M 2828, Scott Bills Papers, WVRHC; [presumably MVMC], *This War Must be Stopped and Soon*, October 1969, A&M

2506, W.V.U. Student Anti-War Movement Collection, WVRHC; James Buchanan to Faculty, October 6, 1969, Shaw Papers, Series III, Box 3, Folder 119, ASC; "CBS News Covers WVU Moratorium Meeting," *Daily Athenaeum*, October 9, 1969.

3. Bob Berlan, "Moratorium Requests Denied as Harlow Refuses 'U' Stand," *Daily Athenaeum*, September 26, 1969; Julianne Shedd, "Moratorium Motion Tabled," *Daily Athenaeum*, October 14, 1969.

4. "Moratorium Events Schedule," *Daily Athenaeum*, October 15, 1969; Terry Belck, "Moratorium to Climax with Walk," *Morgantown Post*, October 15, 1969; Eirik Blom, "A Long, Cold Night on Oglebay Plaza," *Morgantown Post*, October 15, 1969 Al Hardesty, "Moratorium Seen as Enemy Support," *Daily Athenaeum*, October 15, 1969; Mike Fisenchia and Bob Berlan, "Rally Called 'Beautiful'," *Daily Athenaeum*, October 16, 1969; David Thompson and Mary Miello, "Townspeople Share Their Protest Views," *Daily Athenaeum*, October 16, 1969; Wendell R. Cochran, "'A Chill Wind Blew' at Square," *Dominion News* [Morgantown, WV], October 16, 1969; Ray Martin, "'Walk Extra Mile for Peace,'—Wells," *Dominion News*, October 16, 1969; Terry Belck, "'. . . And in One Moment He was Dead—DEAD!'," *Morgantown Post*, October 16, 1969; Eirik Blom, "Moratorium: There is a Place for Peaceful Dissent," *Morgantown Post*, October 16, 1969; Ray Martin, "Local Moratorium Day is Declared Success," *Dominion News*, October 17, 1969.

What is interesting is that women threw the epithets and heckled the assembled peace demonstrators. Perhaps this suggests a sense of women shaming those men who they saw as deficient in their exercise of manly duties, such as military service; in other words, challenging their manhood by mocking them. It may also indicate a need to re-evaluate assumptions about the masculine nature of pro-war support and to question whether support for the war existed more strongly amongst segments of the population that had little or no likelihood of personally seeing combat. In any case, these questions of gender lay beyond the scope of this analysis, though they suggest some interesting paths for future study.

5. David Blumberg, "Athens Peace Group Mobilizes," *Post*, September 30, 1969; "Rally, March Planned by Local Peace Group," *Post*, October 3, 1969; "Workshops, Teach-Ins Set for Moratorium," *Post*, October 9, 1969.

6. DeBenedetti, *An American Ordeal*, 256.

7. Claudia Bernard, "No Class Cancellation on Moratorium Date," *Post*, October 9, 1969.

8. Bernard, "No Class Cancellation on Moratorium Date," *Post*, October 9, 1969.

9. Bernard, "No Class Cancellation on Moratorium Day," *Post*, October 9, 1969.

10. Bill Rosen, "Demands Presented to Chancellor Posvar," *Pitt News*, February 10, 1969; "Opposition to Fleming Bill Mounting as Students, Faculty and Voters Unite," *Duquesne Duke*, March 14, 1969; Robert C. Alberts, *Pitt: The Story of the University of Pittsburgh, 1787–1987* (Pittsburgh, PA: University of Pittsburgh Press, 1986), 392–93

11. "Views of M-Day, Oct. 15," *Pittsburgh Draft Resistance Newsletter*, DWRM, Series I, Box 2, Folder 1, ASC; "Vietnam Moratorium," *Pitt News*, October 13, 1969; "Peaceful Demonstration," *Pitt News*, October 13, 1969; Kathy Joyce, "Stage Set for Wed.," *Pitt News*, October 15, 1969; Bob Ging, "Pre-Moratorium Falters," *Pitt News*, October 15, 1969.

12. Zaroulis and Sullivan, *Who Spoke Up?* 269.

13. "Views of M-Day, Oct. 15," *Pittsburgh Draft Resistance Newsletter*, DWRM, Series I, Box 2, Folder 1, ASC. *Pitt News* ran an entire edition dedicated to the Moratorium on October

17, 1969. The *Duquesne Duke* also ran several articles in both the October 17 and October 24, 1969, editions about the Moratorium. In both cases, the student papers provided images of the activities, as well as commentary from students, professors, and administrator. The front page of the October 16, 1969, edition of the *Pittsburgh Post–Gazette* contained a half–dozen stories about the Moratorium locally, nationally, and its effect in Vietnam. David R. Morrison, "The October 15 Moratorium March," November 20, 1969, DWRM, Series I, Box 1, Folder 12, ASC.

In Paul Hoffman's book, written and published only a few months after the Moratorium, he discusses the sense of deflation felt as the optimism of October 1969 confronted continued war; see Hoffman, *Moratorium*, 200–1.

14. David R. Morrison, "The October 15 Moratorium March," November 20, 1969, DWRM, Series I, Box 1, Folder 12, ASC.

15. Hoffman, *Moratorium*, 204.

16. Scott L. Bills, *Kent State/May 4: Echoes through a Decade* (Kent, OH: Kent State University Press, 1982), xi, 10–18; Kenneth J. Heineman, *Campus Wars: The Peace Movement at American State Universities in the Vietnam Era* (New York: New York University Press, 1993), 248–49; Tom Wells, *The War Within: America's Battle over Vietnam* (Berkeley, CA: University of California Press, 1994), 424–30; Terry H. Anderson, *The Movement and the Sixties: Protest in America from Greensboro to Wounded Knee* (New York: Oxford University Press, 1995), 350–53; Lytle, *America's Uncivil Wars*, 353–56; Gerard J. DeGroot, *The Sixties Unplugged: A Kaleidoscopic History of a Disorderly Decade* (Cambridge, MA: Harvard University Press, 2008), 381–35; Ken Light and Melanie Light, *What's Going On?: 1969–1974* (Light Squared Media, 2015), 178–80; Thomas M. Grace, *Kent State: Death and Dissent in the Long Sixties* (Amherst: University of Massachusetts Press, 2016); Craig S. Simpson and Gregory S. Wilson, *Above the Shots: An Oral History of the Kent State Shootings* (Kent, OH: Kent State University, 2016).

The President's Commission on Campus Unrest painstakingly reconstructs the events of that day, and the days leading up to the shootings; the commission's report details not only what happened in Kent (and, later in Jackson, MS) but also explores the underlying causes of student protests. For a detailed explanation of the day's events and images from Kent, see U.S. President's Commission on Campus Unrest, *Report of the President's Commission on Campus Unrest; Including Special Reports: The Killings at Jackson State, the Kent State Tragedy* (Washington, D.C.: Government Printing Office, 1970), 259–82, 293–410.

17. Neil Young, "Ohio," Crosby, Stills, Nash, & Young, *So Far*, Atlantic, 1970.

18. Bill Gormley, "Kent Deaths, Cambodia, Spur Protests," *Pitt News*, May 8, 1970; Virginia Joyce, "Peaceful Market Square Rally Held," *Pitt News*, May 12, 1970.

19. "Pitt Graduates 4800," *Pitt News*, May 5, 1970; Bill Gormley, "Kent Deaths, Cambodia, Spur Protests," *Pitt News*, May 8, 1970; Bob Bonn, "Klavonic and Officials Meet," *Pitt News*, May 8, 1970; Virginia Joyce, "Peaceful Market Square Rally Held," *Pitt News*, May 12, 1970; Wesley W. Posvar, Edward Eddy, Rev. Henry J. McNulty, Sister Jane Scully, Arthur M. Blum, and H. Guyford Stever, "Presidents' Stand," *Pitt News*, May 12, 1970.

20. "Peace–nik Returns," *Post*, May 4, 1970; Wm. Charles Culp, *Security Report May 4*, CSA, Campus Security Reports, OU; David Blumberg, "Massive Rally Votes to Strike," *Post*, May 5, 1970; Editorial, "On Strike," *Post*, May 5, 1970; Jackson, *Go Back, You Didn't Say "May I"*, 80.

21. Zaroulis and Sullivan, *Who Spoke Up?*, 320; Gitlin, *The Sixties*, 410; DeBenedetti, *An*

American Ordeal, 279–80; Anderson, *The Movement and the Sixties*, 350; Lytle, *America's Uncivil Wars*, 353–55; Isserman and Kazin, *America Divided*, 280.

22. David Blumberg, "'March' Set as Strike Continues," *Post*, May 6, 1970; Monica deStephano, Letter to the Editor, *Post*, May 6, 1970.

23. Wm. Charles Culp, *Security Report*, May 6, 1970, CSA, Campus Security Reports, OU; Charles R. Sowle, "Meeting of President Sowle with Representatives of the Press," May 6, 1970, Alan Geiger Papers (1965–2010) Collection, Box 32, Student Demonstrations Folder [hereafter referred to as: Geiger], OU; Andrew Alexander, "Campus in Confused State Following March, Meeting," *Post*, May 7, 1970; William Kane, "Security Report, May 7, 1970," CSA, Campus Security Reports, OU; Janis Burton, Lydia Parchment, and B.K. Perkins, Letter to the Editor, *Post*, May 8, 1970; Andrew Alexander, "'Peace' Emphasis Calms Campus," *Post*, May 8, 1970; Jackson, *Go Back, You Didn't Say "May I"*, 85–86, 88.

24. "Sowle Airs Views," *Post*, May 9, 1970; Mark Custis and Julie Snider, "Sowle May Meet Group Today," *Post*, May 9, 1970; Andrew Alexander and Eric Fralick, "Speakers for Rally Banned by University," *Post*, May 10, 1970.

25. Andrew Alexander and Eric Fralick, "Speakers for Rally Banned by University," *Post*, May 11, 1970; Editorial, "Freedom of Speech?" *Post*, May 11, 1970; Robert Guinn, William Kane, James Westfall, and Wm. Charles Culp, *Security Report*, Monday, May 11, 1970, CSA, Campus Security Reports, OU; "University Still Open—But Barely," *Post*, May 12, 1970; "Demands," *Post*, May 12, 1970.

26. Editorial, "University Still Open . . ." *Post*, May 12, 1970.

27. William Kane, Robert Guinn, James Westfall, and Wm. Charles Culp, *Security Report*, Tuesday, May, 12, 1970, CSA, Campus Security Reports, Mahn Center; Andrew Alexander, "University Struggling to Stay Open," *Post*, May 13, 1970; Wm. Charles Culp, James Westfall, Robert Guinn, and William Kane, *Security Report*, May 13, 1970, CSA, Campus Security Reports, OU; Wm. Charles Culp, James Westfall, Robert Guinn, and William Kane, *Security Report*, May 14, 1970, CSA, Campus Security Reports, OU; Andrew Alexander, "School Kept Open on 24-Hour Basis," *Post*, May 14, 1970; Wm. Charles Culp, James Westfall, Robert Guinn, and William Kane, *Security Report*, May 15, 1970, CSA, January 1970 Student Disturbances Folder, OU; Andrew Alexander, "School Closed," *Post*, May 14, 1970; Andrew Alexander, 'School Closed," *Post*, May 15, 1970; Charles R. Sowle, Press Release, May 15, 1970, CSA, Sowle Papers, OU; "Month of Campus Tension Results in Violent Closing," *Ohio University Alumni Journal*, August 1970.

28. Claude R. Sowle to University Community, May 12, 1970, Geiger, OU; Office of the President, "Important Announcement," May 12, 1970, Geiger, OU; Claude R. Sowle, "Important Announcement," May 12, 1970, Geiger, OU; Meeting of President Sowle with Representatives of the Press, May 13, 1970, Geiger, OU; Tom Price, "Sowle Suspends Seven Students," *Athens Messenger*, May 13, 1970; *Keep O. U. Open*, May 14, 1970, CSA, Student Flyers, OU; Charles R. Sowle, "Meeting of President Sowle with Representatives of the Press," May 15, 1970, Geiger, OU.

29. "Anti-war Protests, Riots Hit Campuses Over Ohio," *Post*, May 5, 1970; Lytle, *America's Uncivil Wars*, 355.

30. The *Daily Athenaeum* ran a special edition on May 7, 1970, detailing all of the events to that point; local papers also chronicled events, see Glenn Sumpter, "Troopers, WVU Stu-

dents Make Truce," *Dominion News*, May 8, 1970; "Demonstrators Stage 'Victory' Celebration," *Morgantown Post*, May 8, 1970; *Morgantown Assembly Opposes Cambodia Invasion*, May 1970, A&M 2506, W.V.U. Student Anti–war Movement Collection, WVRHC; Jeffrey A. Drobney, "Generation in Revolt: Student Dissent and Political Repression at West Virginia University," *West Virginia History* 54, no. 6 (1995), 105–22.

31. Zaroulis and Sullivan, *Who Spoke Up?*, 320; Gitlin, *The Sixties*, 410; Anderson, *The Movement and the Sixties*, 350; Isserman and Kazin, *America Divided*, 280.

32. James G. Harlow, *Statement by James G. Harlow*, May 7, 1970, Incident Week of 08 May 1970 File, WVRHC; Sumpter, "Troopers, WVU Students Make Truce," *Dominion News*, May 8, 1970; "Demonstrators Stage 'Victory' Celebration," *Morgantown Post*, May 8, 1970; Drobney, "Generation in Revolt," 105–22.

33. WVU Committee on Student Discipline, *Notice of Hearing Before West Virginia University Committee on Student Discipline*, June 3, 1970, A&M 161, Miscellaneous Controversial Literature Collection and A&M 2828, Scott Bills Papers, WVRHC; *The Case of the Morgantown 6; Or, Up Against the Wall Commie–Hippie Agitators*, summer 1970, A&M 2828, Scott Bills Papers, WVRHC; Glenn Sumpter, "Student Radicals," *Morgantown Post*, June 21, 1970; "Civil Authorities Hesitant to Prosecute Accused," *Daily Athenaeum*, July 9, 1970.

As far as outside pressure, it may not have come in a direct form of taxpayers or contractors demanding action; rather, Harlow and others may have sensed a general impression. By 1970, there was a distinct mood in the country of disgust with continued unrest on campuses and a fear that such unrest could transform into riots. Thus fearing an unexpressed backlash for failing to act, the Harlow administration may have sought pre–emptively to assuage any fears.

34. "Students' Hearing Delayed to August," *Dominion News*, June 25, 1970; "Morgantown Six Petition; No University Reply Yet," *Daily Athenaeum*, July 2, 1970; "Six Demand Hearing or Dropping of Charges," *Daily Athenaeum*, July 16, 1970; Robert C. Jenkins to Joseph C. Gluck, June 23, 1970, Incident Week File, WVRHC; Joseph C. Gluck to Robert C. Jenkins, June 23, 1970, Incident Week File, WVRHC.

35. MFP, Teach–in/Rally, June 1970, A&M 161, Miscellaneous Controversial Literature Collection and A&M 2828, Scott Bills Paper, WVRHC; MFP, Untitled Flyer [re: June 24 teach-in], June 1970, A&M 161, Miscellaneous Controversial Literature Collection and A&M 2828, Scott Bills Papers, WVRHC; MFP, *Information*, June 1970, A&M 161, Miscellaneous Controversial Literature Collection and A&M 2828, Scott Bills Paper, WVRHC; MFP, *Strike June 24!*, June 1970, A&M 161, Miscellaneous Controversial Literature Collection, WVRHC; Joseph C. Gluck to Herbert J. Rogers, July 9, 1970, Incident Week File, WVRHC; Scott Bills, Dan Bucca, Mike Weber, and Steve Stepto to James G. Harlow, July 15, 1970, Incident Week File and A&M 2828, Scott Bills Papers, WVRHC; Herbert J. Rogers to James G. Harlow, August 7, 1970, Incident Week File, WVRHC; Joseph C. Gluck to John Brisbane, August 13, 1970, Incident Week File, WVRHC; Scott Bills to Harry Heflin, August 18, 1970, Incident Week File, WVRHC; Stephen Stepto to Harry Heflin, August 18, 1970, Incident Week File, WVRHC; Joseph C. Gluck to William Miller, August 27, 1970, Incident Week File, WVRHC; Joseph C. Gluck to James G. Harlow, August 31, 1970, Incident Week File, WVRHC; James G. Harlow to Herbert J. Rogers, September 10, 1970, Incident Week File, WVRHC; Howard W. Butler to

James G. Harlow, October 6, 1970, Incident Week File, WVRHC; Howard W. Butler to James G. Harlow, October 6, 1970, Incident Week File, WVRHC.

Interestingly Bills left WVU to attend graduate school at KSU where he earned both an MA and a PhD in history.

36. Christopher L. Connery, "Marches Through the Institutions: University Activism in the Sixties and Present," *Representations* 116, 1 (Fall 2011): 88–89.

37. Edward M. Kennedy, "Senator Kennedy Testifies on Reducing the Voting Age to 18 by Statute," March 9, 1970, Edward M. Kennedy Institute for the United States Senate [https://www.emkinstitute.org], http://cfadm.3cdn.net.

38. J. Ford Huffman, "Analysis of Voting Age," *Daily Athenaeum*, January 27, 1971; Lee Eils, "Voter Registration Day Draws 1244 Students," *Pitt News*, March 8, 1971; "Senate Ratifies 18-Year-Old Vote," *Daily Athenaeum*, April 29, 1971; Richard M. Nixon, "Statement About Ratification of the 26th Amendment to the Constitution – June 30, 1971," in *Public Papers of the Presidents of the United States: Richard Nixon; Containing the Public Messages, Speeches, and Statements of the President; 1971* (Washington, D.C.: United States Government Printing Office, 1972), 793; "Student Vote Impact Argued," *Pitt News*, September 10, 1971; Paul Allen Beck, "Impact of Youth Vote '72 Probed," *Pitt News*, October 8, 1971; Wendell W. Cultice, *Youth's Battle for the Ballot: A History of Voting Age in America* (Santa Barbara, CA: Greenwood Press, 1992); Anderson, *The Movement and the Sixties*, 392–404; Glenn H. Utter, *Youth and Political Participation: A Reference Handbook* (Santa Barbara, CA: ABC-CLIO, 2011), 20–27; Eric S. Fish, "The Twenty-Sixth Amendment Enforcement Power," *The Yale Law Journal* 121, no. 5 (March 2012), 1182–95.

39. Joshua M. Glasser, *The Eighteen–Day Running Mate: McGovern, Eagleton, and a Campaign in Crisis* (New Haven, CT: Yale University Press, 2012), 286–93.

40. Sharon Sexton, "Survey Shows Student Election Apathy," *Pitt News*, November 6, 1972.

41. "Students Deem Voter's Registration Difficult," *Daily Athenaeum*, September 3, 1971; "Student Vote Troubles," *Daily Athenaeum*, September 8, 1971; "Pa. Attorney Gen. Rules Campus Vote for Students," *Pitt News*, September 13, 1971; Johanna Fisher, "Rejected Voters to Appeal," *Daily Athenaeum*, September 21, 1971; "Browning on Student Vote," *Daily Athenaeum*, September 22, 1971; Editorial, "Electoral Equity," *Post*, September 22, 1971; "Rockefeller Disappointed in Young Vote," *Daily Athenaeum*, November 5, 1971; Bruce Estes, "Residency Questioned," *Post*, January 13, 1972; P.J. Bednarski, "Voter Poll Shows Student Apathy; Only 18 Per Cent Return Survey," *Post*, February 14, 1972; "Voter Registration Said Slim," *Daily Athenaeum*, February 17, 1972; Editorial, "Voting in Athens," *Post*, February 29, 1972; "Eagleton Discloses Past," *Daily Athenaeum*, July 27, 1972; Sharon Sexton, "Survey Shows Student Election Apathy," *Pitt News*, November 6, 1972; Anderson, *The Movement and the Sixties*, 399–404; Isserman and Kazin, *America Divided*, 292; Utter, *Youth and Political Participation*, 27.

42. Editorial, "Mock Convention," *Post*, October 4, 1971.

43. Bill Choyke, "Police Arrest 80 in Lindley Takeover," *Post*, May 10, 1972; "Campus Protests Peaceful Through Meetings, March," *Post*, May 11, 1972; P.J. Bednarski, "Pre–Hearing Slated to Discuss HB 1219," *Post*, May 11, 1972; Editorial, "Grave Mistake. . ." *Post*, May 11, 1972; Editorial, ". . . No Help Either," *Post*, May 11, 1972; Dave Gossett, "Court Processes

Protesters; All Enter Plea for Continuance," *Post*, May 11, 1972; "Non–Court Hearings Under Way for 77 Protestors," *Athens Messenger*, May 11, 1972; People's Coalition for Peace and Justice, *List of Demands*, May 12, 1972, CSA, Miscellaneous Folder, OU.

44. Paul M. Scott, "House Bill 1219: A Study," *Akron Law Review* 5, no. 1 (Winter 1972), 93–116; Bill Choyke and Dave Gossett, "Pre-Hearings Held, Rally Planned Today," *Post*, May 12, 1972; Editorial, "React Now," *Post*, May 12, 1972; "Demonstrators' Hearings Begin," *Post*, May 15, 1972; P.J. Bednarski, "SGB Supports Charge Drop," *Post*, May 15, 1972; Art Silverman, "ACLU Challenges 1219 Constitutionality," *Post*, May 17, 1972; Editorial, "Squelching Effect," *Post*, May 17, 1972; Steven D. Fought, "Civil Disobedience," *Post*, May 17, 1972; Richard Kaser, "ACLU Explains Stand on Suit," *Athens Messenger*, May 17, 1972; Tom Price, "Sowle Asks 1219 Hearings Delay Pending Ruling," *Athens Messenger*, May 17, 1972; Bill Choyke and Ira Fine, "Referee Halts Bill Hearings, Awaits Ruling on Injunction," *Post*, May 18, 1972; Editorial, "Banish Banishment," *Post*, May 19, 1972; Neal Pattison, "Court Hearings Begin," *Post*, May 30, 1972; "Hearing on 1219 Set," *Athens Messenger*, May 30, 1972; "Campus Disruption Case Slated for Trial Wednesday," *Athens Messenger*, September 21, 1972; "Athens 75 Jury Selection Starts; Sheeter Refuses Delay Request," *Post*, September 27, 1972; Editorial, "Athens 75," *Post*, September 27, 1972; Neal Pattison, "Burns Battles with Defense as Athens 75 Trials Proceed," *Post*, September 28, 1972; Herb Amey, "Sowle Recalls 1970 Riots in Campus Disruption Trial," *Athens Messenger*, September 28, 1972; Dave Gossett, "Sowle Testifies in Second Day of Athens 75 Trial," *Post*, September 29, 1972; Herb Amey, "Defense Rests in Protest Trial," *Athens Messenger*, September 29, 1972; Dave Gossett, "Smith Verdict Appeal Expected, Second Trial Begins Wednesday," *Post*, October 2, 1972; Herb Amey, "Jury Selection Begins Again," *Athens Messenger*, October 4, 1972; Dave Gossett, "Athens 75 Trials Proceed Amid Legal Confusion," *Post*, October 5, 1972; Randy Rieland, "Sowle Offers Outlet for 1219 Convictions," *Post*, October 5, 1972; Editorial, "Loopholes in HB 1219," *Post*, October 5, 1972; Dave Gossett, "Defendants Reject Charge Reduction Proposal," *Post*, October 6, 1972; Dave Gossett, "Schwartz Found Guilty on Non–HB 1219 Charge," *Post*, October 9, 1972; "Hunt Deal Could Bring Early End to '75' Trials," *Post*, October 18, 1972; Herb Amey, "Break Possible in Trials," *Athens Messenger*, October 18, 1972; "Hunt Pleads Guilt to Trespass; Prosecution Drops 1219 Charge," *Post*, October 19, 1972; "Guilty Pleas Entered in Athens 75 Trials," *Post*, October 26, 1972; Herb Amey, "Athens 77: The End is In Sight," *Athens Messenger*, November 12, 1972.

45. Gordon L. Weil, *The Long Shot: George McGovern Runs for President* (New York: W. W. Norton & Company, 1973), 156–94; Zaroulis and Sullivan, *Who Spoke Up?*, 390; Bruce Miroff, *The Liberals' Moment: The McGovern Insurgency and the Identity Crisis of the Democratic Party* (Lawrence, KS: University Press of Kansas, 2007), 89–97; Isserman and Kazin, *America Divided*, 292; Glasser, *The Eighteen–Day Running Mate*, 286–93.

46. Arthur Pearl, *Landslide: The How & Why of Nixon's Victory* (Secaucus, NJ: The Citadel Press, 1973); Miroff, *The Liberals' Moment*, 249–59; Glasser, *The Eighteen–Day Running Mate*, 286; Ken Hughes, *Fatal Politics: The Nixon Tapes, the Vietnam War, and the Casualties of Reelection* (Charlottesville, VA: University of Virginia Press, 2015), 81–83, 143–45.

47. "Rockefeller Disappointed in Young Vote," *Daily Athenaeum*, November 5, 1971; Bednarski, "Voter Poll Shows Student Apathy; Only 18 Percent Return Survey," *Post*, February

14, 1972; Editorial, "George McGovern," *Post*, April 6, 1972; "McGovern Well-Received at Pittsburgh Street Rally," *Daily Athenaeum*, September 14, 1972; Jamie Kirkwood, "McGovern, Kennedy Rally Crowd in Market Square," *Pitt News*, September 15, 1972; Ohio University McGovern Committee, *Register to Vote in Athens*, September 26, 1972, CSA, Student Voting Flyers Folder, OU; "McGovern, Rockefeller Lead Opponents in Student Poll," *Daily Athenaeum*, September 29, 1972; Editorial, "New Voters," *Post*, October 11, 1972; "McGovern Supporters Plan Canvasses," *Daily Athenaeum*, October 12, 1972; Rich Cerilli, "Student Legislature Endorses McGovern," *Daily Athenaeum*, October 17, 1972; Editorial, "McGovern for President," *Post*, October 26, 1972; "McGovern Workers Push on Despite Polls," *Post*, November 6, 1972; Ron Brown and Jim Prozzi, "Let Us be Blunt About McGovern," *Pitt News*, November 6, 1972; "Polls See McGovern Doom," *Post*, November 7, 1972; Anderson, *The Movement and the Sixties*, 396, 401, 404; Miroff, *The Liberals' Moment*, 19–24.

Conclusion

1. Untitled Flyer, May 17, 1971, CSA, Student Flyers, OU.

2. *Athens Justice*, May 17, 1971, CSA, Kim Levitch—Charles Cochran Incident Folder, [hereafter referred to as: Levitch], OU; *Protest the Police State*, May 17, 1971, CSA, Levitch, OU; "Draft Protester Free on Bond," *Athens Messenger*, May 18, 1971.

3. *Protest the Police State*, May 17, 1971, CSA, Levitch, OU.

4. See Chapter Eight

5. Thomas Kiffmeyer, *Reformers to Radicals: The Appalachian Volunteers and the War on Poverty* (Lexington, KY: University Press of Kentucky, 2008).

6. Kenneth J. Heineman, *Campus Wars: The Peace Movement at American State Universities in the Vietnam Era* (New York: New York University Press, 1992); Marc J. Gilbert, *The Vietnam War on Campus: Other Voice, More Distant Drums* (New York: Praeger, 2000); Robbie Lieberman, *Prairie Power: Voices of 1960s Midwestern Protest* (Columbia, MO: University of Missouri Press, 2004); Andrew Grose, "Voices of Southern Protest during the Vietnam War Era: The University of South Carolina as a Case Study," *Peace & Change* 32, 2 (April 2007): 153–67.

7. "National Day of Draft Resistance," *Tartan*, December 6, 1967; John Caywood, "Ministry Peace Service Finds Probable Arson Amidst 'Friendliness'," *Pitt News*, December 6, 1967; "Two Youths Turn in Draft Cards," *Morgantown Post*, April 3, 1968; Evelyn Ryan, "Draft Cards Sent Back to Hershey in Protest," *Daily Athenaeum*, April 4, 1968.

8. Frank Couvares, "Obligation to Dissent," *Pitt News*, June 13, 1966.

9. John T. Nixon, Letter to the Editor, *Post*, April 6, 1967.

10. Martin Coy, "Osage Homes Pilot Project," *Daily Athenaeum*, January 17, 1967; Sue Serenlla, "SDS Denounces Vietnam Conflict," *Daily Athenaeum*, February 28, 1967; "Program May Cause SDS Demonstration," *Daily Athenaeum*, March 10, 1967; "SDS Petition to Place Barbers 'Under Fire'," *Daily Athenaeum*, March 15, 1967; "Student Cabinet Offers SDS Representative," *Daily Athenaeum*, March 21, 1967; Joan O'Connor, "Stump Speaker States SDS Stand on War," *Daily Athenaeum*, April 13, 1967; Allan Brick, *Shaw as Vietnam Volunteer*, August 28, 1967, Shaw Papers, Series III: Organizations, AFSC—Peace Education Committee, 1967–1968, Box 1, Folder 29, ASC; Harry Shaw to National Mobilization Committee,

September 25, 1967, Shaw Papers, Series III, Box 1, Folder 29, ASC; Letter, Harry Shaw to Central Committee for Conscientious Objection, September 27, 1967, Shaw Papers, Series III, Box 1, Folder 29, ASC; "Biographical Sketch," Shaw Papers, Series I: Harry F. Shaw, Jr. Personal Files, Biographical Sketch and Bus/Airline Ticket Receipts, Box 1, Folder 1, ASC; David Morrison to Harry Shaw, March 22, 1968, Shaw Papers, Series III: Organizations, Pittsburgh Draft Information Center, (United Oakland Ministry) correspondence, leaflets, and pamphlets regarding the draft and draft counseling, 1968, Box 2, Folder 84, ASC; Evelyn Ryan, "Draft Cards Sent Back to Hershey in Protest," *Daily Athenaeum*, April 4, 1968; Harry F. Shaw, *Letter of Resistance to the Selective Service*, April 1968, A&M 2828, Scott Bills Papers, WVRHC.

Bibliography

Primary Sources

Archives

Ohio University

Robert E. and Jean R. Mahn Center for Archives and Special Collections, Ohio University, Athens, OH

Alan Geiger Papers (1965–2010)

James J. Whalen, Executive Vice-President Records

Collection on Student Activism

University of Pittsburgh

Archives of Industrial Society, University of Pittsburgh, Pittsburgh, PA

Chancellor of the University of Pittsburgh, David H. Kurtzman (Acting), Administrative Files

Draft and War Resistance Movement Records, Pittsburgh, Pa., 1966–1972

Harry F. Shaw, Jr. Papers

Peace and Freedom Center of Pittsburgh Records

Young Friends of North America, Committee on Conscription Records

Swarthmore College

Swarthmore College Peace Collection, Swarthmore College, Swarthmore, PA

David R. Morrison Papers

West Virginia University

West Virginia and Regional History Collection, West Virginia University, Morgantown, WV

Incident of Week 08 May 1970 File

Miscellaneous Controversial Literature Collection

Scott Bills Papers

WVU Discrimination Petition

WVU Office of Student Life Collection

W.V.U. Student Anti-War Movement Collection

Music

Boyce, Tommy, and Bobby Hart. "(Theme from) The Monkees." The Monkees. *The Monkees*. Colgems. 1967.

Young, Neil. "Ohio." Crosby, Stills, Nash, & Young. *So Far*. Atlantic. 1970.

Newspapers

Athens Messenger
Boston Globe
Chillicothe Gazette [Chillicothe, OH]
Daily Athenaeum [Morgantown, WV]
Dominion News [Morgantown, WV]
Duquesne Duke [Pittsburgh, PA]
Morgantown Post
New York Times
Ohio University Alumni Journal
Pitt News [Pittsburgh, PA]
Pittsburgh Peace and Freedom News
Pittsburgh Point
Pittsburgh Post-Gazette
Pittsburgh Press
Post [Athens, OH]
Spokane-Review, The [Spokane, WA]
Star-News [Wilmington, NC]
Tartan [Pittsburgh, PA]
University Bulletin [Morgantown, WV]

Published Primary

"A Young $10 Billion Power: The US Teen-age Consumer Has Become a major Factor in the Nation's Economy." *Life*, August 31, 1959, 78–84.

Appalachian Regional Commission. "Subregions of Appalachia." Accessed on February 10, 2013. http://www.arc.gov.

Auburn, Norman P. *The First Hundred Years Are the Hardest: The Story of The University of Akron*. New York: Newcomen Society in North America, 1970.

Berger, Ed, Larry Flatley, John Frisch, Mayda Gottlieb, Judy Haisley, Peter Karsten, Larry Rexton, and William Worrest. "ROTC, Mylai and the Volunteer Army." *Foreign Policy*, 2 (Spring 1971): 135–60.

Bloom, Alexander, and Wini Breines, eds. *"Takin' it to the Streets": A Sixties Reader*. New York: Oxford University Press, 2003.

Capp, Glenn R., ed. *The Great Society: A Sourcebook of Speeches*. Belmont, CA: Dickenson Publishing, 1967.

Caudill, Harry M. *Night Comes to the Cumberlands: A Biography of a Depressed Area.* Boston, MA: Little, Brown, and Co., 1963.

Central Committee for Conscientious Objection. *CCCO Draft Counselor's Manual.* 1972.

Committee on Un-American Activities, U.S. House of Representatives. *Communist Origin and Manipulation of Vietnam Wek (April 8–15, 1967).* 90th Congress, 1st session. March 31, 1967.

DeNicola, Daniel, email message to author, 6/1/2015.

Farber, Jerry. *The Students Nigger: Essays and Stories.* New York: Pocket Books, 1970.

Ferber, Michael, and Staughton Lynd. *The Resistance.* New York: Beacon Press, 1971.

Ford, Thomas R., ed. *The Southern Appalachian Region: A Survey.* Lexington, KY: University of Kentucky Press, 1962.

Friedman, John. "Poor Regions and Poor Nations: Perspectives on the Problem of Appalachia." *Southern Economic Journal* 32, 4 (April 1966): 165–75.

Fulbright, J. William. *The Arrogance of Power.* New York: Vintage Books, 1966.

Goertzel, Ted, and Acco Hengst. "The Military Socialization of University Students." *Social Problems* 19, 2 (Autumn 1971): 258–67.

Hoffman, Paul. *Moratorium: An American Protest.* New York: Tower Public Affairs, 1970.

Holmes, Robert L. "University Neutrality and ROTC." *Ethics* 83, 3 (April 1973): 177–95.

Horowitz, Irving Louis, and William H. Friedland. *The Knowledge Factory: Student Power and Academic Politics in America.* Chicago, IL: Aldine Publishing, 1970.

Jackson, Thomas. *Go Back, You Didn't Say "May I": The Diary of a Young Priest.* New York: Seabury Press, 1974.

Johnson, Lyndon B. "Remarks in Athens at Ohio University, May 7, 1964." http://presidency.uscb.edu.

Keniston, Kenneth. "Youth Culture as Enforced Alienation." In *The Cult of Youth in Middle-Class America*, 85–87. Edited by Richard L. Rapson. Lexington, MA: D.C. Heath and Company, 1971.

Kennedy, Edward M. Press Release. "Senator Kennedy Testifies on Reducing the Voting Age to 18 by Statute," March 9, 1970. Edward M. Kennedy Institute for the United States Senate. http://cfadm.3cdn.net.

Kennedy, Robert F. "Address by Attorney General Robert F. Kennedy to a Joint Meeting of the Kanawha County Parent-Teachers Council and Members of Action for Appalachian Youth, Inc." Charleston, West Virginia, April 29, 1965. https://www.justice.gov.

———. "Day of Affirmation—South Africa." University of Capetown, South Africa, June 6, 1966. http://rfkcenter.org.

Kerr, Clark. *The Uses of the University.* Fifth Edition. Cambridge, MA: Harvard University Press, 2001.

Knipfing, Vincent P. "Attitudes of Seniors Toward the ROTC Program at a State University." Master's Thesis, Ohio University, 1966.

Luria, S. E., and Zella Luria. "The Role of the University: Ivory Tower, Service Station, or Frontier Post?" In *The Embattled University*, edited by Stephen R. Graubard and Gino A. Ballotti, 75–83. New York: George Braziller, 1970.

Ohio University. *Ohio University Bulletin: For the Biennium, 1958–1960*. Athens, OH: Ohio University, 1958. http://www.archive.org.

Ohio University. *Ohio University Bulletin: For the Biennium, 1964–1966*. Athens, OH: Ohio University, 1964. http://www.archive.org.

Ohio University. *Ohio University Bulletin: General Catalog Issue 1966–1967*. Athens, OH: Ohio University Printing Office, 1966.

Ohio Valley Region Peace Conference. *Campus Handbook for Vietnam Week*. Cleveland, OH: Regional Coordinating Committee for the Spring Mobilization, 1967.

Mahn, Robert E. *The Presidency of Claude R. Sowle: August 1, 1969 to September 1, 1974*. Volume II. Athens, OH: Ohio University Libraries, 2007.

McNeal, James U. *Children as Consumers*. Austin, TX: Bureau of Business Research University of Texas, 1964.

Nixon, John T. Email correspondence, February 8–9, 2018.

Nixon, Richard M. "Executive Order 11497—Amending the Selective Service Regulation to Prescribe Random Selection." November 26, 1969. http://www.presidency.ucsb.edu.

———. "Statement About the Ratification of the 26th Amendment to the Constitution—June 30, 1971." In *Public Papers of the Presidents of the United States: Richard Nixon; Containing the Public Messages, Speeches, and Statements of the President; 1971*. Washington, DC: United States Government Printing Office, 1972.

Pearl, Arthur. *Landslide: The How & Why of Nixon's Victory*. Secaucus, NJ: The Citadel Press, 1973.

President's Appalachian Regional Commission. *Appalachia: A Report By the President's Appalachian Regional Commission, 1964*. Washington, D.C.: Government Printing Office, 1964.

Ruppen, Diane, ed. *The Owl [1966]: The Annual of the University of Pittsburgh*. Pittsburgh, PA: University of Pittsburgh Press, 1966. http://digital.library.pitt.edu.

Scott, Paul M. "House Bill 1219: A Study." *Akron Law Review* 5, 1 (Winter 1972): 93–116.

Selective Service System. "Induction Statistics." https://www.sss.gov.

Selective Service System. "The Vietnam Lotteries." https://www.sss.gov.

Shaw, Paul C. "The Urban University Student: A Political Profile." *Research in Higher Education* 2, 1 (March 1974): 65–79.

Special Committee on ROTC Program and George C. S. Benson. *Report of the Special Committee on ROTC to the Secretary of Defense*. Washington, D.C.: U.S. Department of Defense, 1969.

"Studs Terkel on 'The Good War'," *NBC Today Show*. New York: NBC Universal, October 22, 1984. https://archives.nbclearn.com.

Thoreau, Henry David. "Civil Disobedience." In *Walden & Civil Disobedience*. New York: Barnes & Noble Classics, 2003.

Tunley, Roul. "The Strange Case of West Virginia." *The Saturday Evening Post*, February 6, 1960, 19–20, 64–66.

U.S. Census of Population, 1960: Vol. I, Characteristics of the Population, Number of Inhabitants, General Population Characteristics, General Social and Economic Characteristics, and Detailed Characteristics: Part I, United States Summary. Washington, D.C.: Government Printing Office, 1962.

U.S. Census of Population, 1970: Vol. I, Characteristics of the Population: Part 1, United States Summary: Section 1. Washington, D.C.: Government Printing Office, 1973.

U.S. President's Commission on Campus Unrest. *The Report of the President's Commission on Campus Unrest; Including Special Reports: The Killings at Jackson State, the Kent State Tragedies.* Washington, D.C.: Government Printing Office, 1970.

von Hoffman, Nicholas. *The Multiversity: A Personal Report of What Happens to Today's Students at American Universities.* New York: Holt, Rinehart, and Winston, 1966.

Wagner, Patricia, ed. *The Owl [1968]: The Annual of the University of Pittsburgh.* Pittsburgh, PA: University of Pittsburgh Press, 1968. Available from: http://digital .library.pitt.edu/cgi-bin/t/text/text-idx?c=pittyearbooks&idno=1968e49702. (Accessed on January 19, 2010).

Weil, Gordon L. *The Long Shot: George McGovern Runs for President.* New York: W. W. Norton & Company, 1973.

Weller, Jack E. *Yesterday's People: Life in Contemporary Appalachia.* Lexington, KY: University of Kentucky Press, 1965.

Secondary Sources

Books/Articles

Alberts, Robert C. *Pitt: The Story of the University of Pittsburgh, 1787–1987.* Pittsburgh, PA: University of Pittsburgh Press, 1986.

Altschuler, Glenn C., and Stuart M. Blumin. *The GI Bill: A New Deal for Veterans.* New York: Oxford University Press, 2009.

Anderson, Benedict. *Imagined Communities: Reflections on the Origins and Spread of Nationalism.* New York: Verso, 1991.

Anderson, Terry H. *The Movement and the Sixties: Protest in America from Greensboro to Wounded Knee.* New York: Oxford University Press, 1995.

Andrew, III, John A. *The Other Side of the Sixties: Young Americans for Freedom and the Rise of Conservative Politics.* New Brunswick, NJ: Rutgers University Press, 1997.

Bailey, Beth. *Sex in the Heartland.* Cambridge, MA: Harvard University Press, 1999.

Batteau, Allen. *The Invention of Appalachia*. Tucson, AZ: University of Arizona Press, 1990.

Billings, Dwight B., and Kathleen M. Blee. *The Road to Poverty: The Making of Wealth and Hardship in Appalachia*. New York: Cambridge University Press, 2000.

Billingsley, William J. *Communists on Campus: Race, Politics, and the Public University in Sixties North Carolina*. Athens, GA: University of Georgia Press, 1999.

Bills, Scott L. *Kent State/May 4: Echoes through a Decade*. Kent, OH: Kent State University Press, 1982.

Biondi, Martha. *To Stand and Fight: The Struggle for Civil Rights in Postwar New York City*. Cambridge, MA: Harvard University Press, 2003.

Blight, David W. *Race and Reunion: The Civil War in American Memory*. Cambridge, MA: Belknap Press of Harvard University Press, 2001.

Brooks, Victor D. *Boomers: The Cold War Generation Grows Up*. Chicago: Ivan R. Dee, 2009.

Burns, Stewart. *Social Movements of the 1960s: Searching for Democracy*. Boston, MA: Twayne Publishers, 1990.

Caute, David. *The Year of the Barricades: A Journey through 1968*. New York: Harper & Row, 1988.

Centers for Disease Central and Prevention. "Vital Statistics of the United States, 2003, Volume I, Natality." Table I-I "Live Births, Birth Rates, and Fertility Rates, by Race: United States, 1909–2003." Washington, D.C.: Government Printing Officer, 2003.

Chapman, Berlin Basil. *West Virginia University: A Memoir*. Parsons, WV: McClain Publishing, 1975.

Chomsky, Noam, Laura Nader, Immanuel Wallerstein, R. C. Lewontin, Richard Ohmann, Ira Katznelson, David Montgomery, Ray Siver, and Howard Zinn, eds. *The Cold War & the University: Toward an Intellectual History of the Postwar Years*. New York: New Press, 1997.

Clark, Daniel A. "'The Two Joes Meet—Joe College, Joe Veteran': The G.I. Bill, College Education, and Postwar American Culture." *History of Education Quarterly* 38, 2 (Summer 1998): 165–89.

Cohen, Lizabeth. *A Consumer's Republic: The Politics of Mass Consumption in Postwar America*. New York: Alfred A. Knopf, 2003.

Cohen, Michael A. *American Maelstrom: The 1968 Election and the Politics of Division*. New York: Oxford University Press, 2016.

Cohen, Robert. *When the Old Left was Young: Student Radicals and America's First Mass Student Movement, 1929–1941.* New York: Oxford University Press, 1993.

Colby, Sandra L. and Jennifer M. Ortman. *The Baby Boom Cohort in the United States: 2012 to 2060*. Current Population Reports P25-1141. Washington, D.C.: U.S. Census Bureau, 2014.

Connery, Christopher L. "Marches Through the Institutions: University Activism in the Sixties and Present." *Representations* 116, 1 (Fall 2011): 88–101.

Coontz, Stephanie. *The War We Never Were: American Families and the Nostalgia Trap*. New York: Basic Books, 2000.

———. *A Strange Stirring: The Feminine Mystique and American Women at the Dawn of the 1960s*. New York: Basic Books, 2012.

Countryman, Matthew J. *Up South: Civil Rights and Black Power in Philadelphia*. Philadelphia, PA: University of Pennsylvania Press, 2007.

Cultice, Wendell W. *Youth's Battle for the Ballot: A History of Voting Age in America*. Santa Barbara, CA: Greenwood Press, 1992.

Dallek, Robert. *Flawed Giant: Lyndon Johnson and His Times, 1961–1973*. New York: Oxford University Press, 1998.

Dawson, James. *WVU: An Early Portrait*. Morgantown, WV: 1971.

DeBenedetti, Charles. "Peace History, in the American Manner." *History Teacher* 18, 1 (November 1984): 75–110.

———. *An American Ordeal: The Antiwar Movement of the Vietnam Era*. Syracuse, NY: Syracuse University Press, 1990.

DeGroot, Gerard J. *The Sixties Unplugged: A Kaleidoscopic History of a Disorderly Decade*. Cambridge, MA: Harvard University Press, 2008.

Diamond, Sigmund. *Compromise Campus: The Collaboration of Universities with the Intelligence Community, 1945–1955*. New York: Oxford University Press, 1992.

Dittmer, John. *Local People: The Struggle for Civil Rights in Mississippi*. Urbana, IL: University of Illinois Press, 1994.

Doenecke, Justus. *Storm on the Horizon: The Challenge to American Intervention, 1939–1941*. Lanham, MD: Rowman & Littlefield, 2000.

Douglas, J. William. *The School of Physical Education at West Virginia University: An Historical Perspective, 1891–1999*. Morgantown, WV: West Virginia University School of Physical Education, 2000).

Drake, Richard B. *A History of Appalachia*. Lexington, KY: University Press of Kentucky, 2001.

Drobney, Jeffrey A. "A Generation in Revolt: Student Dissent and Political Repression at West Virginia University." *West Virginia History* 54, 6 (1995): 105–22.

Dudziak, Mary L. *Cold War Civil Rights: Race and the Image of American Democracy*. Princeton, NJ: Princeton University Press, 2000.

Eagan, Eileen. *Class, Culture, and the Classroom: The Student Peace Movement of the 1930s*. Philadelphia, PA: Temple University Press, 1981.

Eller, Ronald D. *Miners, Millhands, and Mountaineers: Industrialization of the Appalachian South, 1880–1930*. Knoxville, TN: University of Tennessee Press, 1982.

———. *Uneven Ground: Appalachia since 1945*. Lexington, KY: University Press of Kentucky, 2008.

Ergood, Bruce, and Bruce E. Kuhre, eds. *Appalachia: Social Context Past and Present*. Second Edition. Dubuque, IA: Kendall/Hunt, 1983.

Fairclough, Adam. *Better Day Coming: Blacks and Equality, 1890–2000*. New York: Penguin Books, 2001.

Fenton, Edwin. *Carnegie Mellon, 1900–2000: A Centennial History*. Pittsburgh, PA: Carnegie Mellon University Press, 2000.

Fish, Eric S. "The Twenty-Sixth Amendment Enforcement Power." *The Yale Law Journal* 121, 5 (March 2012): 1182–95.

Flynn, George Q. *The Draft, 1940–1973*. Lawrence, KS: University Press of Kansas, 1993.

Foley, Michael S. *Confronting the War Machine: Draft Resistance during the Vietnam War*. Chapel Hill, NC: University of North Carolina Press, 2004.

Friedland, Michael B. *Lift Up Your Voice Like a Trumpet: White Clergy and the Civil Rights and Antiwar Movement, 1954–1973*. Chapel Hill, NC: University of North Carolina Press, 1998.

Gaventa, John. *Power and Powerlessness: Quiescence and Rebellion in an Appalachian Valley*. Urbana, IL: University of Illinois Press, 1980.

Gilbert, Marc J., ed. *The Vietnam War on Campus: Other Voices, More Distant Drums*. New York: Praeger, 2000.

Giroux, Henry A. *The University in Chains: Confronting the Military-Industrial-Academic Complex*. Boulder, CO: Paradigm, 2007.

Gitlin, Todd. *The Sixties: Years of Hope, Days of Rage*. Revised Edition. New York: Bantam Books, 1993.

Glasser, Joshua M. *The Eighteen-Day Running Mate: McGovern, Eagleton, and a Campaign in Crisis*. New Haven, CT: Yale University Press, 2012.

Grace, Thomas M. *Kent State: Death and Dissent in the Long Sixties*. Amherst, MA: University of Massachusetts Press, 2016.

Graham, Hugh Davis, and Nancy Diamond. *The Rise of American Research Universities: Elites and Challenges in the Postwar Era*. Baltimore, MD: Johns Hopkins University Press, 1997.

Grieve, Victoria M. *Little Cold Warriors: American Childhood in the 1950s*. New York: Oxford University Press, 2018.

Grose, Andrew. "Voices of Southern Protest during the Vietnam War Era: The University of South Carolina as a Case Study." *Peace & Change* 32, 2 (April 2007): 153–67.

Hall, Simon. *Peace and Freedom: The Civil Rights and Antiwar Movements in the 1960s*. Philadelphia, PA: University of Pennsylvania Press, 2005.

———. *Rethinking the American Anti-War Movement*. New York: Routledge, 2012.

Halstead, Fred. *Out Now! A Participant's Account of the American Movement Against the Vietnam War*. New York: Monad Press, 1978.

Harkins, Anthony, and Meredith McCarroll, eds. *Appalachian Reckoning: A Region Responds to* Hillbilly Elegy. Morgantown, WV: West Virginia University Press, 2019.

Hayden, Tom. *Reunion: A Memoir*. New York: Random House, 1988.

Haynes, Ada F. *Poverty in Central Appalachia: Underdevelopment and Exploitation*. New York: Garland Publishing, 1997.

Heater, Derek. *What is Citizenship?* Malden, MA: Polity Press, 1999.

Heineman, Kenneth J. *Campus Wars: The Peace Movement of American State Universities in the Vietnam Era*. New York: New York University Press, 1992.

Herring, George C. *America's Longest War: The United States and Vietnam, 1950–1975*. Fourth Edition. Boston, MA: McGraw Hill, 2002.

Hill, Lance. *The Deacons for Defense: Armed Resistance and the Civil Rights Movement*. Chapel Hill, NC: University of North Carolina Press, 2004.

Hollow, Betty. *Ohio University, 1804–2004: The Spirit of a Singular Place*. Athens, OH: Ohio University Press, 2003.

Hoover, Thomas N. *The History of Ohio University*. Athens, OH: Ohio University Press, 1954.

Horowitz, Helen Lefkowitz. *Campus Life: Undergraduate Cultures from the End of the Eighteenth Century to the Present*. New York: Alfred A. Knopf, 1987.

Howe, Barbara J. *Tales from the Tower: If Woodburn Hall Could Speak*. Morgantown, WV: West Virginia University Eberley College of Arts and Sciences, 1997.

Hughes, Ken. *Fatal Politics: The Nixon Tapes, the Vietnam War, and the Casualties of Reelection*. Charlottesville, VA: University of Virginia Press, 2015.

Isserman, Maurice. *If I Had a Hammer . . . : The Death of the Old Left and the Birth of the New Left*. New York: Basic Books, 1987.

Isserman, Maurice, and Michael Kazin. *America Divided: The Civil War of the 1960s*. Third Edition. New York: Oxford University Press, 2008.

Jackson, Kenneth T. *Crabgrass Frontiers: The Suburbanization of the United States*. New York: Oxford University Press, 1985.

Jeffreys-Jones, Rhodri. *Peace Now! American Society and the Ending of the Vietnam War*. New Haven, CT: Yale University Press, 1999.

Kennedy, David M. *Freedom from Fear: The American People in Depression and War, 1929–1945*. New York: Oxford University Press, 1999.

Kennett, Lee. *G.I.: The American Soldier in World War II*. New York: Charles Scribners' Sons, 1987.

Kiffmeyer, Thomas. "From Self-Help to Sedition: The Appalachian Volunteers in Eastern Kentucky, 1964–1970." *Journal of Southern History* 64, 1 (February 1998): 65–94.

———. *Reformers to Radicals: The Appalachian Volunteers and the War on Poverty.* Lexington, KY: University Press of Kentucky, 2008.

———. "Looking Back to the City in the Hills: The Council of the Southern Mountains and a Longer View of the War on Poverty in the Appalachian South, 1913-1970." In *The War on Poverty: A New Grassroots History, 1964–1980*, edited by Annelise Orlick and Lisa Gayle Hazirjian, 359–86. Athens, GA: University of Georgia Press, 2011.

Klatch, Rebecca E. *A Generation Divided: The New Left, the New Right, and the 1960s.* Berkeley, CA: University of California Press, 1999.

Knepper, George W. *New Lamps for Old: One Hundred Years of Urban Education at The University of Akron.* Akron, OH: University of Akron Press, 1970.

Kohn, Stephen M. *Jailed for Peace: The History of American Draft Law Violators, 1658–1985.* Westport, CT: Greenwood Press, 1986.

Kurlansky, Mark. *1968: The Year That Rocked the World.* New York: Random House, 2005.

Latham, Michael E. *Modernization as Ideology: American Social Science and "Nation Building" in the Kennedy Era.* Chapel Hill, NC: University of North Carolina Press, 2000.

Ledbetter, James. *Unwarranted Influence: Dwight D. Eisenhower and the Military-Industrial Complex.* New Haven, CT: Yale University Press, 2011.

Lewis, Lionel S. *Cold War on Campus: A Study of the Politics of Organizational Control.* New Brunswick, NJ: Transaction Books, 1988.

Lewis, Ronald L. *Aspiring to Greatness: West Virginia University since World War II.* Morgantown, WV: West Virginia University Press, 2013.

Lieberman, Robbie. *Prairie Power: Voices of 1960s Midwestern Protest.* Columbia, MO: University of Missouri Press, 2004.

Light, Ken, and Melanie Light. *What's Going On?: 1969–1974.* Light Squared Media, 2015.

Lyons, Paul. *New Left, New Right, and the Legacy of the Sixties.* Philadelphia, PA: Temple University Press, 1996.

Lytle, Mark Hamilton. *America's Uncivil Wars: The Sixties Era from Elvis to the Fall of Richard Nixon.* New York: Oxford University Press, 2006.

MacLean, Nancy. *Freedom Is Not Enough: The Opening of the American Workplace.* Cambridge, MA: Harvard University Press, 2006.

Marshall, Anne E. *Creating a Confederate Kentucky: The Lost Cause and Civil War Memory in a Border State.* Chapel Hill, NC: University of North Carolina Press, 2010.

May, Elaine Tyler. *Homeward Bound: American Families in the Cold War Era.* New York: Basic Books, 1999.

McAdam, Doug. *Freedom Summer.* New York: Oxford University Press, 1988.

McCormick, Charles H. *This Nest of Vipers: McCarthyism and Higher Education in the Mundel Affair, 1951–52.* Champaign, IL: University of Illinois Press, 1989.

McGeever, Patrick J. *Rev. Charles Owen Rice: Apostle of Contradiction*. Pittsburgh, PA: Duquesne University Press, 1989.

McKinnon, Catriona, and Iain Hampsher-Monk, eds. *The Demands of Citizenship*. New York: Continuum, 2000.

Mettler, Suzanne. *Soldiers to Citizens: The G.I. Bill and the Making of the Greatest Generation*. New York: Oxford University Press, 2005.

Miroff, Bruce. *The Liberals' Moment: The McGovern Insurgency and the Identity Crisis of the Democratic Party*. Lawrence, KS: University Press of Kansas, 2007.

Moise, Edwin E. *Tonkin Gulf and the Escalation of the Vietnam War*. Chapel Hill, NC: University of North Carolina Press, 1996.

Monhollon, Rusty L. *"This is America?" The Sixties in Lawrence, Kansas*. New York: Palgrave, 2002.

Neiberg, Michael S. *Making Citizen Soldiers: ROTC and the Ideology of American Military Service*. Cambridge, MA: Harvard University Press, 2000.

Oglesby, Carl. *Ravens in the Storm: A Personal History of the 1960s Antiwar Movement*. New York: Scribner, 2008.

Proctor, Ralph. *Voices from the Firing Line: A Personal Account of the Pittsburgh Civil Rights Movement*. Pittsburgh, PA: Introspect Press, 2013.

Rorabaugh, W. J. *Berkeley at War: The 1960s*. New York: Oxford University Press, 1989.

Rose, Kenneth D. *Myth and the Greatest Generation: A Social History of Americans in World War II*. New York: Routledge, 2008.

Rossinow, Doug. *The Politics of Authenticity: Liberalism, Christianity, and the New Left in America*. New York: Columbia University Press, 1998.

Sale, Kirkpatrick. *SDS: The Rise and Development of the Students for a Democratic Society*. New York: Vintage Books, 1973.

Salstrom, Paul. *Appalachia's Path to Dependency: Rethinking a Region's Economic History, 1730–1940*. Lexington, KY: University Press of Kentucky, 1994.

Sanders, Jane. *Cold War on Campus: Academic Freedom at the University of Washington, 1946–1964*. Seattle, WA: University of Washington Press, 1979.

Schrecker, Ellen W. *No Ivory Tower: McCarthyism and the Universities*. New York: Oxford University Press, 1986.

Schumacher, Michael. *The Contest: The 1968 Election and the War for America's Soul*. Minneapolis, MN: University of Minnesota Press, 2018.

Scott, John C. "The Mission of the University: Medieval to Postmodern Transformation." *Journal of Higher Education* 77, 1 (Jan.-Feb. 2006): 1–39.

Shapiro, Henry D. *Appalachia on Our Minds: The Southern Mountains and Mountaineers in American Consciousness, 1870–1920*. Chapel Hill, NC: University of North Carolina Press, 1978.

Sibley, Mulford Q., and Philip E. Jacob. *Conscription of Conscience: The American State and the Conscientious Objector, 1940–1947*. Ithaca, NY: Cornell University Press, 1952.

Sicakkan, Hakan G., and Yngve Lithman, eds. *Changing the Basis of Citizenship in the Modern State: Political Theory and the Politics of Diversity*. Lewiston, NY: Edwin Mellen Press, 2005.

Simpson, Craig S., and Gregory S. Wilson. *Above the Shots: An Oral History of the Kent State Shootings*. Kent, OH: Kent State University Press, 2016.

Singh, Nikhil Pal. *Black is a Country: Race and the Unfinished Struggle for Democracy*. Cambridge, MA: Harvard University Press, 2004.

Small, Melvin. *Antiwarriors: The Vietnam War and the Battle for America's Hearts and Minds*. New York: SR Books, 2002.

Small, Melvin, and William Hoover, eds. *Give Peace a Chance: Exploring the Vietnam Antiwar Movement*. Syracuse, NY: Syracuse University Press, 1992.

Straw, Richard A., and H. Tyler Blethen, eds. *High Mountain Rising: Appalachia in Time and Place*. Urbana, IL: University of Illinois Press, 2004.

Terkel, Studs. *"The Good War": An Oral History of World War II*. New York: Pantheon Books, 1984.

Thelin, John R. *A History of American Higher Education*. Baltimore, MD: Johns Hopkins University Press, 2004.

Thomas, Jerry Bruce. *An Appalachian Reawakening: West Virginia and the Perils of the Machine Age, 1945–1972*. Morgantown, WV: West Virginia University Press, 2010.

Trotter, Jr., Joe William, and Eric Ledell Smith. *African Americans in Pennsylvania: Shifting Historical Perspectives*. University Park, PA: Pennsylvania State University Press, 1997.

Trotter, Jr., Joe William, and Jared N. Day. *Race and Renaissance: African Americans in Pittsburgh Since World War II*. Pittsburgh, PA: University of Pittsburgh, Press, 2010.

Tyson, Timothy B. *Radio Free Dixie: Robert F. Williams and the Roots of Black Power*. Chapel Hill, NC: University of North Carolina Press, 1999.

Unger, Irwin, and Debi Unger. *Turning Point, 1968*. New York: Scribner, 1988.

Utter, Glenn H. *Youth and Political Participation: A Reference Handbook*. Santa Barbara, CA: ABC-CLIO, 2011.

Vance, J.D. *Hillbilly Elegy: A Memoir of a Family and Culture in Crisis*. New York: Harper, 2016.

Vexler, Robert I., ed. *Pittsburgh: A Chronological & Documentary History, 1682–1976*. New York: Oceana Publications, 1977.

Wells, Tom. *The War Within: America's Battle Over Vietnam*. Berkeley, CA: University of California Press, 1994.

Weyant, Thomas. "Pittsburgh in the Time of Protest: Draft Resistance and Contending Definitions of Patriotism during the Vietnam Era," in *Lesser Civil Wars: Civilians*

Defining War and the Memory of War, 151–73. Edited by Marsha R. Robinson. Newcastle, UK: Cambridge Scholars Press, 2012.

Whisant, David E. *Modernizing the Mountaineer: People, Power, and Planning in Appalachia*. Revised Edition. Knoxville, TN: University of Tennessee Press, 1994.

Williams, John Alexander. *West Virginia: A History*. Morgantown, WV: West Virginia University Press, 2001.

———. *Appalachia: A History*. Chapel Hill, NC: University of North Carolina Press, 2002.

Wilson, Gregory S. *Communities Left Behind: The Area Redevelopment Administration, 1945–1965*. Knoxville, TN: University of Tennessee Press, 2009.

Wittner, Lawrence S. *Rebels Against War: The American Peace Movement, 1933–1983*. Philadelphia, PA: Temple University Press, 1984.

Wynkoop, Mary Ann. *Dissent in the Heartland: The Sixties at Indiana University*. Bloomington, IN: Indiana University Press, 2002.

Young, Marilyn B. *The Vietnam Wars, 1945–1990*. New York: HarperCollins, 1991.

Zaroulis, Nancy, and Gerald Sullivan. *Who Spoke Up? American Protest Against the War in Vietnam, 1963–1975*. New York: Doubleday, 1984.

Index

Black Unity Organization (West Virginia University), 96

Bleed-In (Ohio University), 29, 68–70, 77, 160, 208n12

campus issues. *See* students' rights activism

Carnegie Mellon University/Carnegie Tech, 46, 111, 116–17, 119, 161, 163, 214n4; *Tartan*, 116, 119

Caudill, Harry, 5, 55, 57

Center for Appalachian Studies and Development (West Virginia University), 55–56

Chasan, Joshua, 114–15, 117–18, 121, 150, 162

Chatham College, 111, 163

Choice '68, 122

citizenship, 2, 12–14, 27, 29, 31, 33, 51, 54, 70, 80, 84, 117, 179, 182–84; dual student citizenship, 12–13, 32, 73, 80, 87–107, 155, 169, 183; of the nation, 1, 31, 84, 110, 184; student citizenship, 11–12, 14, 28–30, 33, 40, 42, 53, 59, 77, 83, 85–88, 91, 93, 114, 120, 141–42, 145, 148, 150, 155, 170, 172–73, 177–78, 182–84; of the university, 1–2, 13, 32, 40, 43, 83–85, 92, 97, 99, 173, 184

civil disobedience, 61, 76, 94, 96, 104, 111–12, 153–54

civil rights activism, 11–12, 43, 45–46, 49, 52–54, 58, 83, 87, 104, 144, 179–80, 183–84; 1964 to 1967, 30, 45–54, 58, 62, 65, 76; 1967 to 1968, 83, 87, 96–99; 1968 to 1972, 140, 143–45, 155; in Athens, OH, 51; in Morgantown, WV, 97; at Ohio University, 46, 48, 51–52, 97–98, 144, 197n21; in Pittsburgh, PA, 47–48; at University of Pittsburgh, 46–49, 70, 97–98, 118, 143–45, 194n21; at West Virginia University, 47, 52–53, 97, 144

Cochran, Charles, 177

Cold War, 3, 7–9, 15–19, 23, 25–26, 28–29, 38, 46, 63, 76, 92, 100; universities, 15, 26, 31

Communism/communists, 9, 17–18, 24, 31, 63–64, 70, 75, 78–79, 114

Confrontation with the Warmakers (1967). *See* October Mobilization

conscription. *See* Selective Service System

conservatives, 11, 53, 67, 71, 78, 80, 120, 167, 180

Couvares, Frank, 40, 182

Defense Department research, 18, 165

democracy, 13, 28, 30, 38, 40, 43, 49, 66–67, 70, 75–76, 87, 120, 145, 150–51, 155, 164; participatory democracy, 13, 23, 30, 38, 76

DeNicola, Daniel, 41

D'Ippolito, Alex, 63–65

dissent, 12, 23, 29, 61, 65–70, 72–75, 77–81, 87, 89, 103, 106, 113, 116, 118, 120, 148, 161, 166

Dow Chemical Company protests, 76–77, 109, 114–15, 123

draft. *See* Selective Service System

Duquesne University, 111, 118, 161, 163; *Duquesne Duke*, 118

Eagleton, Thomas, 171, 173

Freedom Summer. *See* Mississippi Freedom Summer Project

Fromm, Peter, 121–22

Fuller, Ed, 117, 162

Garfinkle, Irv, 63–65, 70

G.I. Bill. *See* Servicemen's Readjustment Act of 1944

Gitlin, Todd, 141

Gluck, Joseph, 153, 167

Goldwater, Barry, 38, 49

Great Society, 42

Greek social societies, 17, 19–20, 27, 31–32, 41, 47, 53, 71

Gulf of Tonkin Incident, 62, 100–101, 164, 201n3

Guy, Bonnie, 48

Harlow, James G., 92, 115, 153–54, 158–61, 167–68, 227n33

Harrington, Michael, 55

Heineman, Kenneth, 3, 179

Herald, Elaine, 74–76, 112

Hershey, Lewis B., 71, 116–19

Hill Education Project (HEP) (University of Pittsburgh), 47, 58, 98, 194n21

Hoffman, Paul, 140–41, 158, 162

Horacek, Louis, 115, 119–22

Humphrey, Hubert H., 72–73

in loco parentis, 12, 25, 28–29, 31–37, 68, 83–85, 88–89, 145, 153, 178, 184

International Student Strike and Boycott, 109, 113, 122, 215n9

Jackson, Thomas, 164–65

Johnson, Lyndon B., 21, 38, 45–46, 52, 54, 62, 65, 70, 74–75, 79, 109, 112, 116, 138, 143

Kennedy, Edward, 140

Kennedy, John F., 1, 3, 5, 21, 45

Kennedy, Robert F., 28, 55, 95, 123, 179

Kent State University shooting, 139, 147, 155, 157, 163–75, 177, 179–81, 184

Kerr, Clark, 9, 18, 92. *See also* multiversity

Kiffmeyer, Thomas, 4, 54, 57, 99, 179, 211n35

King, Jr., Martin Luther, 2, 46, 53, 95–97, 113, 119–20, 132, 143–44, 179

Kurtzman, David H., 1, 118

Levitch, Kim, 177

Lewis, John, 46, 49

liberal/liberalism, 8, 11, 17, 38, 43, 46, 53– 54, 57–58, 65, 88, 96, 99, 102–4, 120, 158, 162

Litchfield, Edward H., 23–24

March on Washington to End the War in Vietnam, 61, 64, 110

Marsh, Ted, 117–18

McAdam, Doug, 45, 48, 50, 54, 59

McGovern, George, 171–74

middle class, 2–3, 17, 31, 42, 57, 63, 161

military-industrial-academic complex, 8, 15, 18–19, 28, 31, 71, 92, 115

Miller, Paul A., 27–28, 56

Mississippi Freedom Summer Project (Freedom Summer), 1, 45–55, 58–59, 62, 180, 197n13

Mitchell, David, 66–67, 202n13

mock political conventions, 28, 172; mock Republican convention (1964), 37–38, 122, 171, 193n17

Montgomery, AL, 50–51

Morgantown, WV, 4, 38, 78, 153, 159, 167; antiwar activities, 158–59, 181; civil rights activities, 53–54, 97; West Virginia University, 24–26, 158

Morgantown Six, 168–69

Morrill Land Grant Act (1862), 20, 24, 100

Morrison, David, 118–19, 122, 162

Mountaineer Freedom Party (West Virginia University), 151, 220, 222

multiversity, 9, 15, 17–19, 21, 26, 29, 31, 42, 92; and Clark Kerr, 9, 18, 92

National Guard, 91, 96, 136, 163

New Left, 3, 10–11, 13, 28, 30, 113, 119, 148–50, 171, 188n33, 205n40

Nixon, John T., 42, 182

Nixon, Richard, 125, 140, 143, 149, 158, 161–65, 169, 174

October Mobilization (1967), 109–12

October Moratorium (1969), 113, 127, 133, 139–41, 157–64, 169, 174, 181, 184